FAIRNESS IN ANTITRUST

What drives popular support for state-enforced competition policy? What is it about antitrust law that garners approval from both the public and courts, to the point of demonizing large firms convicted of antitrust offences? In this book Adi Ayal argues that the populist roots of antitrust are still with us, guiding sentiment towards a legal regime that has otherwise shifted towards economic analysis. Antitrust is very much about fairness and morality; this book assesses how modern policy has hijacked popular support—based on traditional conceptions of political and economic power—to combat market power in narrowly defined micro-markets.

Beginning with history, but delving into moral and political philosophy, Professor Ayal shows how arguments concerning fairness in antitrust apply both to monopolists and their victims. Fairness thus requires a balancing test based on context and respecting the rights of all parties involved. While traditionally fairness arguments were used to justify intervention where economic analysis did not, this book assesses them from first principles, to show that pure efficiency analysis is flawed from a moral standpoint when the state intervenes. Protecting weak consumers from strong monopolists may carry rhetorical weight, but the reality of antitrust is that the state is much more powerful than almost all firms it regulates. Protecting the strong from the weak, especially when 'weak' consumers hold legal power and influence, might very well be a moral imperative.

This book offers a philosophical account of the conundrum facing competition policy which challenges widely-held yet often implicit and unfounded beliefs.

Volume 7 in the series Hart Studies in Competition Law

Hart Studies in Competition Law

Volume 1: *Intellectual Property, Antitrust and Cumulative Innovation in the EU and the US*
Thorsten Käseberg

Volume 2: *State Aid and the European Economic Constitution*
Francesco de Cecco

Volume 3: *The Private Enforcement of Competition Law in Ireland*
David McFadden

Volume 4: *Cross-Border EU Competition Law Actions*
Edited by Mihail Danov, Florian Becker and Paul Beaumont

Volume 5: *European Merger Remedies: Law and Policy*
Dorte Hoeg

Volume 6: *Sanctions in EU Competition Law: Principles and Practice*
Michael Frese

Fairness in Antitrust

Protecting the Strong from the Weak

Adi Ayal

• HART •
PUBLISHING
OXFORD AND PORTLAND, OREGON
2016

Published in the United Kingdom by Hart Publishing Ltd
16C Worcester Place, Oxford, OX1 2JW
Telephone: +44 (0)1865 517530
Fax: +44 (0)1865 510710
E-mail: mail@hartpub.co.uk
Website: http://www.hartpub.co.uk

Published in North America (US and Canada) by
Hart Publishing
c/o International Specialized Book Services
920 NE 58th Avenue, Suite 300
Portland, OR 97213-3786
USA
Tel: +1 503 287 3093 or toll-free: (1) 800 944 6190
Fax: +1 503 280 8832
E-mail: orders@isbs.com
Website: http://www.isbs.com

First published in hardback 2014
Paperback edition, 2016

Hart Publishing is an imprint of Bloomsbury Publishing plc.

British Library Cataloguing in Publication Data
Data Available

ISBN: HB: 978-1-84946-515-1
PB: 978-1-50990-706-9

Typeset by Compuscript Ltd, Shannon
Printed and bound in Great Britain by
Lightning Source UK Ltd

PREFACE

This book is about antitrust, but I intend to engage not only those versed in the legal and economic details of antitrust law, but also those interested in the morality of matters between the individual and the state. At issue is whether an important social function currently being regulated in a certain manner is, or is not, respectful of rights we as a society consider basic, indeed almost sacred. If my analysis of antitrust holds true, this body of law errs in assuming only one side in the debate has rights. What matters is not merely if antitrust doctrine is good or bad (or can be improved), but what we can learn through querying what has hitherto gone unaddressed, assumed away. Through exploration of the moral and economic justifications for the body of law we call antitrust, I delve into the subconscious bias favouring 'consumers'—even when we do not really know what the word means. Through putting both producers and consumers side by side, each is examined in light of the other, seeing through the categories to the underlying assumptions and mental images guiding them. Furthermore, by placing 'those we love to hate' on equal footing with those we empathize with and see ourselves in, we can discipline ourselves into exposing what we are really saying—and why it might mean something different than initially presumed.

The thesis of this book is that antitrust law as practiced today blends together two themes, contradictory in nature. On one hand, there is a widely-held belief that competition is right, indeed a moral right we are entitled to—as well as an economically sound policy. On the other hand there is an assumption that consumers deserve to be protected, that high prices are at best a temporary phenomenon drawing in competition to lower them, and at worst—a social evil to be combated by courts and state agencies. The *rights* of consumers assume a moral content to antitrust, while the *efficiency* of competition assumes objective and value-neutral criteria for state intervention. *Producers' rights* are seen (if at all) as instrumental. I hope to show that moral-neutrality is not an option in antitrust, that the current economic focus is not value-free and consumer-centrality is just one more explicit step in a direction already existing implicitly in the antitrust-as-efficiency paradigm. It not against the result that I argue, as society has a right to choose which rights to protect, but I do argue that current doctrine implicitly assumes away producers' rights and leads to intellectual dishonesty. By misleading ourselves about antitrust being both moral and right, we avoid the hard work of balancing between competing claims. Through antitrust we support intervention and governmental takings that would never have garnered such support were they framed in other contexts.

In the interest of engaging a broad audience, I give a background for and explain the main terms antitrust debate requires. Those familiar with the literature will find, I hope, a novel outlook in the descriptive parts. Efficiency analysis is presented and assessed, but it is not the main thrust of the book—morality is. Efficiency is one of the various goals society seeks to achieve through antitrust, central in its application, but requiring moral justification just as does any other reason for governmental intervention. The main discussion is of rights: specifically, the rights of those harmed by monopolistic practices as well as the rights of antitrust offenders.

I separate between rights that can be argued to be vested in specific individuals, or groups of individuals, and the aggregate interests of society at large. In the end, courts decide on issues where rights clash, and my main argument is that antitrust is precisely such a case—though current doctrine often sidesteps the issue. Similarly to other cases where the state infringes upon an individual's rights, or where two parties claim rights whose implications clash, it is constitutional discourse which interjects. I aim to bring antitrust law to such constitutional review and argue for a standard according to which courts, regulators, and legislators can balance between the competing claims. The issues debated are not just which practice is 'competitive' and which not, but which standard of care the state should use when affecting individuals' rights. The question is of the morality of actions that government carries out in our name, with a broad consensus assuming such conduct is both right and fair. I hope to show that it is not that simple.

The current focus in antitrust enforcement towards economically-oriented rules applied by technocratic administrative agencies avoids philosophical disputes regarding rights by focusing on scientific economic principles applied by supposedly value-neutral professionals. I hope to show that such value-neutrality is a myth, and underlying the technocratic rules are implicit assumptions regarding the basic rights of those involved. Were efficiency-maximizing rules to be applied in other contexts as they are in antitrust, we would have a rebellion on our hands by those claiming infringement of their rights to governmental respect of property and freedom of contract. The fact that these issues remain unaddressed in the realm of antitrust is explained by its history and gradual evolution, as the type of 'monopoly' which initially justified antitrust legislation (and still underlies popular conceptions of its subject matter) is very far from today's implementation of the same terms.

The ultimate goal to which I aspire is not that antitrust be altered in one specific way or another, but that we as a society take more care in exercising our power; that even when force or compulsion are necessary and justified, we employ them with respect for those whose conduct requires limiting. Through true recognition of the various rights, and true effort in balancing them correctly, we can better ourselves as a society which collectively wields great power through the state and its legal system.

CONTENTS

Introduction

Antitrust is a fascinating subject. Broad in application and rhetoric, almost all can rally around the popular themes of competition, economic efficiency, and consumer protection. Standard antitrust rhetoric envisions the state intervening in order to protect the many from the few, the weak from the strong and the 'common people' from 'monopolists'. But perhaps this view exists more in theory than in practice; an illusion of wholesomeness kept in place by avoiding the hard issues of protectionism, of populism, of promoting an implicit view of property very different from the one guiding other legal topics and public opinion generally.

The general and broadly-accepted theme of antitrust can be stated thus: that it is government's duty to ensure effective competition, protect the marketplace from monopolization and collaboration among competitors, in order to facilitate economic growth and protect consumers; that both economics and basic moral values support society's regulation of excessive power in the marketplace and that the unilateral and coordinated effects of monopolistic phenomena are justly curtailed; that there is a right to compete, but not to monopolize, a right to expand, but not to overpower.

It should be stated at the outset, that this intuitive guideline is precisely what I hope to show is wrong with current antitrust doctrine. What has become the commonsensical view masks a hidden assumption—that monopolists as such are to be limited unless *others* benefit from their practices. This assumption, while not always clearly stated in the literature, is a necessary one for many of the standard arguments, and the text below will aim to flush out its underlying existence as well as where it is dead wrong. I focus on 'monopolists', although the argument is broader. It relates also to actual and potential possessors of unilateral market power, as well as businesses wishing to coordinate by agreement or merger. In general, the term 'monopolist' throughout the book should be understood not as a term of art, but as a broad description of those that antitrust law aims to regulate. Where monopolies, cartels and mergers require differentiation, I shall explore their distinctions as these apply to legal and economic policy. While the argument is general, applying to possessors of market power more generally (or those hoping to achieve it), I use the term 'monopolists' for the simple reason that arguing for their protection is the hardest case to make. I thus focus on the extreme, since if my argument proves true there—it will be easier to apply elsewhere. Once monopolists' rights are accepted as a key feature of the antitrust debate, applying similar arguments to less extreme cases, where market power is less clearly an issue, will follow. It should be clear, though, that my argument is broader than some current commentators' arguments in defence of monopoly. It is not just that monopoly is sometimes efficient (eg, due to innovation or 'winner-take-all' competition), and it is not just that some monopolists 'deserve' their supra-competitive gains (as some have argued following *Microsoft* and *Trinko*). I hope to justify a broader contention—that monopolists are to be treated with a priori respect, as bearers of protected rights, until these are shown to be justifiably overcome by other concerns. Defining what 'justifiably' means in this context, and how balancing is to be achieved, are the main tasks before us.

The question this book aims to answer is a seemingly simple one: what are the justifications for the existence of antitrust law and how coherent is existing doctrine with its underlying justifications? This basic question leads us down a path of research ranging from the initial concerns that gave rise to antitrust legislation some one hundred years ago, to the latest developments in ongoing economic research reassessing actual effects of the law's implementation. This book aims to incorporate the different facets of antitrust research, from the highly theoretical arguments of philosophy, law and economics, to the empirical research witnessing sometimes mixed effects of current legal regimes. While true justice to the disciplines this book draws from demands many volumes devoted to each sub-topic, my hope is that the interest in focus and conciseness will not detract from the quality of the debate.

Most commentators on antitrust begin with a simple and endearing premise: monopoly as such distorts the balance of power between buyers and sellers, allowing the latter to raise prices above the competitive level. The negative effects discerned are both with regard to the total welfare created by trade, and with regard to the distribution of surplus between those directly affected. The analysis called for by this basic premise is already multifaceted: economic analysis of the relevant business practices and their effects in different circumstances, philosophical assessment of the rights and duties of those involved and legal analysis of the definitions used and the institutions involved with implementation. What seemed at first a consensual premise for justifying state intervention in monopolistic practices thus develops into a series of related debates, each highlighting the differing effects of specific circumstances and theoretical conceptions. The 'monopolists' studied here are all those whose conduct is to be limited by antitrust law, whether true holders of a unique selling position, firms proposing a merger which might be forbidden, or business people engaged in what might be construed as an antitrust offence. In all cases, antitrust law plays a limiting role, constraining the freedom of those hoping to achieve their own aims, presumably with legal doctrine operating in the interest of society at large. It is precisely this public interest which I challenge, examining the rights infringed upon and the justification for state intervention.

This book offers a model that draws from different viewpoints and aims to build one coherent framework. In a nutshell, the argument may be presented as follows: in order to argue that a specific rule of antitrust is appropriate, that rule must rely on coherent principles. These principles, in turn, must present a complete picture of the relevant circumstances, ie, take into consideration all those affected with no one left out. Obviously, different parties will have different interests, thus we cannot hope for one 'correct' answer that will satisfy everyone. Thus, a model must be devised that will create a standard for judging among the competing interests—whether lexically preferring one side over the other, or balancing them in some other way.

Any proposed standard must be built 'from the bottom up', meaning that we begin by defining the relevant parties and defending or rebutting their claimed interests in the matter. Each interest is assessed not only as to its importance to the party claiming it, but also as to the moral justification of protecting such an interest in the first place—separating material interests from vested rights.

The philosophical distinction between interests and rights will prove central in our debate regarding the protection that each side to the debate may claim from outside intervention. It is here that the crux of the matter lies regarding antitrust law: the devising of rules, and especially their implementation, is aimed at initiating state intervention that will ultimately limit one side (monopolists) and protect the other (consumers). The balancing of limitation and protection employed exposes the legal system's underlying assumptions regarding the rights involved, their relative weight and the appropriate balance to be struck when both sides have competing claims.

If a balancing test is to be complete, it must consider not only the party suffering from the opposed business practices, but also those to be limited by state intervention—the monopolists themselves. While the need to assess monopolists' rights may seem self-evident when presented in the context of devising a balancing test, it is illuminating to note that the great majority of antitrust scholars have very little to say on the subject. Below, we shall see that most of the literature regarding the core principles of antitrust deal extensively with the rights of consumers and other groups harmed by monopolistic business practices, but analysis of 'the monopolists' side' focuses almost exclusively on claims that 'no harm was done', or efficiency justifications claiming benefits exceeding costs. What is missing from the debate is a strong positive statement on behalf of monopolists: that even if harm was done, or the practices concerned are inefficient, monopolists are sometimes well within their rights to do so. One of the initial contributions this book seeks to make is in substantiating the need for a rights-based analysis of monopolists as well as their victims, before judgement may be passed on any conception of antitrust law, or rule thereof.

On this basis, I offer a specific balancing test drawn from basic tenets of constitutional law—that similarly to a democracy's right to protect itself from non-democratic elements, a capitalistic society has the right to protect itself from economic power aimed at subverting the market process. In both cases, the framework provided by the state relies on an ideology of political restraint allowing free exchange of opinions and goods, and both provide means for misuse of the freedoms granted.

An established constitutional frame for this type of issue is the extent of freedom of speech granted to non-democratic elements, where a balance must be struck between an affected individual's rights in promulgating their views and society's interest in self-preservation. Constitutional discourse examines this in the extreme, such as cases where anti-democratic groups seek protection of their right to freedom of speech and assembly. It is at this extreme that clarity is sought in differentiating what exactly we mean when the term 'rights' is used, and how these rights have standing independent of our moral judgement regarding the party claiming them. The text below will show striking resemblances between this case and the framework of the free market (though the latter is obviously a much less extreme example), where monopolists claim a right to choose with whom and on what terms to conduct their business.

The right to free trade, similarly to the right to free expression, is not without its limits—especially where actions usually protected by such a right may lead to its limitation for others whom the system must protect as well. On a practical level, once the need for assessing monopolists' rights is made clear, and the balancing test spelled out, I will show that the current focus in antitrust implementation and scholarship is inappropriate. The current trend towards professional application of 'scientific' rules based on economic analysis belies the moral content implicitly assumed, and the focus on market power assessed on a case-by-case basis inappropriately biases application away from the values for which antitrust was initially enacted and currently supported. If we are to take the moral content of antitrust seriously, practical significance points toward an emphasis on economic, rather than market, power.

Looking into the underlying social agreement which legitimizes antirust requires focus on its effect on a macro level, rather than a micro scale. Succinctly put, the analysis below may lead to a context-sensitive application of antitrust rules—more intervention in politically sensitive arenas such as media and information (as well as basic and essential goods) and less intervention in markets less worthy of collective support, such as luxury items and those producing social harms. Contextual application, while intuitive in some respects, is problematic in others—namely that value judgements must be made, and antitrust agencies are not necessarily the best situated to make them. I thus explore institutional issues raised by this option, and the difficulties which are bound to arise. Here as before, my focus is not solely on the final result and policy recommendations, but on the in-depth analysis preceding them. My hope is that even those opposing my conclusions can gain from the discussion, and that the need for a balancing test is substantiated—even if its application is disputed. Since it is values and beliefs about society which require balancing, differing views are to be expected and I hope to set out a method for deliberation which would force us to take the competing claims into account. The process, rather than the result, is key.

The book's thesis is developed in three parts: in the first part, the contextual setting of antitrust is presented—both legal and economic. In the second part, the goals of antitrust are presented and discussed. I differentiate between aggregate goals that society as a whole pursues, and fairness claims made on behalf of the direct parties to the debate: monopolists on one hand, and their victims on the other. In part three, the case for a constitutional balancing test is made—both its justification and its content. Examples of implementation and general conclusions wrap up.

PART I: THE SETTING OF ANTITRUST

Chapter one, 'The Legal and Rhetorical Context of Antitrust', begins with history—the social and legal setting in which antitrust arose and reached its current prominence. Common law antecedents are reviewed, from the rise of monopolies, through restrictions of trade by consensual means, to the enactment of specific statutes dealing with the problems stemming from economic and market power (including the distinction between the two). Historical review allows for differentiation between the themes which led to initial antitrust legislation and those guiding today's implementation. While labels (such as 'monopoly') remain the same, I show that content changed considerably. This distinction allows for an observation which proves key later on—that many supporters of antitrust have specific mental images regarding the monopolistic phenomena enjoined, images based on the evolution of the field and far from today's practice.

The basic goals of antitrust (as stated by legislators, courts and scholars worldwide) are presented, setting the stage for in-depth discussion in later chapters. I then present American and European antitrust doctrines, in each case focusing on one central issue to allow for a deeper understanding of the legal systems where implementation of the proposed model is later to take place. Finally, I examine the role of competition, arguing that while rhetoric abounds regarding its status as an independent goal, this unduly masks its instrumental role in serving underlying interests—mainly the protection of consumers or economic efficiency (and a few others to be considered below). Competition, I argue, is used mostly as a proxy—a means justified only when the ends are worthwhile. This is not the only option. Competition can be valued as an independent good, although delving into the justifications therefore shows that application should differ greatly from current practice—giving it prominence in specific contexts, while limiting it in others.

PART II: THE GOALS OF ANTITRUST

Chapter two, 'The Societal Goals of Antitrust', begins the mission of presenting the different interests affected by monopoly and antitrust, focusing on aggregate concerns. The societal goal most often referred to in antitrust debate is that of economic efficiency, thus it is assessed first. I define the different conceptions of economic efficiency and assess each, both as to its use in justifying antitrust intervention and as to contrary considerations, ie, the efficiency reasons for favouring non-intervention. Since the basic economic models justifying antitrust are well known, I sketch them out concisely and concentrate on their critique and qualification, as well as introducing arguments not previously considered. Consequently, this chapter is more focused on raising objections to accepted antitrust doctrine than on justifying it.

Objections to antitrust follow one of two basic routes: first, economic analyses shows where previous models overstated the inefficiency resulting from monopolistic practices, as well as showing alternative efficiency gains from practices previously considered aggregately inefficient. Most students of antitrust might find it baffling that anyone would seriously argue that monopoly is efficient, yet serious commentators contend precisely that—albeit within limited circumstances. I present the main arguments in this vein, and present empirical evidence supporting such conclusions. In addition to such 'efficient monopolization' arguments, more mundane analyses are presented as well, showing the limitations of accepted economic theories regarding monopoly's inefficiency. While the inefficiency of monopolistic practices is often irrefutable, its scale may be much smaller than commonly perceived.

The second type of objection to antitrust's efficiency, contends that even if monopoly as such is inefficient, the actions taken in order to combat its evils may be harmful in themselves. A distinction is made between direct costs of antitrust enforcement and the indirect costs thereof. While the direct costs are quite easily pointed out, the indirect costs are more often ignored. Here, I focus on the 'public choice' literature which sheds new light on an old subject, and use empirical studies to emphasize the theoretical arguments made.

After an extensive review of the efficiency arguments, of different types and persuasions, I turn to other societal goals, of a non-economic sort. Two main arguments of this type are presented and critiqued: the claim that antitrust is aimed at facilitating a society of entrepreneurs or small businesses (the 'Jeffersonian ideal'), and that antitrust exists to protect democracy from the accumulation of economic power in the hands of the few (the problem of bigness). Both have been historically significant in the development of antitrust doctrine, despite currently giving way to the focus on economic efficiency. As previously, I stress limitations rather than strengths of claims made on behalf of societal protection of its interests, keeping in mind that even when society has a legitimate interest, the question remains of who is to benefit and what rights may be claimed by those paying the price therefore. Nonetheless, the history of societal concern with economic (rather than market) power and the effect of 'bigness' on democracy is important, and this chapter lays the groundwork for the return to these issues later on, in the discussion of the balancing test and the values considered within it.

Chapter three, 'Monopoly's Victims', moves our debate to the realm of fairness and individual rights. As stated above, the rights of those suffering from monopolistic practices have long played a central role in the justification of antitrust law designed to protect them. Consumers have long been assumed to be the paradigmatic victims of monopoly, but they are not alone. Competitors, small businesses and local communities are also among those whom antitrust purports to protect. Each of these groups is separately assessed, with special emphasis on discerning the interests of each group distinctly from their vested rights. The result is a critical assessment of some of the most commonly assumed justifications for antitrust law. The famous 'wealth transfer' argument in particular is analyzed at length as to its philosophic assumptions, and different conceptions of justice are reviewed that might warrant antitrust intervention for the protection of individual rights.

Given the consumer-centrality of current antitrust debate, I delve into the question of their vested rights, underlying the common 'protect the weak from the strong' conception of antitrust. While multiple prongs of research are presented and assessed, I stress Rawls' 'veil of ignorance' criterion, both due to its centrality in moral and political philosophy, and due to its ability to transcend biases and preconceptions we might bring to the debate. The question which social agreement might be reached when each of us is blind to our own preferences and circumstances allows for a new outlook regarding consumer rights and the justification of antitrust.

Chapter four, 'Monopolists' Rights', is the first in-depth look at monopolists as bearers of rights. I rely on the basic formulation used in chapter three, and apply a similar framework to the other side. Since monopolists have traditionally received less attention in the rights debate (more often seen as the 'bad guys' whose conduct is to be limited), I begin with justifying the very need to review their rights in a manner comparable with their victims. Despite their being potential perpetrators of evil, I show that no debate of antitrust's basic concepts can be complete without all affected parties being equally assessed as to their rights-based claims. Once the need for assessment is made clear, the interests and rights of monopolists are subjected to careful analysis, in line with that of monopoly's victims.

Next we turn to taking apart the vague term of 'monopolists' to see who it is that is adversely affected by antitrust enforcement. Shareholders, workers, creditors and local communities are each separately assessed as to interests and rights claimed. Finally, the question of firms as bearers of rights is addressed. Since almost all antitrust suits are directed at firms rather than individuals, and the debate here focuses on both interests and rights, we must delve into the question of firms' moral standing, either as proxies for distinct individuals, or as independent bearers of rights on their own. On this point, as on others preceding it, I make it a point to assess the arguments directly, as well as showing where the same issues arose when assessing monopoly's victims. The 'consumers' protected by antitrust enforcement are often firms involved in commercial transactions, precisely of the same sort populating the producers' side. Furthermore, the *indirect purchaser rule* posits direct consumers as the paradigmatic plaintiffs—leading almost all private antitrust litigation to be brought on behalf of firms, and directed against other firms. The issue of firms' rights is tackled, including questions basic to corporate law and the evolution of commercial speech. Still, since firms reside on both sides of the antitrust divide, the issue of their moral standing is non-determinative of the end result. Even antitrust commentators who 'agree to disagree' on firms' rights (assuming they pay attention to the issue at all), cannot escape the fact that both sides to this debate rely on firms, thus leading to the necessity of a balancing test—precisely where my argument is heading.

PART III: THE BALANCING ACT OF ANTITRUST

This part is where push comes to shove. After laying the groundwork by debating the different grounds for antitrust intervention, here they are combined to offer a coherent standard that antitrust law must live up to.

Chapter five, 'Towards a Constitutional Balance in Antitrust', begins by assessing the arguments both for and against using a balancing test in the first place, and then moves on to the intellectual setting fitting it best. Since the focus is not on any specific rule, but on the very basis for justifying antitrust altogether, I turn to constitutional law for guidance. While perhaps not self-evident for those practiced in the economic and technical jargon of current antitrust debate, constitutional law is appropriate due to the need to assess rights of different parties, and especially when examining clashes between them. I show that the theoretical conception that antitrust must draw from has a much broader basis in the question of state intervention versus minimalism, the right to property and the very ground rules guiding social life in capitalist societies.

In order to develop the standard for balancing among the different parties' rights, I examine both public and private interests in antitrust, and define relevant differences between private action and state action, with special emphasis on considerations that law enforcement agencies in particular must respect. Constitutional law, and evaluation of state-protected rights and interests more generally, depend on philosophical distinctions regarding which values are to be given prominence. Many alternatives exist as to assessing these, and I rely mostly on the Rawlsian framework of a hypothetical social agreement which can be argued to represent what most, if not all, members of society would have agreed to—had they been able to assess and deliberate these issues in a disinterested manner. Within this framework, I return to the issue of the values which should guide antitrust enforcement, and the distinction between economic power on a macro level and market power assessed by microeconomic technical and context free rules. I argue that the former aligns more closely with dominant social views, while the latter represents current antitrust doctrine. I thus propose a reassessment of antitrust enforcement along these lines.

Chapter six, 'Formalization of Fairness and Envy-Freeness', offers an intellectual detour prior to the final implementation of the proposed balancing test. My hope is that this less familiar form of analysis, developed by economists seeking to employ mathematical tools in order to assess arguments of fair division, will allow examination of the issues presented above in a different light and affirm the direction taken. While the more philosophically minded will find the very idea of 'numerical fairness' surprising, this form of analysis is well grounded, and offers substantial insights relevant to our debate. An extensive review of the literature, together with its critique, is presented and then applied to the realm of antitrust. Since antitrust analysis has to do with economic concepts, the connection here is natural, building on the wealth transfer arguments presented in chapter three and dominating much of the fairness-oriented antitrust literature. I use these models of fairness to illuminate chasms in the standard conceptions of wealth transfers and consumer surplus, raising the question of what right a consumer might have in a surplus he did not create, indeed one which never existed prior to, or independent of, the trade he now seeks to modify. Issues of freedom, endowments and forced labour are tackled, using theoretical constructs to tease apart what common arguments overlook.

Chapter seven, 'The "Clear and Present Danger" Standard for Antitrust', brings together all the foundational effort to develop a standard drawing directly from the constitutional treatment of clashing rights in other contexts. I develop the idea implied above, that monopolists arguing for a right to trade unimpeded by the state, are relying on free-market conceptions that they themselves are undermining. While a natural gut reaction would be to deny their legitimacy in such a claim, a striking similarity can be found in other examples considered in-depth by constitutional discourse. Non-democratic groups claiming a right to free speech, in part in order to promote social change which would negate that very right, are an extreme case of a similar claim—that even those burrowing under a system are to be afforded protection, up to a point. The point, in the free speech context, is where their actions constitute 'clear and present danger' to society or specific members thereof, and it is that standard which I seek to learn from and apply to antitrust.

Trade and speech are thus compared, and their similarities and differences noted, in order to assess the claim that standards developed in one arena are relevant to the other. I argue on behalf of monopolists for protection of their rights to property and freedom of contract, noting that their actions might impede on others' ability to exercise the same. Since the claim and its result are counterintuitive for those used to consider victims' rights alone, I go to great lengths to substantiate my claims and to raise (and answer) a wide variety of potential objections to the proposed standard. The balancing test is shown to incorporate the lengthy analysis that preceded its formulation, so that the whole book comes together into one coherent model upon which future policy can be built and thought provoked.

The *process* of balancing (rather than merely its result) is stressed, as a society required to address these issues head-on within a juridical balancing test will be forced to consider competing claims—thus unable to ignore the rights of monopolists even when ultimately choosing to overrule them in specific cases. It is the *act of balancing* itself which keeps us aware and maintains a healthy need for empathy—taking into account not only those with whom we easily identify, but also those initially deemed unworthy of consideration. It is this uneasy empathy which keeps us honest, and it is the task of legal standards (among other things) to thrust society beyond its comfort zone and protect not just the weak from the strong, but occasionally also protect the strong from the weak, especially when the latter combine under the auspices of (and employ the power of) the state.

Part I

The Setting of Antitrust

1

The Legal and Rhetorical Context of Antitrust

State regulation protecting competition may seem obvious today, but its history as a distinct topic is a relatively short one, most notably beginning in 1890 with the enactment of the Sherman Act in the US.[1] Since then, the regulation of competition has become commonplace, and so widely practised that arguments against it may seem heretical, if not nonsensical. Nonetheless, in order to understand current paradigms, it is important to assess the backdrop against which modern law and policy developed and the problems addressed by historical legislators. While much has changed over the years, in both economic understanding and in legal application, dominant paradigms stem from historical attitudes towards economic power.[2] As shall be clarified below, current abhorrence of monopoly and its abuse stems largely from metaphors created during the formative era of antitrust and used to this day, despite major changes in their application. I thus begin with history—though obviously a small selection of it—aiming for exposition rather than survey.

Since the regulation of competition is today an international endeavour, one struggles with terminology: I shall thus employ the terms 'antitrust' and 'competition law' interchangeably, hoping the European reader will forgive the former, while the American reader forgives the latter. My goal is theoretical analysis, assessing 'what is right' rather than current law, thus discussion of existing law will necessarily be brief and incomplete. I do hope to portray current legal paradigms in a manner doing them justice, while focusing on the normative underpinnings of current policy. This chapter thus aims at showing how current views rely on historical ones, while giving some context for the discussion ahead. American history offers a clear dividing line between legal traditions; thus it allows a clear view into common attitudes regarding our subject. After giving some historical context for the development of American antitrust law in section I, section II does the same for EU competition law, stressing the differences between the regimes

[1] Canada and New Jersey enacted similar statutes in 1889, although the Sherman Act is, by far, better known and more widely discussed.

[2] Economic power is a more traditional and more general term than 'market power' which is the focus of modern competition policy. The distinction between the two, as well as the implicit policy assumptions stemming from each, shall be addressed in ch 2.

and the interaction between the goals of competition and the industrial policy of European integration. Section III then moves on to set up the normative discussion of antitrust's goals, including both efficiency and fairness, but also broader social conceptions of the common good to be served. 'Competition', a term used ubiquitously and presumed to be self-explanatory, is deconstructed to separate between its different meanings. Scholars and jurists use the same term to refer sometimes to the end-result of efficient allocations and sometimes to processes of rivalry thought to be inherently worthy. I thus enumerate the ways in which competition is considered an independent viable social goal, as well as the underlying primary goods for which it serves a useful proxy. Separating between the different uses of the term 'competition' allows for greater clarity and intellectual coherence when discussing its applications. Section IV then explains the focus on 'monopolists' as subjects of analysis and bearers of rights. While antitrust governs the activity of many groups and individuals, I focus on monopolists as the extreme example and as a test-case for the main argument regarding their rights. If defendable claims can be made on behalf of the most unlikely candidate, their application to less extreme cases will be much easier later on.

I. THE DEVELOPMENT OF ANTITRUST LAW: COMMON LAW ANTECEDENTS

The origins of competition law can be traced back along two routes. One strand originates with the common law treatment of contracts restraining trade, beginning as far back as fifteenth century England; the other deals with royal grants of monopoly, which bestowed upon their recipients the sole right to deal in a particular good or service, usually due to a special investment or special relationship with the royal family or their entourage.[3] A typical case of the first strand would be an employment contract where the employee promises not to compete in the same business (or town) after employment has been terminated. In the guild system then common, this made the employee's commercial future dependent upon the employer's good will, and thus all but perpetuated their relative positions. Usually, non-competition clauses would not preclude *any* competition, but limit the geographical area the employee may operate in, the specific types of goods he might offer, or some similar market division. Overly broad restrictions

[3] See, eg, W Letwin, 'The English Law Concerning Monopolies' (1954) 21 *University of Chicago Law Review* 355; TB Nachbar, 'Monopoly, Mercantilism and the Politics of Regulation' (2005) 91 *Virginia Law Review* 1313; Yale Brozen famously made the argument that this dynamic of governmental creation of monopoly persists over time and changes mostly in name and form; see Y Brozen, 'Is Government the Source of Monopoly?' (Winter 1968–69) 5 *The Intercollegiate Review* 67. Royal grants were often decreed specifically to guilds, or craft companies, rather than to individuals; see JE Scott, 'Limitations of Gild Monopoly' (1917) 22(3) *The American Historical Review* 586.

were frowned upon by the courts, and often declared void under common law.[4] What is important to note, though, is that such restrictions served not only to limit trade, but also to facilitate prior cooperation that otherwise might not take place. Employers fearing that a current employee will become a future competitor would be hesitant to train him (historically it was usually him, rather than her), and especially fear entrusting him with trade secrets or specific knowledge central to the employers' comparative advantage in the local marketplace. Absent contractual protection, employers would thus likely keep proprietary knowledge to themselves, limiting both private and social benefits from division of labour and growth of business which depend (at least in part) on investment in workers' human capital.

Restraints of trade operated in contracts between actual and potential competitors as well. In such cases, parties' gain from restraining their freedom to trade as they please was the mutual commitment of their counterpart, allowing each a position of market power in the portion of the market allotted to him and with it the ability to increase price without fear of undercutting by competitors. Today, these restraints might be called 'plain-vanilla cartels' targeted for antitrust intervention. It is interesting to note, though, that in the early development of competition law, the method for analyzing such non-competition clauses was that of private law, focusing on the parties to a contract rather than 'the public'. The common denominator of such early judicial cases discussing such cases, was the *parties'* freedom to trade, rather than the interests of an outsider to the contract, or the resulting price. Such a clause could be found—based on specific facts to the case—to be oppressive in nature or essential to the business interaction (employment, joint venture, sale of business, etc). Thus, the courts in England distinguished between 'reasonable restraints' necessary for commerce and bad ones deemed oppressive. Analysis of the parties' interests, though, ignored social consequences and externalizations imposed on others beyond the contractual relations.

The *social* price that monopoly creates was recognized through the second strand of antitrust antecedents, the royal grant. As early as 1602, courts in England dealt with the issue of monopoly by grant, voiding a patent monopoly granted by the Queen as contradicting common law.[5] *Darcy v Allein*, though being often cited as antitrust's first, revolved mostly around constitutional issues and separation of powers in the parliamentary kingdom, as the same patent monopoly granted by the Queen and declared void by the court, was subsequently granted to a local

[4] See Letwin (n 3); E Gellhorn, WE Kovacic and S Calkins, *Antitrust Law and Economics in a Nutshell* 4th edn (St Paul, MN: West, 1994) ch 1. Common law is often relied on as a basis for modern antitrust jurisprudence as well, though with obvious changes over time. Indeed, the broad and ambiguous terms employed by the Sherman Act were argued to draw from terms at common law, and interpreted accordingly. See H Hovenkamp, *Federal Antitrust Policy: The Law of Competition and its Practice*, 2nd edn (St Paul, MN: West, 1999) 51. Senator Sherman himself, while proposing and explaining the Act to bear his name, said the law 'applied old and well recognized principles of the common law to the complicated jurisdiction of our State and Federal Government', 21 Cong Rec 2456 (1890).

[5] *Darcy v Allein* [1602] ER 77 KB 1260.

guild by Parliament.[6] Not a great victory for competition, though Parliament gained both stature and influence. The recognition that the general public was affected by restriction of trade, and that competition was both needing and deserving of protection, had to wait a while longer.

A. Early American Sentiment

The royal grant met its fiercest opposition in the American colonies, where markets were often monopolized by those granted royal favour at the expense of the 'little guy' prevented from trade and forced to purchase at monopoly prices. The issue became so central in colonial American political thought, that in 1641 the Massachusetts Body of Liberties stated unequivocally that 'no Monopolies shall be granted or allowed amongst us'. Similar effects created through different means were also central in American resistance to English rule, as in the case of the Navigation Acts enacted by the English Parliament. These forced colonial goods through English ports and vessels, creating a bottleneck monopoly and inducing open rebellion by American colonists who found themselves commercially constrained. The fact that these Acts were a part of an English power ploy in the context of international maritime trade produced a compound effect on the already discontented colonists, who found themselves limited commercially as well as marginalized politically.

Resistance to monopoly by royal grant was fierce in colonial America, as attested by the strong language in state declarations and constitutions. For example, the Maryland Constitution enacted in 1776 stated that 'monopolies are odious, contrary to the spirit of a free government and the principles of commerce'; the North Carolina Declaration of Rights stated that 'perpetuities and monopolies are contrary to the genius of a free State, and ought not to be allowed'; both the Virginia Declaration of Rights and the Massachusetts Constitution included identical language expounding the principle for such anti-monopoly sentiments: 'no man nor corporation or association of men have any other title to obtain advantages, or particular and exclusive privileges distinct from those of the community, than what rises from the consideration of services rendered to the public'.[7]

All in all, distaste for monopoly in early American political thought is clear and was sufficiently central to appear in the primary legal documents and political proclamations of the time.[8] It is important, though, to note what the term

[6] See Letwin (n 3) 367.

[7] See E Daniels, 'Reversing Course: American Attitudes about Monopolies, 1607–1890' in G Hull (ed), *The Abolition of Antitrust* (New Brunswick, NJ: Transaction, 2005).

[8] Eg, 'monopolies in trade [will be] granted to the favorites of government, by which the spirit of adventure will be destroyed, and the citizens subjected to the extortion of those companies who will have an exclusive right', 13 *Documentary History of the Ratification of the Constitution* 482 (as reported in DA Crane, *The Institutional Structure of Antitrust Enforcement* (Oxford: Oxford University Press, 2011) 7, fn 23.

'monopoly' meant at this time—the grant of exclusivity in trade to one person or group by Regal authority, usually in the interests of a political and economic elite (indeed, cementing these as one). This distaste for monopoly carried over into monopolies later created though associations of trade or wealth irrespective of royal (or even state) authority. However, as we shall see below, the rhetoric of economics displaced that of politics.

B. Shifting Focus: From Grants to Trusts

As time progressed, and the Industrial Revolution generated economies of scale at an ever-increasing rate, economic power began to be seen as real a problem as political power. Economies of scale, the increased efficiency garnered from increasing production or centralizing management, make larger enterprises more efficient and thus able to drive the smaller, less efficient ones, out of business. This may be due to lower costs leading to lower prices, ultimately beneficial to consumers. Alternatively, it may be due to large enterprises controlling essential inputs (including transportation or marketing avenues)—depriving competitors of a needed lifeline. Since real life is messy, it is reasonable to assume that most cases of economic concentration include a mixture of both efficient and inefficient mechanisms. Obviously, extreme cases lead to a monopoly which can afford to raise prices without excessively curbing residual demand—leading to high prices. The public hatred of monopolies, though, was not inhibited by fancy economic analysis pointing out the benefits of size. Louis Brandeis famously declared war on 'the Curse of Bigness', and public sentiment largely followed.[9] As commerce evolved and firms of increasing size became prominent, the populist view declared them large behemoths abusing their power and requiring state action to curb their appetite for profit.[10] Nowhere is this dynamic more apparent than in the classic trusts which gave the Sherman Act its public resonance—and antitrust law its name. The most famous example is Standard Oil, which began as an Ohio Corporation in the oil business and quickly saw economic benefit in increasing its purview to the railroads transporting its product, as well as to out-of-state refineries and oil companies.[11] In economic parlance—which later became standard antitrust terminology—Standard Oil expanded both vertically and horizontally: vertically towards businesses which previously supplied inputs or consumed Standard Oil products, and horizontally towards would-be competitors producing

[9] See LD Brandeis, *Other People's Money and How the Bankers Use It* (New York: Stokes, 1914) ch 8.

[10] See E Foner, *Give Me Liberty! An American History* (New York: WW Norton & Company, 2006) ch 17. Far from today's pejorative connotation, the 'populist' movement was legitimate and viable as a social movement, with leading politicians accepting the title as their own. The populist movement viewed not just big business as a social problem, but political cronyism as well, and especially the confluence of economic and political power.

[11] See R Chernow, *Titan: The Life of John D Rockefeller Sr* (New York: Random House, 1998) ch 6, 7.

similar products. Since the State of Ohio prohibited its companies from owning stock in out-of-state companies, a novel business arrangement was used, using the long-standing legal mechanism of the trust as a vehicle by which the shares of many companies could be controlled in unison by the trustees. Essentially, owners of large blocks of shares would entrust them to the central management of the trust, led by Rockefeller, in return for certificates granting them the right to share in the profit of common assets.

The legal trust created efficiencies as well as less legitimate profit opportunities. Economies of scale and benefits of central management achievable when 40 refineries were operated as one giant enterprise, were passed on in part to consumers enjoying lower prices as well as innovative products (eg, what is today known as 'Vaseline' started out as a synthetic petrochemical derivative competing with then popular beeswax). On the other hand, Standard Oil became known for aggressive moves against competitors, who often complained not just of being priced out of the market, but also of outright bullying.[12] The fact that the trust allowed for vertical expansion also became central, as railroads controlled by the trust (as well as other suppliers of transport services, wary of losing large contracts) were instructed to refuse passage to competitors of Standard Oil. In short, shrewd business combined with economic power created profitable opportunities for the trust's beneficiaries as well as hardship and frustration for those enjoined from competing effectively. The result was increasing public outcry, witnessed and fanned by stories such as Ida Tarbell's series of articles in *McClure's* magazine, which was later assembled as *The History of the Standard Oil Company*, published in 1904.

For those familiar with antitrust law, the Standard Oil name is invariably reminiscent of the 1911 Supreme Court case which required dissolution of the company into 34 separate companies with separate boards of directors (unwittingly increasing their aggregate share price and bestowing upon Rockefeller a windfall profit).[13] This case, which also set the stage for the Rule of Reason employed in most antitrust cases today, will feature in the discussion below. Beyond its legal significance, Standard Oil still looms large in the collective memory of what antitrust is essentially about. Most telling is Chief Justice White's remark within his *Standard Oil* opinion: 'It is remarkable that nowhere at common law can there be found a prohibition against the creation of monopoly by an individual'.[14]

[12] For a contemporary popular account, see Henry Demarest Lloyd, 'The Story of a Great Monopoly' (March, 1881) *The Atlantic Monthly*. On the other hand, see JS McGee, 'Predatory Price Cutting: The Standard Oil (NJ) Case' (1958) 1 *Journal of Law and Economics* 137, arguing that the record does not support the commonly-levelled charge of predatory pricing, and somewhat surprisingly, that such conduct would have *improved* aggregate welfare due to its economizing on the costs of monopolization that ultimately occurred, costs borne by consumers.

[13] See M Reksulak, WF Shughart, RD Tollison and A Basuchoudhary, 'Titan Agonistes: The Wealth Effects of the Standard Oil (NJ) Case' (2004) 21 *Research in Law and Economics* 63.

[14] *Standard Oil Co of NJ v United States*, 221 US 1, 55 (1911).

While originally monopoly was assumed to originate in royal decree alone, modern times have witnessed the expansion of this term to include various economic effects, even when created through (imperfect) market mechanisms. As a result, antitrust evolved to encompass various limitations on individuals' and firms' business behaviour, aimed at curtailing the type of economic power used to drive out competitors or harm consumers. In contrast to early times, antitrust law today is commonly assumed to protect primarily public interests rather than those of individual plaintiffs. '[L]egislative history illuminates congressional concern with the protection of competition, not competitors', Chief Justice Warren famously expounded. This focus on society's gain from competition will loom large in the discussion below.[15]

II. COMPETITION LAW IN EUROPE: BETWEEN NATIONAL AND COMMUNITY GOALS

European competition law is easier named than defined. Is it merely the 'law' in effect through European treaties or should we broaden our perspective to include national competition regimes within Europe as well? The multinational characteristic of present-day Europe does not allow for simple unambiguous statements as to common goals on which we may base our discussion. Thus, when speaking of European competition law, there is a need to include the different perspectives that helped form the 'law' enacted by the relevant treaties, and enforced by both EU and national institutions. In our context, a full comparative review is impossible, thus discussion is limited to some historical context which will help illuminate the difference between EU competition law and that of the US.

The first premonitions of competition law in Europe were parallel to those in the US during the 1890s.[16] The economic developments and growth of cartels in nineteenth-century Austria were the main reasons for a suggestion by Adol Menzel to legislate specific cartel regulation. His innovation, presented at the 1894 'Verein fur Sozialpolitik' conference, was not the fact of regulation itself, but his emphasis on utilizing administrative law, rather than the existing criminal provisions. Through this paradigmatic shift, implementation would be facilitated and economic experts would replace criminal judges so that the harms of price-raising cartels could be avoided while maintaining the social benefits (especially social and economic stability) that they were thought to bestow. Viewing international cartels as friend or foe depended mostly on the beholder, as they both fostered globalization and allowed for reducing volatility while, at the same time,

[15] *Brown Shoe Co, Inc v United States*, 370 US 294, 320 (1962).

[16] While a Bill was submitted to the Austrian legislature in 1897, other political issues prevented its enactment. See DJ Gerber, 'The Origins of the European Competition Law Tradition in *Fin-de-Siecle* Austria' (1992) 36 *American Journal of Legal History* 405.

created monopoly power with the accompanying increase in prices and reduction of output.[17]

In 1923, Germany became the first European country to enact a law designed specifically against cartels ('Regulation Against Abuse of Economic Power Positions') but political developments and lingering economic depression eliminated its effect during the 1930s.[18] This early experience, though, had an important effect on the intellectual development of economic and legal thought on the matter.

The notions of the 'correct' economic framework developed in Europe quite differently from the US. While in the US free trade and competition were considered integral parts of the democratic tradition, continental European thought has traditionally seen industrial policy, aka state intervention in economic matters, more favourably. The 1923 German legislation was important especially due to the wide and forceful debate that ensued. Proponents of cartel restrictions were much more interested in curbing inflation and maintaining economic stability than in idealizing competition itself. Cooperation among competitors was regarded more as a facilitator of economic growth, and even a tool of achieving public interest goals, than a threat to democracy or efficiency.

While the UK stands out for its different approach to competition, most of continental Europe not only allowed industry-wide cartels, but in some cases even mandated them.[19] The most extreme and well known example was, of course, the facilitation of national cartels in Nazi Germany. The Nazi government benefited from the cartels, since concentration lends itself to central planning, and the Nazi regime relied heavily on the manufacturing industry in its war effort, in organizing and exploiting the Jewish captive labour force, and in the genocide by mass extermination they sought to achieve. History sometimes reacts as a pendulum to dominant phenomena, and massive collusion has come to remind many of

[17] The 'cartels as stabilizers' paradigm increased in importance in the 1920s, following the Great War and its wake of unemployment, just as their internationalism lent credence to the claim that they serve to reduce strife between nations and prevent war. Viewing trade policy as war prevention is a distinctly European notion, distinguishing it from the efficiency-centric concept of competition in the US. For discussion and analysis in the context of emerging international competition standards, see DJ Gerber, *Global Competition: Law, Markets, and Globalization* (Oxford: Oxford University Press, 2010) 23–35.

[18] *Verordnung gegen Mißbrauch wirtschaftlicher Machtstellungen*, 1923 *Reichsgesetzblatt* RGBl. IS 1067 (2 November 1923). English version from R Liefmann, *Cartels, Concerns and Trusts*, trans DH MacGregor (London: Methuen, 1932) 351–57. An important aspect of the 'regulation' though, was its temporary and anti-inflationary intent, rather than a full pro-competition vision. The economic depression of 1929 weakened the fragile support that the regulation still had, and in 1930 it was amended to all but eliminate the Cartel Court's powers. See DJ Gerber, *Law and Competition in Twentieth Century Europe: Protecting Prometheus* (Oxford: Clarendon Press, 1998) 124–25; WC Kessler, 'German Cartel Regulation under the Decree of 1923' (1936) 50 *Quarterly Journal of Economics* 680.

[19] In the UK common law held contracts in restraint of trade void, see section I above. The first formal English legislation regarding competition policy was the Monopolies and Restrictive Practices (Inquiry and Control) Act 1948. See DM Raybould and A Firth, *Law of Monopolies: Competition Law and Practice in the USA, EEC, Germany and the UK* (London: Graham & Trotman, 1991) 431–37. For a juxtaposition of the British versus Continental approaches, see G Amato, *Antitrust and the Bounds of Power* (Oxford: Hart Publishing, 1997) 40.

the horrors it made possible.[20] Economic concentration in Axis countries before the war was considerable, and arguably played a large part in pushing towards militaristic policies. In Japan, much of the economy was controlled by *Zaibatsu*, large business groups consisting each of a bank supporting a major industrial firm, together with its network of suppliers. The quest for raw materials for industrial concerns was part of the incentive for war and conquest, as Japanese firms required more than their island could provide. Indeed, one of the main concerns of Allied forces after the war was to enact a competition law, one which was forced on Japan by American occupiers, who also mandated its retention after the occupation ended.[21]

Post-war Europe saw a strong return to the debate over competition laws, with then recent history providing a strong emotional argument towards curbing cartels and privately-held economic power in general. Many European countries introduced competition laws in one form or another, due to internal and external pressures prevalent at the time.[22] Internally, competition was seen as a stimulus to economic development, while externally, the US was prominent with its strong free-market rhetoric and fear of industrial concentration of the sort that facilitated the Nazi war effort. Of course, self-seeking objectives for American concerns were also present, namely the knowledge that for American firms to successfully enter the European markets, the local cartels' power must be curbed.

The theme of administrative control, stemming from early Austrian debate and the subsequent pre-war German law, was widely accepted in Europe as the right balance between the need for intervention and the desire for economic growth. Competition relevant statutes were generally broad in scope, allowing for discretion in their application, and granting the relevant bureaucracies strong negotiation powers with suspect businesses, so that informal 'consent decrees' may be achieved.[23]

[20] See, eg, R Pitofski, 'The Political Content of Antitrust' (1979) 127 *University of Pennsylvania Law Review* 1051, 1055; LB Schwartz, 'Justice and other Non-Economic Goals of Antitrust' (1979) 127 *University of Pennsylvania Law Review* 1076, 1078.

[21] See Gerber, *Global Competition* (n 17) 211–13, as well as T Freyer, *Antitrust and Global Capitalism, 1930–2004* (New York: Cambridge University Press, 2006) 160–83. Interestingly, Gerber and Freyer diverge as to their assessment of the Japanese response to American influence in early competition policy, with Gerber stressing the intra-Japanese pendulum effect and resistance to foreign imposition, while Freyer presents a more nuanced version distinguishing between different Japanese schools of thought.

[22] See SA Riesenfeld, 'The Protection of Competition' in E Stein and T Nicholson (eds), *American Enterprise in the European Common Market: A Legal Profile*, vol 2 (Ann Arbor, MI: University of Michigan Press, 1960); HB Thorelli, 'Antitrust in Europe: National Policies after 1945' (1959) 29 *University of Chicago Law Review* 222.

[23] Thus, the European approach is sometimes categorized as more context-specific than the American, which focuses more on outright prohibition of suspect practices. See WPJ Wils, *Efficiency and Justice in European Antitrust Enforcement* (Oxford: Hart Publishing, 2008) ch 6, as well as Gerber, *Law and Competition in Twentieth Century Europe* (n 18) 164, 174–76. Such characterization may be over-reaching. While it is true that the American 'per se' approach is less flexible and thus does not directly distinguish between beneficial and detrimental practices, it does allow for administrative discretion in filing suits, and in forming consent decrees. Thus, 'per se' rules may sometimes be seen as

The main influence on post-war competition doctrine is usually ascribed to the German Freiburg school. There, during the Nazi regime, a group of economists and lawyers developed a strong critique of market consolidation, and laid the foundations for competitive reform. Understandably, their work was carried out in secrecy for fear of reprisals as 'enemies of the state' (or at least of its chosen representatives at the time). This doctrine was labelled 'Ordoliberal', as it stressed the liberal nature of rights and freedoms, and sought a state-enforced order that would secure those rights.[24] Competition policy was thus aiming at 'the protection of individual economic freedom of action as a value in itself, or vice versa, the restraint of undue economic power'.[25] Public interests, previously considered the raison d'etre for state intervention in the economy, were argued by the Freiburg school to be reflected in individuals' interests and thus competition assured the simultaneous attainment of both state and personal goals.[26]

The Freiburg school attained outside recognition and influence when the Second World War ended and occupied Germany underwent economic reform. The American influence felt so strongly at the time exerted its influence on approaches to competition, but no less important was the fact that the work done by the Freiburg school was ready 'in the right place and at the right time'. Franz Bohm, one of the prominent members of the Freiburg school, went on to become an MP and presented the initial Bill to the Bundestag.[27]

The Freiburg school, while influential in Germany and of scholarly importance, did not bring about similar change in other European countries. Within each country, local and nationalistic aims took precedent, and competition law was sometimes seen as interfering with national firms' ability to compete internationally, or, on the other hand, impeding the state-influenced economy

'exit options' granting the enforcement agency a strong bargaining position so that the relevant firm may be coerced into amending rather than abandoning its practices. Furthermore, 'per se' rules are subject to ongoing interpretation, limiting their application and occasionally refuting their essence.

[24] See DJ Gerber, 'Constitutionalizing the Economy: German Neo-Liberalism, Competition Law and the "New" Europe' (1994) 42 *American Journal of Comparative Law* 25. See also G Schnyder and MM Siems, 'The Ordoliberal Variety of Neoliberalism' in SJ Konzelmann and M Fovargue-Davies (eds), *Banking Systems in the Crisis: The Faces of Liberal Capitalism* (London: Routledge, 2012) for analysis of Ordoliberalism as distinct in its stress on state intervention to secure and protect the system by which liberal values can be sustained.

[25] W Moschel, 'Competition Policy from an Ordo Point of View' in A Peacock and H Willgerodt (eds), *German Neo-Liberals and the Social Market Economy* (Oxford: Oxford University Press, 1998).

[26] See ME Streit, 'Economic Order, Private law and Public Policy: The Freiburg school of Law and Economics in Perspective' (1992) 148 *Journal of Institutional and Theoretical Economics* 675; M Wohlgemuth, 'A European Social Model of State-Market Relations: The Ethics of Competition from a Neo-Liberal Perspective' (2008) 9 *Journal for Business, Economics, and Ethics* 69. See also FA von Hayek, *Individualism and Economic Order* (Chicago, IL: University of Chicago Press, 1948) 77–78, stressing only individual knowledge contains preferences to be satisfied, as well as his 'The Use of Knowledge in Society' (1945) 35 *American Economic Review* 519, explaining competitive price mechanism as the ultimate tool for optimal social allocation, based on flow of information and comparative advantage in its use.

[27] Indeed, in 1957, Germany was the first Continental European country to adopt an antitrust law. See Amato (n 19) 42, as well as Raybould and Firth (n 19) 382–83.

deemed appropriate. It was not until 1957 when the European Common Market was formed, that questions of competition penetrated into most countries.[28] Even today, there are continuing debates regarding the proper balance between non-intervention and other more centralist approaches, seeking to achieve goals beyond competition per se.[29]

A. The Dual Goals of European Competition Law

The Treaty of Rome formed the European Economic Community in 1957, and dealt for the first time with competition law from a pan-European perspective. Its main focus was that of interstate commerce, not unlike the Federalist emphasis in the US Constitution. Competition law in Europe thus poses limitations not only on businesses, but on Member States as well, especially as to their ability to support national organizations and industries to the detriment of other community interests. Since some of the Member States had their own competition laws at this point (and others would enact them later), the interaction between national and pan-European approaches to competition is central to understanding EU competition doctrine. In the words of the Court of Justice:

> [T]he states have acknowledged that Community law has an authority which can be invoked by their nationals before their courts and tribunals. The conclusion to be drawn from this is that the Community constitutes a new legal order of international law for the benefit of which the states have limited their sovereign rights.[30]

The Commission's unilateral power to apply EU competition law is quite extraordinary within EU jurisprudence where, on most occasions, Member States are entrusted with the application and enforcement of community law through their own national authorities.[31] Perhaps it is the nature of competition law,

[28] Germany, France, Holland and Belgium were among the first countries in Europe to adopt competition laws, with Luxembourg, Ireland, Greece and Portugal following suit during the 1970s and 1980s. The Rome Treaty demanded serious changes in some of the countries' competition laws, and the continuing trend towards integration caused a wave of reform to sweep through the Member States during the early 1990s.

[29] See ME Streit and W Mussler, 'The Economic Constitution of the European Community: From "Rome" to "Maastricht"' (1995) 1 *European Law Journal* 5. The use of competition policy to pursue political and economic goals of market integration continued to trouble the Ordoliberals; see W Sauter, *Competition Law and Industrial Policy in the EU* (Oxford: Clarendon Press, 1997) 34–39. Some see the tendency toward a centralist industrial policy rather than a competitive economic framework an unwelcome diversion from the economic goals of the Rome Treaty. See W Molle, *The Economics of European Integration: Theory, Practice, Policy* (Aldershot: Dartmouth Publishing, 1990) 11.

[30] Case 26/62, *Van Gend & Loos* [1963] CMLR 129, 130.

[31] Regulation 1/2003 emphasized this pan-European aspect of competition law, empowering National Competition Authorities to enforce EU law, as well as share information among NCAs and the Commission. This latter aspect is central in facilitating cross-border investigations and regulating international businesses, but is problematic procedurally, as countries differ with respect to investigative powers and the regulation of search and seizure. For discussion of these issues, see Gerber, *Global Competition* (n 17) 200–02, and Wils (n 23).

drastically affecting other economic factors and interests, which accounts for this unique structure. Since states have interests in industrial policy, which affects the fabric of social life and national goals, it is perhaps understandable that a non-partisan institution was needed to surpass local concerns if a community-wide policy was to be successful. Still, it would be overly optimistic to conclude that the clash between local and community goals has no detrimental effect on local enforcement.[32]

Even focusing on the pan-European perspective, EU competition law is not perfectly compatible with that of the US. While the general goals of efficiency and fairness described above are equally pertinent to Europe, their relative weights differ considerably due to the special emphasis on 'community' goals.[33] Such goals include facilitating economic integration with special regard to intra-European interstate commerce and the Member States' national policies towards aiding their local enterprises relative to outside competitors (especially as to 'national champions').[34] Competition policy has thus been largely regarded by many as subrogated to integration objectives,[35] and even those regarding competition as an independent aim often pay lip service to the integration issue as well.[36] Of course, this goes against the grain of Ordoliberal views described above and is thus subject to much debate. Given that political necessity dictates much of legal

[32] The uncertainty critique is set out in I Forrester, 'Modernization of EC Competition Law' (2000) 23 *Fordham International Law Journal* 1028. Others argue that national agencies will be more adept than the courts at discriminating between different economic factors and appropriate policies. See CD Ehlermann, 'Implementation of EC Competition Law by National Anti-trust Authorities' (1996) 17 *European Competition Law Review* 88. The issue was addressed in Council Regulation (EC) No 1/2003 (16 December 2002), on the Implementation of the Rules on Competition Laid Down in Articles 81 and 82 of the Treaty, [2003] OJ L1/1, which has decentralized much of the decision-making process in EU competition policy.

[33] See I Lianos, 'Some Reflections on the Question of the Goals of EU Competition Law' (2013) CLES Working Paper Series 3/2013; RJ Van Den Bergh and PD Camesasca, *European Competition Law and Economics: A Comparative Perspective* (Antwerp: Intersentia, 2001); L Parret, 'The Multiple Personalities of EU Competition Law: Time for a Comprehensive Debate on its Objectives' in D Zimmer (ed), *The Goals of Competition Law* (Cheltenham: Edward Elgar, 2012).

[34] See D Hay, 'The Assessment: Competition Policy' (1993) 9 *Oxford Review of Economic Policy* 1; Sauter (n 29) 119–22 and references therein. But see W Kerber, 'Should Competition Law Promote Efficiency? Some Reflections of an Economist on the Normative Foundations of Competition Law' in J Drexl et al (eds), *Economic Theory and Competition Law* (Cheltenham: Edward Elgar, 2009), regarding the difficulty of promoting non-economic goals within antitrust, including European integration.

[35] H Von der Groeben, *The European Community: The Formative Years. The Struggle to Establish the Common Market and the Political Union (1958–1966)* (Luxembourg: Office for Official Publications of the European Communities, 1985) 60. Others see these aims as complementary: see P Pescatore, 'Public and Private Aspects of European Competition Law' (1987) 10 *Fordham International Law Journal* 373; B Van der Esch, 'EEC Competition Rules: Basic Principles and Policy Aims' (1980) 7 *Legal Issues of European Integration* 75; J-F Verstrynge, 'Current Antitrust Policy Issues in the EEC: Some Reflections on the Second Generation of Competition Policy' in BE Hawk (ed), *Annual Proceedings of the Fordham Corporate Law Institute 1984: Antitrust and Trade Policies in International Trade* (New York: Matthew Bender, 1985).

[36] Eg, while assessing the success of European competition policy, with special emphasis on efficiency and maintaining fair business practices, the introduction to the official report stated that 'competition policy is one of the fundamental means for preserving the unity of the market', EC Commission, *Sixth Report on Competition Policy: 1976* (Brussels, 1977) 9.

implementation the world over, EU competition law is no exception.[37] As starkly stated by Giorgio Monti: 'Since the birth of the Community, competition policy has been used as a mechanism for integrating the EC market'.[38] Though he goes on to list specific measures used to abolish protectionist measures employed by the Member States, the complexity of a competition policy aimed at integration, together with economic freedom *and* the attainment of efficiency, is striking. While the EU is a clear example of multiple goals simultaneously guiding competition policy, we shall see below that a truly unitary competition policy is easier stated than achieved.

III. INTRODUCING THE GOALS OF ANTITRUST: FAIRNESS, EFFICIENCY AND BEYOND

The goals of antitrust are often stated, and even more often presumed, but rarely used as deciding factors in real-world implementation. Many have written on the subject and especially on the shift from early-day normative deliberation towards the modern-day focus on economic efficiency, with a common assumption being that both strands suggest similar policies.[39] Even a whole book would be too limited a

[37] Of course there are those who consider the European Treaty to be a uniquely appropriate economic constitution, dealing well with the complexity of relevant parameters. See CD Ehlermann, 'The Contribution of EC Competition Policy to the Single Market' (1992) 29 *Common Market Law Review* 257.

[38] G Monti, *EC Competition Law* (Cambridge: Cambridge University Press, 2007) 39.

[39] Arguments regarding the Sherman Act abounded since the Act's inception; see JH Benton, 'The Sherman or Anti-trust Act' (1909) 18(5) *Yale Law Journal* 311. Debates regarding its goals persisted over time, leading to numerous symposia and public discourses; see, eg, RH Bork and WS Bowman, 'Goals of Antitrust: A Dialogue on Policy' (1965) 65(3) *Columbia Law Review* 363; JJ Flynn, 'Antitrust Jurisprudence: A Symposium On the Economic, Political and Social Goals of Antitrust Policy' (1976–77) 125 *University of Pennsylvania Law Review* 1182. These later distilled into 'schools of thought' associated with different universities such as Chicago, Harvard and Virginia as leading contenders. For an interesting review of the scene over time, see a series of Herbert Hovenkamp's writings: 'Distributive Justice and the Antitrust Laws' (1982) *51 George Washington Law Review* 1; 'Antitrust Policy after Chicago' (1985) 84 *Michigan Law Review* 213; *The Antitrust Enterprise: Principle and Execution* (Harvard: Harvard University Press, 2005). For a more varied and recent critique, see R Pitofsky (ed), *How the Chicago School Overshot the Mark: The Effect of Conservative Economic Analysis on US Antitrust* (Oxford: Oxford University Press, 2008) which discusses the predominant focus on economic effects and price-theory analysis. Arguments against economic efficiency as the primary goal of antitrust are laid out in EJ Hughes, 'The Left Side of Antitrust: What Fairness Means and Why it Matters' (1994) 77 *Marquette Law Review* 265. The classic argument that Congress intended antitrust as a consumer protection measure rather than maximizing aggregate efficiency is laid out in RH Lande, 'Wealth Transfers as the Original and Primary Concern of Antitrust: The Efficiency Interpretation Challenged' (1982) 34 *Hastings Law Journal* 65. Other notable contributions to historical analysis are RJ Peritz, 'A Counter-History of Antitrust Law' (1990) *Duke Law Journal* 263, as well as his book, *Competition Policy in America: History, Rhetoric, Law*, rev edn (New York: Oxford University Press, 1996); see also AJ Meese, 'Liberty and Antitrust in the Formative Era' (1999) 79 *Boston University Law Review* 1. A review of the competing historical and normative claims can be found in W Page, 'Ideological Conflict and the Origins of Antitrust Policy' (1991) 66 *Tulane Law Review* 1. Maurice Stucke, in 'Reconsidering Antitrust's Goals' (2012) 53 *Boston College Law Review* 551, recently argued that economic efficiency was never successful as a unifying goal for antitrust. Instead, he suggests a

venue for full review, thus I refer the interested reader to the many good works cited in the footnotes. My aim here is to delineate antitrust goals pertaining to aggregate societal concerns from those pertaining to fairness—a distinction following chapters will rely on. Chapter two will then introduce societal goals in more detail, while chapters three and four will delve into the meaning of fairness in antitrust, and why current treatment thereof suffers from a bias that must be corrected.

Antitrust is often said to serve several goals simultaneously, and though some dwell on the different sources of these goals and their relative importance, most assume they do not contradict each other in either theory or practice, thus avoiding a need to select between them. Present antitrust scholarship stresses economic efficiency, which reflects aggregate welfare for society at large. Some scholars go as far as arguing that this is (or should be) the *sole* goal of antitrust, while others focus not on aggregate measures, but on distinct groups which may be harmed by monopoly in a way requiring intervention by the state.[40] Protection of consumers is often cited, protection of competitors less so (though this used to be an accepted goal as well), with workers and local communities being mentioned in passing, but rarely central in application.

As shall be argued in chapter two, aggregate concerns go beyond economics, as social *processes* are often no less important than their end results. Protection of democracy comes to mind (as monopoly is thought to create concentrations of power threatening the state's sovereignty), as does the Jeffersonian ideal of facilitating a society of independent entrepreneurs, rather than allowing economic agglomeration in which large firms employ many workers who labour under centrally controlled management. Protection of competition itself, as an independent goal reflecting the importance granted to this economic process, is often used as a place holder for a variety of interests. These include innovation, market dynamics inducing economic growth and even the social ideal of a free marketplace in which each can earn his own and vie for a bigger slice of the pie.[41] While competition may be seen as a separate and independent goal of antitrust, it is often used as a proxy—beneficial due to its results rather than its inherent worth. Even when focused on economic effects, modern-day antitrust litigation is often portrayed as 'good versus evil', with monopolistic power and practices being the obvious culprits.[42] How appropriate this truly is, and how much such value judgements can be independently substantiated, is the subject of our investigation below.

non-unitary 'blended' approach provides a better policy tool as well as more accurately defining what society 'wants' from its antitrust endeavour, though this is far from uniformly accepted. For a compilation of recent debates on the subject, see Symposium (2013) 81 *Fordham Law Review*.

[40] Indeed, some declare the question moot and consensus achieved. See, eg, SL Dogan and MA Lemley, 'Antitrust Law and Regulatory Gaming' (2008) 87 *Texas Law Review* 685: 'The law and the scholarship have converged with respect to both the proper goals of Antitrust and the general rules that will achieve those goals'.

[41] GJ Sidak and DJ Teece, 'Dynamic Competition in Antitrust Law' (2009) 5 *Journal of Competition Law and Economics* 581.

[42] See, eg, Crane, *The Institutional Structure of Antitrust Enforcement* (n 8) 100.

Broadly speaking, we may divide the goals antitrust law is said to serve into two general categories: the protection of individuals and firms harmed by suspect business practices, and the enhancement of total societal welfare (however that may be measured). The first focuses on individuals: the state protecting some from the power of others, thus invoking 'fairness' considerations. The second focuses on aggregate concerns thought to be of interest to all community members alike. This category is easiest exemplified by 'efficiency', but aggregate concerns go further. Economic efficiency is aggregate in nature since each individual's utility is measured and taken into consideration (or rather, approximated, as we are far from being able to truly measure all relevant parameters). But beyond efficiency, other societal goals exist as well. For instance, the view that antitrust law is important in order to counteract tendencies towards concentration of economic power focuses on aggregate society-wide concerns, though political–democratic concerns are emphasized rather than economic ones. Similarly, the Jeffersonian ideal that society is improved when commerce involves mainly small businessmen and entrepreneurs and extols antitrust as a force against the ever-increasing role of large firms in the modern economy.[43] Also, the view that competition generates more innovation or social mobility when guarded by a fierce antitrust policy stems from a concern with the type of society we want to live in, rather than the benefit of any specific group harmed by monopoly, or even the aggregate wealth created in such an economy.

Antitrust law varies across both nations and time, thus no one ideology may be said to pertain to all enacted regimes. Widespread agreement does exist regarding the most common aims of antitrust (if not their relative importance). A common ground can thus be stated, with differences between regimes discussed thereafter. While the focus will be on American and European conceptions of antitrust, commonalities across jurisdictions regarding goals outweigh differences by far, and most of what follows is applicable to almost all discussions of antitrust worldwide.[44] Different regimes enact antitrust laws for different reasons, each applying their own reasoning and implementation, but almost all relate to the general terms of protecting consumer welfare and enhancing competition (even if the meaning ascribed to these general terms varies). As we shall see shortly,

[43] Justice Peckham famously remarked: 'It is not for the real prosperity of any country that such changes should occur which result in transferring an independent business man, the head of his establishment, small though it might be, into a mere servant or agent of a corporation … having no voice in shaping the business policy of the company and bound to obey orders issued by others'; see *US v Trans-Missouri Freight Association*, 166 US 290, 322–23 (1897). These words resonate with Learned Hand's ideological statement that antitrust aims to 'perpetuate and preserve, *for its own sake and in spite of possible cost*, an organization of industry in small units which can effectively compete with each other' (emphasis added), *US v Aluminum Co of America (ALCOA)*, 148 F 2d 416, 425 (CCA 2d, 1945). Of course, these sentiments do not guide current antitrust policy, nor do they fit well with current admonitions that aggregate economic efficiency is the key goal of antitrust.

[44] See, generally, RA Epstein and MS Greve (eds), *Competition Laws in Conflict: Antitrust Jurisdiction in the Global Economy* (Washington DC: AEI Press, 2004), as well as the ICN Report on the Objectives of the Unilateral Conduct Laws at: www.internationalcompetitionnetwork.org/uploads/library/doc353.pdf.

more specific political and social goals have been suggested as well, creating some dispute among antitrust adherents. Most disagreements remain in the realm of theory, as often the same policies can be justified in different ways, yet implementation may be affected as well. This book aims to assess these differences by exploring the first principles underlying them, hopefully flushing out hidden assumptions and potential inconsistencies.

Modern antitrust law is a worldwide phenomenon, and multinational corporations, as well as national ones marketing or producing internationally, created a necessity of cooperation between antitrust agencies worldwide. The result is a drive towards 'harmonization' of antitrust law to facilitate enforcement as well as create a common basis upon which firms can effectively plan their international operations.[45] The international harmonization movement is mostly led by the US and European Union, competing for dominance in shaping smaller countries' antitrust policy in their own form and flavour. International organizations, such as the ICN (International Competition Network), and the OECD (Organization of Economically Developed Countries) play a role as well, both as fields where the US and EU interact and as independent actors with a stake in the game.

While implementation and practical significance are important, the discussion below begins with the normative, assessing what is morally right rather than describing current law or policies. After investigating philosophy we can turn to politics, and after understanding the intellectual basis of antitrust, implementation of its principles in the real world may be better understood.

Beyond economic efficiency, as the main (but not only) societal goal competition is said to serve, different classes of individuals are argued to deserve special protection due to their specific vulnerability. Such protection, if granted, is distributional in nature, ie, may not affect (or sometime even adversely affect) the aggregate benefits society enjoys, focusing instead on the distribution of such benefits among different parties within society. It is here that fairness analysis is most potent, focusing on rights of individuals and their claim to state protection for their own sake, rather than as a by-product of societal wealth. Consumers are the most prominent such party in antitrust analysis, partly because of the 'obviousness' of a society committed to democracy protecting everyone—as everyone consumes. Nonetheless, it is important to maintain a distinction between aggregate concerns of 'everyone', and a focus on consumer versus producers which includes a distributional bent. Sometimes this is referred to as the debate between 'consumer welfare' and 'total welfare', though as we shall see, the ambiguity of terms leads to many misunderstandings and arguments over legislative purpose.[46] Below we shall see that even the focus on total welfare does not absolve

[45] See SW Waller, 'The Internationalization of Antitrust Enforcement' (1997) 77 *Boston University Law Review* 343, though see DP Wood, 'International Harmonization of Antitrust Law: The Tortoise or the Hare?' (2002) 3 *Chicago Journal of International Law* 39, for a more reserved view.

[46] Some go as far as to state: 'Consumer welfare is the most abused term in modern antitrust analysis'; see JF Brodley, 'The Economic Goals of Antitrust: Efficiency, Consumer Welfare, and Technological Progress' (1987) 62 *New York University Law Review* 1020, 1032.

the antitrust scholar from distributional issues, and even a focus on aggregate efficiency may mask underlying biases in favour of some members of society and against others.

In order to avoid confusion and keep the distinction stark, I distinguish between two classes of goals. The first is 'societal goals' where the relevant parameters are those of *aggregate* utility of society at large, in some cases measured by monetary gains (encompassed in the 'efficiency' rhetoric in antitrust) and in other cases referring to different classes of 'social goods' to be enumerated and assessed below. The second class of goals includes 'fairness goals'. These goals share the characteristic of considering one class of individuals as competing with another, and antitrust law as determining the extent of the protection granted to each.[47] Since monopoly's victims are assumed to be economically weak when compared with powerful monopolies, the state intervenes on their behalf. Later chapters will explore both assumptions: whether monopoly's victims are truly weak, and whether state intervention on their behalf is justified. As we shall see below, both are debatable, and even where relative strength is far from equal, state intervention is not automatically warranted.

Beginning with the judicial review of contracts restraining trade, antitrust law took as its aim to protect the weak against the strong, lest the marketplace allow de facto servitude that the state sought to abolish. While all antitrust regimes are routinely justified both on the basis of efficiency considerations and on those of fairness, different scholars place different emphases on the two archetypes. Since in many cases arguments of the two types lead to concurring results, it is not uncommon for them to be stated together, indeed sometimes intertwined.[48] This tendency of praising antitrust as simultaneously fair and efficient is so entrenched in popular and academic discourse that cases where the two types of goals conflict often escape review. The discussion below will maintain the distinction as strictly as possible, both since different forms of arguments are appropriate for each, and since it is precisely those cases where fairness and efficiency collide which pose practical and philosophical challenges. In short, I propose to repudiate Herbert Hovenkamp's claim that 'antitrust is an economic, not a moral, enterprise'.[49]

[47] Protection of consumers on fairness grounds must be kept distinct from the economic term 'consumer welfare'. Consumer welfare is sometimes used to denote all benefits created from trade, thus enlarging it is akin to promoting aggregate efficiency, which can sometimes be achieved *at the expense* of an individual consumer (or class thereof). The economic term denoting the welfare of consumers as a whole, is 'consumer surplus'. The distinction between consumer surplus and total welfare is the subject of many scholarly debates, mostly due to Robert Bork's ambiguous use of the term 'consumer welfare' in his famous book, *The Antitrust Paradox: A Policy at War with Itself* (New York: Basic Books, 1978). Recent writings have focused on this issue, eg, S Salop, 'Question: What is the Real and Proper Antitrust Welfare Standard? Answer: The *True* Consumer Welfare Standard' (2009) 22 *Loyola Consumer Law Review* 336 and many others cited below. What constitutes the *true* standard, rather than 'other' consumer welfare standards is precisely the issue addressed. In order to avoid the ambiguity associated with different meanings ascribed to the same term, I shall avoid it altogether.

[48] See, eg, Lande (n 39); Peritz (n 39). See also Meese (n 39), offering such an interpretation of case law in the early days of American antitrust.

[49] Hovenkamp, *The Antitrust Enterprise* (n 39) 10.

I shall argue that the public support of antitrust and the broad consensus it enjoys, relies mainly on moral grounds—that competition is 'right' rather than merely beneficial. The distinction between aggregate utility and fairness will allow both for clarifying the moral justifications underlying antitrust, and their limitations—showing where current policy oversteps its appropriate boundaries. What these boundaries are, and from whence they are derived, is the subject of our investigation below.

IV. TERMINOLOGY AND FOCUS: WHAT IS MEANT BY 'MONOPOLIST' AND WHICH RIGHTS ARE ASSESSED?

Since the purpose of this book is to critically assess the philosophical basis underlying antitrust law's basic tenets and especially current implementation, I begin by lumping together true monopolists, oligopolists and even members of actual or potential cartels. The term 'monopolist' is used broadly below, referring not only to a single seller of a distinct good, but to all holders of market power, or those who would use means scrutinized by antitrust law to achieve or maintain market power. Those limited by antitrust law are (for most purposes) united in arguing that they deserve more consideration than currently afforded them, thus I bracket them as 'monopolists' unless context requires differentiation.

A 'monopolist' might be Rockefeller and his Standard Oil empire, or the firm holding a valuable input without which others may not enter the market, or a group of individuals seeking to cooperate in order to achieve monopoly. Since the focus of this book is on the rights of parties to the antitrust debate, I do not begin with a prejudice against monopoly as such, or an automatic assumption that cartels are evil. Monopolists of all sorts (including those hoping for yet unachieved monopoly status) will receive similar attention to that afforded their victims, reserving moral judgement until analysis is complete. Distinctions between different types of monopoly and different types of antitrust offenders will similarly wait their turn, until after discussion of the main arguments relevant to them all. My choice of terms is not coincidental. The term 'monopoly' carries with it a negative connotation and is difficult to defend and precisely for this reason I choose to engage it. If monopolists as such have a viable claim for consideration, the lighter shades of anticompetitive conduct may rely on the general defence afforded the most extreme example and perhaps add more of their own later on. In other words, I hope to challenge antitrust at its core, rather than chip away at outer fringes. After the main task is clear, I shall delve into distinctions between different cases and difficulties of implementation.

The legal treatment of competition is both a highly technical endeavour based on economic modelling and legal distinctions, and a public interest legal arena where offenders are criminally charged as well as often publicly disparaged. The Standard Oil case referred to above is a telling example. Rockefeller was considered by many to be paradigmatic of the 'robber barons' associated with accumulating enormous wealth and power through business combinations covering multiple industries, and the type of economic power he possessed was central in achieving the broad public support antitrust enjoyed. The fact that his influence spread over multiple industries as well as political and financial institutions served to cement in public opinion the need for government intervention. Antitrust enforcement was thus deemed necessary not merely (or even mainly) for the attainment of economic efficiency, but for the protection of democracy and the 'little guy' steamrollered by powerful firms.[50] Competition, thus, was seen as a democratic process rather than merely an efficient one.

Most telling in this regard is a famous caricature published in 1904 depicting the reach and influence of Rockerfeller's Standard Oil empire. The octopus' tentacles reach (and strangle!) political and industrial powers, symbolizing contemporary fears of economic power and political influence.[51]

[50] Some describe the entire populist and progressive movements as a counter-movement to misuse of power, both economic and political: 'The traditional progressive agenda of the late 19th and early 20th centuries was in large part a response to the cronyism and corruption of state legislatures and Congress. These deliberative bodies were dominated by representatives beholden to the trusts, corporations, and robber barons, but the government bureaucracies were even worse', SL Arxer, M Babcock and W Borges, 'Progressivism and Economics' in L Finley and L Esposito (eds), *Grading the 44th President: A Report Card on Barack Obama's First Term as a Progressive Leader* (Santa Barbara, CA: Praeger, 2012). This view relies on an assumption that material success owes more to societal infrastructure than individual merit, an assumption that we shall return to below.

[51] Published in *Puck magazine* (7 September 1904). Octopi have been a common metaphor in monopoly-related journalism, probably due to fears of far-reaching economic power and political clout held by powerful firms. See for contemporary application, eg, D Gilson, 'Octopi Wall Street' (6 October 2011) *Mother Jones*: www.motherjones.com/mixed-media/2011/10/occupy-wall-street-octopus-vampire-squid.

As I shall show below, the public support that legal protection of competition enjoys stems from this view of the monopolist as a danger to society at large, and those daring to challenge its business dealings in particular. Exploitation of monopoly power is targeted as a criminal endeavour, demonstrating its centrality not merely as economic policy, but as morally repugnant and contrary to the underlying social contract on which modern democracies rely.[52] It is this aspect—of the implicit assumption of unfairness and normative repugnancy—that I focus on here.

The fact that competition law stems from moral and democratic (rather than merely economic) principles, shall be central in the analysis below, with my aim being the differentiation between those cases where such moral indignation is appropriate from those where the same legal principles apply but their ideological underpinnings differ. Competition law is enforced today by the state both criminally and administratively, but also by private actors relying on the same rules.[53] Such private enforcement is obviously beneficial as a facilitator of deterrence, but may also be misused by firms hoping to stymie competition.[54] Beyond the potential for misuse of public proceedings competition law shares with other legal arenas, a context-specific problem is at work—that the rules of competition law were determined with the paradigmatic monopolist in mind, leading not only to misapplication in select cases, but to inappropriateness on a normative level when the monopoly in question is of a different sort. By initially focusing on 'monopolists', we shall delve below into the implicit assumptions guiding competition law insofar as these affect intuitive moral judgments guiding antitrust implementation. Assessing these will be the focus of the fairness analysis in chapters three and four.

A central example to be developed below is the current focus on narrow market definition that characterizes current enforcement. This type of micro-market focus, coupled with technical economic analysis and implicit assumptions that all 'monopoly' should be treated equally, create problems that are more readily addressed once context is taken into account. The breadth covered by the ubiquitous term 'monopolist' can and should be differentiated into cases of differing extremity, precisely the aim of this book. We shall thus begin with broad generalizations as to what a 'monopolist' is, in order to more narrowly define it according to context in chapter four, and apply an appropriate balancing test in chapter seven. Both public and private enforcement will then be addressed and subjected

[52] Of course, the content of such 'exploitation' differs among jurisdictions, most famously between the American version of 'monopolization' and the European term 'abuse of monopoly power'. Both versions, though, share a common implicit assumption that the forbidden conduct is unfair and violates their victims' *rights*, the subject of our normative analysis below.

[53] Private enforcement can far outweigh public as a factual matter, on a scale of 10 to 1, or perhaps even 20 to 1 in the US. See Hovenkamp, *The Antitrust Enterprise* (n 39) and Crane, *The Institutional Structure of Antitrust Enforcement* (n 8).

[54] See, eg, WJ Baumol and JA Ordover, 'The Use of Antitrust to Subvert Competition' (1985) 28 *Journal of Law and Economics* 247; DD Sokol, 'The Strategic Use of Public and Private Litigation in Antitrust as Business Strategy' (2012) 85 *Southern California Law Review*; DA Crane, 'Optimizing Private Antitrust Enforcement' (2010) 63 *Vanderbilt Law Review*. 675.

to the test defined, allowing for context-specific implementation lacking in today's practice. It should be stressed that when public agencies of the state enforce competition rules, they benefit from discretion as to application, thus the problem of overly broad rules is alleviated. When private enforcement is based on the same rules, such discretion is absent, as only the economic incentives of the parties to litigation determine legal application. This distinction between private and public enforcement will be revisited after developing the normative arguments behind the proposed balancing test. One might expect that private enforcement will thus be subject to more narrowly construed rules than those applied by public state agencies, though this is but one of the distinctions assessed below.

Later on in the book, I make extensive use of the rights to property and freedom of contract, leading up to the necessity of balancing the rights claimed by different parties. Both property and contract are initially used as broad catchphrases before being clearly defined. The legal literature is replete with sub-divisions and specific connotations for each, and only some of these conceptual differences will be attended to, due to space constraints and a wish for clarity of exposition. The focus of this book is on the application of a balancing test within antitrust, and where rights pertaining to property and contract are claimed on behalf of both monopolists and their victims, sub-divisions and limitations become less important. Where application differs across categories of affected individuals, such particularities will be addressed.

The generality of terms used will thus allow us to set up the argument that even a clear-cut monopolist possessing market power may claim legal and moral protection. The extent of this protection, and its interaction with similar claims made on behalf of those suffering from his monopoly and seeking state protection, can only be assessed through the balancing test argued for in chapter five and outlined in chapter seven. In order to substantiate my claim that balancing is needed, I must first convince the reader that both monopolist and consumer (as well as others) have defendable claims to state protection, and this shall be done by attending to both sides' moral and legal standing. Chapters three and four expound each party's claims, showing their common ground in the fairness debate, after chapter two outlines society's interests as independent grounds for intervention. But prior to immersing ourselves in the debate ahead, a brief introduction may be required for the uninitiated. The following chapter sketches out the main paradigms employed in competition law scholarship, both in the US and European Union. Readers versed in the literature may wish to skip ahead, though I hope even they will find the exposition illuminating.

Part II

The Goals of Antitrust

2

The Societal Goals of Antitrust

Competition benefits society. This truism is so ingrained in our legal and economic education that arguments for and against seem unnecessary, and views to the contrary—disingenuous. Yet I hope to show that beyond the well known (and mostly true) justifications for competition and its protection by the state, lie caveats and exceptions that must be addressed. Sometimes competition comes at a cost, and as a society we have to decide whether we want to pay it. Sometimes competition fails to produce the benefits normally associated with it, and we must choose between protecting competition for its own sake and aiming for the primary goods competition proxies. The attainment of economic efficiency, protection of democracy or facilitation of a particular type of 'good life' or society, are all associated with competition, though not always served well by it. This chapter focuses on society's interests, the primary *aggregate* goods competition policy is said to promote. They shall be outlined and assessed, stressing the cases often ignored where competition fails or poses difficult choices between clashing interests. Even where competition is beneficial to society as a whole, individuals and groups within society may be harmed, and these instances will be addressed in chapters three and four as part of our discussion of fairness.

We begin with an assessment of competition law's most touted goal—economic efficiency. After assessing the types of efficiency usually associated with competition, we turn to the role of competition *beyond* economics, facilitating the production of other social goods. In all cases, society as a whole is addressed, assuming there is such a thing as 'a better society' and that as a group, we have both the right and the duty to strive for its attainment—including difficult questions of pluralistic conceptions of what 'good' entails and how democratic societies resolve such differences.

Since 'the good of society' is an elusive term to define, our task would be much easier if we could point to antitrust making *everyone* better off, with no one left out (Pareto superiority). The problem is that as with most realistic contentions, Pareto superior moves are severely limited in a society where every move affects many individuals with clashing interests. Both aggregate concerns and distributional issues must then be addressed, though the latter will be more fully specified in chapters three and four as part of the fairness criteria. Our path is thus to assess first what society gains from antitrust, and then which specific individuals and groups gain or lose in the process. Efficiency, in the economic sense of maximizing total welfare, is one attribute of the social good, and obviously a central one in antitrust scholarship. Nonetheless, it is not the only one; other social goals will thus be addressed as well, such as protection of democracy, and competition as fostering a society of entrepreneurs or enhancing individual freedom. Since much of the scholarship regarding the goals of antitrust conflates these issues, I shall be careful to distinguish between them. What will first be addressed as philosophical distinctions will later pave the way for practical implementation.

I. THE EFFICIENCY MODEL OF ANTITRUST

The argument that antitrust is best understood as a system enhancing aggregate efficiency needs no introduction. Fierce debate exists as to its *uniqueness* in justifying and guiding antitrust policy (ie, is it the *only* goal or merely an important one) but its importance cannot be overstated. Efficiency is defined as maximizing social welfare, often confounding welfare and wealth (ruling out non-economic social goods). Moreover, one needs to address the conflict between maximization and distribution. Attempting to *solve* this debate is somewhat presumptuous, thus I define and assess the various effects that competition law may have on society, without at this time suggesting a standard of comparing between them (that will come later in the book, within chapters five and seven). I separate social goods from fairness considerations, since fairness focuses on distinct individuals affected and protects them as ends, rather than means. Social goods, on the other hand, take a broad view of society as a whole aiming for aggregate or common benefits that in some cases may come at the expense of specific individuals or classes thereof.

Much has been said and written regarding antitrust as wealth maximization, and precisely which type of 'wealth' counts. I thus begin with a delineation of terms, separating between different types of efficiency, in order to later on tackle normative questions regarding preference between them and their relation to other goals competition is said to serve. I begin with a general explanation of the three main prongs of efficiency (allocative, productive and innovative—sometimes grouped as static versus dynamic), and focus on circumstances bringing exceptions to the rule that competition enhances efficiency.[1] This is not in

[1] This debate is often framed as one stemming from adherence to specific schools of thought thus the literature abounds with references to the 'Chicago School' versus others. It seems that even time is separated accordingly—thus 'post-Chicago' scholarship denotes economic analyses relying on models more complex than the simple price-theoretic ones that 'Chicago' scholars used to show antitrust intervention is often unwarranted. As substantive debate has been supplanted with reference to schools of thought and generalizations, terminology has also become important and contentious. See DA Crane, 'Chicago, Post-Chicago, and Neo-Chicago' (2009) 76 *University of Chicago Law Review* 1911; B Kobayashi and T Muris, 'Chicago, Post-Chicago, and Beyond: Time to Let Go of the 20th Century' (2012) 78 *Antitrust Law Journal* 147.

order to downplay competition or antitrust, but to stress their limitations and the need for a more general guiding rule than merely 'promoting competition'. This section thus plays both a definitional and normative part. Definitional, as antitrust scholarship is replete with confusing misuse of terms regarding which efficiencies are relevant for which circumstances (for example, 'consumer welfare' as a goal denoting both total welfare and a specific sub-part thereof). Precise definitions are thus necessary to ensure my arguments are understood as intended. Normative, as efficiency, is assumed to rely on competition, and I wish to separate the two to examine when one can be attained without the other. Nonetheless, the discussion will be condensed, as most readers are very familiar with the terms, and I refer those less versed in the literature to sources where exposition is more complete. Hopefully, the terms and modes of analysis surveyed here will help focus the main arguments made throughout the book while avoiding misunderstandings as to the terms used.

Some argue that efficiency should be considered the *sole* aim of antitrust, a view most famously associated with Robert Bork.[2] Bork's work, beyond analysis of the efficiency loss caused by monopolistic practices, focused on historical analysis of the US Congress' intent while enacting the Sherman Act. Since our focus is normative rather than historical, we need not delve into that debate, though its practical effect should not be understated. Through coincidence or causation, the enforcement of antitrust in the US in the 1980s followed Bork's tune. The political and ideological views of the Reagan Administration called for less government involvement in the marketplace, and Bork supplied the scholarly basis for implementation in antitrust. His work granted support both of economic reasoning and of legislative intent, both very important in legitimizing legal institutions.[3] Others have argued vehemently against this one-dimensional focus on economic efficiency as the sole goal of antitrust, both as normatively wrong due to its blindness to important fairness considerations, and historically, as misconstruing legislative intent.[4] Of course, the term 'consumer welfare' lends itself to misunderstanding,

[2] See R Bork, *The Antitrust Paradox: A Policy at War with Itself* (New York: Basic Books, 1978).

[3] Many have written on the Reagan Administration's limitation of antitrust enforcement. For a specific analysis of Bork's impact, see WE Kovacic, 'The Antitrust Paradox Revisited: Robert Bork and the Transformation of Modern Antitrust Policy' (1990) 36 *Wayne Law Review* 1413.

[4] See, especially, the work of RH Lande: 'Wealth Transfers as the Original and Primary Concern of Antitrust: The Efficiency Interpretation Challenged' (1982) 34 *Hastings Law Journal* 65; 'The Rise and (Coming) Fall of Efficiency as a Rule of Antitrust' (1988) 33 *Antitrust Bulletin* 429; 'Chicago's False Foundation: Wealth Transfers (Not Just Efficiency) Should Guide Antitrust' (1989) 58 *Antitrust Law Journal* 631; NW Averitt and RH Lande, 'Consumer Sovereignty: A Unified Theory of Antitrust and Consumer Protection Law' (1997) 65 *Antitrust Law Journal* 713. Lande, of course, is not alone in his misgivings. Other representative works include: H Hovenkamp, 'Antitrust Policy After Chicago' (1985) 84 *Michigan Law Review* 213 and those cited in ch 4 below, especially nn 1 and 3. For practical implementation and a variety of approaches regarding the goals of competition law, see International Competition Network, *Competition Enforcement and Consumer Welfare—Setting the Agenda* (The Hague: Tenth Annual ICN Conference Discussion Paper, 2011); Organization of Economically Developed Countries, *Policy Brief: What is Competition on the Merits?* (OECD Policy Roundtable, 2006). Maurice Stucke gathers much evidence and sources regarding the multiplicity of

since many take it to denote allocative efficiency generally (synonymous with 'total welfare'), while others may embrace it as a focus on consumers rather than producers (synonymous with consumer surplus).[5] Here, we need not take a side in that debate, as economic efficiency is treated as an *appropriate* concern of antitrust, one of many, not necessarily exclusive or trumping other concerns.

A word of warning might be necessary: economic efficiency tends to crowd out other concerns in antitrust scholarship, with arguments for and against regarding the extent of intervention, types of suspect practices and social gains. Here, the point is not full explication of the economic arguments within antitrust, but placing them *within* the array of arguments relevant for the assessment of antitrust policy and its normative standing. I focus on qualifications to the standard arguments and the costs of antitrust enforcement. This is not to insinuate that society gains nothing from antitrust enforcement (a claim I consider false), but to point out the need for careful balancing, not just on a case-by-case basis, but as part of the justification argument—when and how much intervention is warranted, and who should bear the burden of proof. In the end, it is the fairness arguments, the rights infringed upon, which carry more weight in my opinion than the economic effects. These right-based arguments will be the focus of the following chapters, and balancing between them, and between rights-issues and economic issues, are the end to which I hope to lead.

The place of efficiency within the full debate depends on the way in which we come to view 'the rest of the world' of antitrust justifications. If we are serious in our endeavour to truly assess what is right, and not settle for what is familiar or easily known, we will see efficiency as 'the good of society' in its totality. Similar to other 'good of society' improvements, we should appreciate their complexity and strive to know whether anyone was hurt in the process, any rights infringed upon. The focus on efficiency allows for professionalization, an objectification of the issues in a way that allows them to be assessed dispassionately, as scientists trying

goals competition policy serves, see ME Stucke, 'Reconsidering Antitrust's Goals' (2012) 53 *Boston College Law Review* 551. Christopher Grandy argues that Congress was intent on protecting competitors, but only insofar as they are harmed by anticompetitive measures, rather than focusing on their utility directly; see C Grandy, 'Original Intent and the Sherman Antitrust Act: A Re-examination of the Consumer-Welfare Hypothesis' (1993) 53 *Journal of Economic History* 359.

[5] See Kovacic (n 3) 1449–50, explaining that while the Supreme Court accepted Bork's 'consumer welfare' goal, welfare transfers were considered to be included as well. Others argue that agencies and courts do, and should, take consumer surplus into account, but not since they matter more than total welfare, but as a corrective measure against the selection bias which occurs when lobbying is producer-centric due to their rational investment in it and their organizational advantage over consumer interests. See DJ Neven and LH Röller, 'Consumer Surplus vs Welfare Standard in a Political Economy Model of Merger Control' (2005) 23 *International Journal of Industrial Organization* 829. See also H Hovenkamp, 'Knowledge About Welfare: Legal Realism and the Separation of Law and Economics' (2000) 4 *Minnesota Law Review* 805, offering a dim view of any kind of welfare analysis that incorporates economics.

to measure the result. This might lead to preferring cool detachment over messy details, thus creating a bias towards pronouncing the efficient result the *right* one as well. While in some cases it is, the answer depends on our acceptance of the rights argument, and the result of balancing between competing rights as well as between the realm of personal effects and that of aggregate ones. That will be our focus in the formulation and implementation of the balancing test, but first, let us delve into efficiency.

A. Allocative Efficiency

Allocative efficiency gets its name from its focus on the allocation of goods: simply put—that efficiency is achieved by allocating each good to its 'most efficient user'—the person (or firm) valuing the good more highly than anyone else. Such valuation can be due to personal preferences (the one garnering the most enjoyment from the good's consumption) or due to comparative advantage in utilizing the good (the one best able to use it as an input for further production). Assuming away (for the moment) problems of information, transaction costs, and unequal access to capital, both subjective preferences and comparative advantage in utilization are relevant in making the best use of every good—benefiting society as a whole. The converse is also true, that if goods fail to reach their most efficient user, something has been lost, an opportunity for gain missed. This type of efficiency is also referred to as 'static efficiency' due to its focus on point-in-time analysis, taking existing goods and production methods as given. Dynamic considerations, including production, innovation and formative effect on markets, will be considered below.

Antitrust is considered a central tool in achieving allocative efficiency, since unfettered competition allows all beneficial transactions to take place while monopoly restricts output in order to raise prices (or vice versa), effectively making a profit on an artificially created shortage. In a competitive market, firms might *wish* to do the same, but any one firm attempting to do so would be undercut by another firm supplying the product. Since profit is created in the difference between the buyers' willingness to pay and the firms' cost of production, a monopoly might be willing to exchange quantity for profit, but when competitors exist, they could always offer to sell at a slightly reduced price, shifting demand towards them and making markups unprofitable. Since monopoly profit can be made through any form of market power, whether the source is true monopoly (lack of competitors), strategic mergers (structurally eliminating competitors), or cartels (behaviourally eliminating competitors)—all are grouped under the short title of 'monopolists' for the moment.

Two classic sources of societal waste are connected with monopoly: the 'deadweight loss triangle' and the 'rent-seeking rectangle'. Both are easier understood in their graphic formulation:

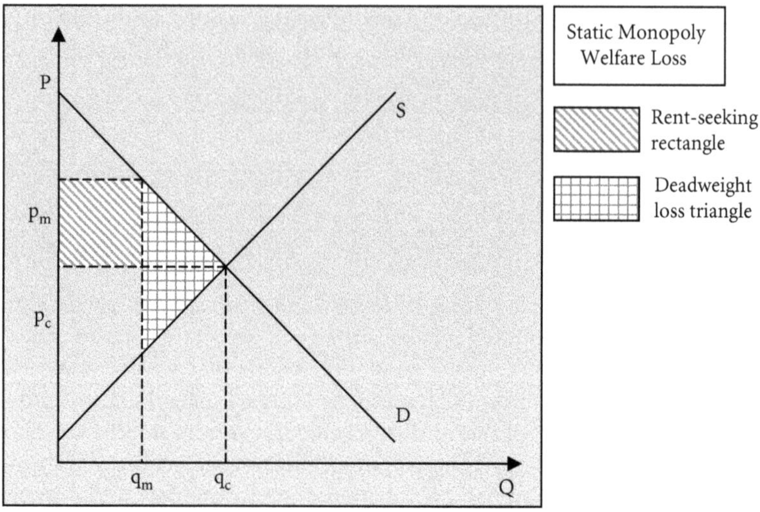

Figure 1: Static Monopoly Welfare Loss

The basic idea is simple and familiar to students of economics or antitrust: the monopolist profits from raising prices above the competitive level (from p_c to p_m), but this causes consumers to reduce consumption (from q_c to q_m). Thus, the chequered triangle represents deadweight loss—products never made or sold, despite the fact that they cost less to produce than their value to consumers. The total loss is borne by society as a whole, consumers and producers alike. This is easily demonstrated by focusing on the horizontal line at p_c which cuts the triangle into two: the top half showing lost consumer surplus (benefit from purchasing at p_c what consumers would have paid up to D), and the bottom half showing producer surplus (profit from selling at p_c what cost S to produce).

The striped rectangle represents the extra profit made by monopolists by raising price, essentially transferring what would be consumers' surplus in competition, to themselves. Thus, the rectangle is usually referred to as a 'wealth transfer', representing the inherent *unfairness* of monopoly. This section focuses on efficiency rather than fairness (the latter will be addressed in the next chapter), and the rectangle is problematic in this respect as well: since producers can anticipate this additional profit awaiting those successful at achieving monopoly, they would rationally invest in the race to be first. Obviously a gross simplification for explicative purposes, but the rectangle can be seen as representing gains from monopoly (subtracting from it their lost share in the deadweight triangle) and thus also the amount invested in achieving it by firms seeking the rents achievable through market power.[6] Of course, these investments might also turn out to be welfare enhancing in part, such as innovative processes and products created by what Joseph Schumpeter described as a process of 'creative destruction' whereby firms race to achieve monopoly, displacing previous market leaders and replacing older technologies with new.[7]

In general, measuring the welfare gains and losses stemming from monopoly is easier in theory than in practice, with prominent scholars disagreeing even on the basic question whether the benefits from having an antitrust policy outweigh its costs. Dennis Carlton, while serving as the Chief Economist of the Department of Justice Antitrust Division, stated 'for the United States, no comprehensive study yet exists that quantifies the benefits (or costs) of our current antitrust policies compared to other possible policy regimes'.[8] Since the intuitive case for welfare losses from antitrust is strong, and the picture painted by graphs similar to Figure 1 is stark, it is important to outline counter-arguments and qualifications to the general argument. This is not intended as an argument *against* the efficiency justification for antitrust, but more as a cautionary note regarding its automatic acceptance, as is all too common in public (as well as scholarly) discussions of antitrust. This might seem one-sided at first, but as my aim is developing a balancing test that will take into account caveats and special circumstances, considerations contrary to standard wisdom are afforded more attention than repeating it.

i. Qualifications and Misgivings regarding the General Principle

Questioning the common assumption of antitrust as promoting efficiency proceeds in three parts: qualifications on arguments as they are presented, discussion of empirical evidence regarding antitrust intervention and delving into the costs of antitrust—both direct and indirect. We shall thus proceed with qualifications on the rent-seeking rectangle, then delve into the other prongs of efficiency associated with antitrust, productive and innovative efficiencies (outlining their arguments and qualifying them in turn, including arguments for potential *efficiencies* of collusion), and then turn to empirical validation and discussion of costs.

[6] Gordon Tullock made this point as early as 1967 in what became a base point for the 'public choice' literature, analyzing political processes through the same cost-benefit prism as other economic activities, and Richard Posner expanded upon it in the realm of antitrust, leading some to remember it by his name, 'the Posner rectangle'. See G Tullock, 'The Welfare Costs of Tariffs, Monopolies, and Theft' (1967) 7 *Western Economic Journal* 224; R Posner, 'Theories of Economic Regulation' (1974) 5 *Bell Journal of Economics and Management Science* 335; R Posner, 'The Social Cost of Monopoly and Regulation' (1975) 83 *Journal of Political Economy* 807.

[7] See JA Schumpeter, *Capitalism, Socialism and Democracy*, 2nd edn (New York: Harper & Bros, 1947) ch 8. For a recent exposition of Schumpeter's scholarship and intellectual development, see TK McGraw, *Prophet of Innovation: Joseph Schumpeter and Creative Destruction* (Cambridge, MA: Harvard University Press, 2007).

[8] D Carlton, 'Does Antitrust need to be Modernized?' (2007) 21(3) *Journal of Economic Perspectives* 155, 174. A good example of the problem can be seen in the Fall 2003 volume of the *Journal of Economic Perspectives*, where Jonathan Baker debated this issue with Robert Crandall and Clifford Winston.

Since the rent-seeking rectangle can also be seen as the wealth-transfer rectangle, I should stress that here I focus on the former interpretation, while the latter will be discussed in the next chapter as a fairness issue, focusing on consumers' interests in avoiding wealth transfers.

The standard argument regarding the rent-seeking rectangle assumes all monopoly profit will be dissipated by the 'race for monopoly' that firms will rationally engage in. Since costs are borne by many firms, and only one attains monopoly profits, all others' costs are pure waste, while the successful monopolist will have expended most (if not all) expected earnings in order to come out first, retaining zero profit. Furthermore, since the race involves many firms, and only one wins, the costs cumulatively borne may be higher than the entire monopoly profit.

Several qualifications may be stated:

1. **Winner Spends All:** When firms differ, the winning firm need not expend all potential benefits in the rent-seeking race. The maximum individual expenditure, even within the model, will be that of second best firm, since once past that point, the winning firm no longer needs to continue the race. This is similar to the popular story of two friends encountering a lion in the jungle (or a bear in the woods): one stops to put on running shoes and is asked by the other whether he really thinks he has a chance of outrunning a predator. 'No' the first replies, 'but I don't have to. All that I need is to run faster than you'.
2. **Heterogeneity of Firms:** The model assumed that firms' costs are equal, while this may not be the case. The 'winning' firm may have qualities granting it an advantage over others in cost-to-benefit ratio. In such a case, the costs expended in order to secure a monopoly position need not necessarily be equal (or close) to the monopoly profit. A firm that can utilize unique advantages in the contest for monopoly position may spend much less on attaining it.[9] Thus, in conjunction with the previous qualification, the firm will spend the minimum necessary to achieve a slightly better *position* than the second in line, and this amount may be much smaller than the expected return. What remains of the rent-seeking rectangle, then, is a maximum limit on spending that no firm will pass, though none will necessarily reach it. Of course, aggregate spending may still be very large (even higher than expected monopoly profit), due to the stated fact that many firms engage in the race for monopoly, with only one winning.

[9] Eg, in a simple case of attaining monopoly position through acquiring the single available plant in the region, the first-mover has a distinct advantage and may end up paying very little for a large profit potential. Classic analysis would have other competitors bidding for the same plant, raising its price to the level anticipated by Posner. Informational inefficiencies though, or other market failures, may limit competition for monopoly, thus the first owner enjoys all monopoly profit. This, of course, is but a simple example, but it is not difficult to think of other cases in which market failures allowing for monopoly to be profitable, constrain initial competition for that position as well.

3. **Limits on Spending:** The assumption that costs of achieving a monopoly are comparable to the benefits of achieving it depends on unlimited avenues for profitable spending. Where the set of feasible actions supporting rent-seeking (ie, those that actually raise probability of monopoly being achieved) is limited, a firm rationally willing to spend more might find its options constrained. Thus, the race might end at a relatively early stage with positive economic profit remaining for the winning firm. Obviously, this is also a case-specific argument, depending on circumstances. Thus, it reminds us that the general argument itself should be qualified according to context of application.
4. **Quitting when Behind:** Firms will rationally invest in attaining monopoly only as long as potential benefits *discounted by the chances of success* exceed current expenditures. At a certain stage, one firm's advantage is observed by others. At that point, while the race is theoretically open, the disadvantaged firms perceive a lower chance of success, and may prefer to quit. Since first-mover advantages are often substantial, this type of unravelling may occur at an early stage. The earlier unravelling occurs, the less aggregate costs are expended in rent-seeking.
5. **Antitrust as Preventing the Race for Monopoly?** Regarding the rectangle as a cost associated with monopoly, assumes that antitrust law can avoid these costs. Even with antitrust law in place, monopoly positions may be attainable, either through realistically expected imperfections in deterrence and enforcement, or through legal means of attaining monopoly (including lobbying for political protection and specific exemptions, to be addressed in the section on public choice below). The existence of antitrust law may actually *exacerbate* the problem, rather than diminish it, since firms will rationally invest in legal and political battles to protect their coveted monopoly status or raise their chances of attaining it.
6. **Costs of Antitrust:** Any costs remaining after all of the above, must be compared to the costs associated with enacting, refining and enforcing antitrust law itself. Since this is a general argument, not relevant to the rent-seeking rectangle alone, we shall defer discussion until all efficiency considerations are raised.

As the above qualifications make clear, there are still many questions of fact to be answered before the rent-seeking rectangle can be taken as a convincing argument for the efficiency enhancement of antitrust law as a whole, at least to the *extent* argued. It may be, for instance, that some industries allow for more spending than others, or that certain market conditions limit the implementation of this argument. More precise and case-specific analysis is thus warranted.

B. Productive Efficiency

A common argument is that in the presence of monopoly, productive inefficiencies occur, due to lack of competitive pressure on the monopolist. This argument assumes that when competitive pressures are lessened, monopolists' incentive to reduce costs is likewise reduced, since they will be able to sell at a higher price anyway. The phenomenon is occasionally referred to as the 'fat cat' effect, or X-inefficiency.[10] The former term is intuitive, referring to the common notion that those not threatened with competition have less of an incentive to improve their wares or procedures. The latter alludes to the opaqueness of the argument that such inefficiency will in fact occur, as its source is unclear and incentives for economizing on costs exist wherever lower costs lead to higher profits, beneficial to competitive and monopolistic firms alike.

How are we then to explain the productive inefficiency ascribed to monopoly? One possibility is to reject it altogether as mistaken and unfounded. Another is to regard the empirical evidence cited as evidence of phenomena other than simple disregard for cost savings. Informational inefficiencies may lead to a signalling effect, so that firms wishing to maintain their market power would benefit from potential entrants perceiving costs as high and profits normal. This explanation would work only in cases where circumstances allowed for magnified *perception* of existing costs. If it were necessary to allow productive inefficiency to lower *actual profits* to normal, the incentive for monopoly itself would erode.

Another possibility may be that exogenous effects interact with monopoly position, such as the large bureaucracy likely in a single monopolistic firm is in itself inefficient. This explanation is equally relevant for similar sized and situated firms, regardless of their monopolistic status. It also does nothing to explain cases where monopoly persists in small, narrowly defined, markets where no large bureaucracy is necessary to dominate sales.

Focusing on productive efficiency brings into question previous arguments for the inefficiency of monopoly as well, outlined above as part of the deadweight triangle. Good arguments exist for actually *preferring* monopoly to competition, at least as to some goods in some markets. Natural monopolies are well known, usually seen as inevitable and aggregately more beneficial to society in cases where average cost of production falls with an increase in quantity. These are common and accepted in markets where large investments in infrastructure are necessary, but here I want to make a stronger case—that beyond natural monopoly, sometimes *collusion itself* is preferable to the competitive alternative. Again, this is not intended as a general argument against antitrust, but as a qualification requiring

[10] See, originally, H Liebenstein, 'Allocative Efficiency vs X-Efficiency' (1966) 56 *American Economic Review* 392. The postulate that monopoly leads to X-inefficiency is based primarily on the lower incentives for managers (and through them, workers) to reach the efficiency production frontier, economizing on costs and utilizing all opportunities to maximize profit. This contention has been vigorously debated, beginning with George Stigler; G Stigler, 'The Xistence of X-Efficiency' (1976) 66 *American Economic Review* 213 and in numerous other papers. For a survey of the debate, see Symposium: 'X-Inefficiency after a Quarter of a Century' (1992) 82 *American Economic Review* 428. For a modern application under a different name, see ME Porter, *The Competitive Advantage of Nations* (Basingstoke: Macmillan, 1998). This mirrors Judge Learned Hand's famous quote that unchallenged power 'deadens initiative', while 'rivalry is a stimulant', in *US v Aluminum Co of America (ALCOA)*, 148 F 2d 427 (2d Cir, 1945).

attention before accepting the intuitive (and overly broad) condemnation of monopolistic practices.

C. Innovative Efficiency

Innovative efficiency generally refers to the pressure competition creates on firms in the market to produce new goods as well as reduce the costs (and/or improve the quality) of existing goods. Furthermore, competition is associated with new firms entering the market, often using innovative procedures in order to overcome their 'latecomer' disadvantage or carve out their own niche. For our purposes here, a double-tier assessment is necessary: first as to the desirability of innovative efficiency as an independent goal of antitrust and second as to the effect of antitrust enforcement on innovation. The first assumption will be questioned and qualified as to appropriate levels of 'socially optimal innovation' and the second will allow for implementation and questions as to the extent that antitrust law spurs innovation above and beyond what would exist without it. We should bear in mind that even absent antitrust enforcement, markets are not easily monopolized, or monopoly easily maintained. Since our issue is not with competition itself, but the benefits (and costs) of its legal protection, qualifications as to the effectiveness of antitrust in securing socially optimal levels of competition and innovation will follow.

Innovation is a public good. Many social and cultural advances are based on technological innovation, with both personal rewards for innovators and positive externalities benefiting others. Furthermore, innovation is not merely technological. When firms seek material rewards, they explore new ways of satisfying their customers' desires, and invent many procedures and methods of communicating along the way. One may view the internet or social networks as innovative products, as innovation inducing infrastructure, or as facilitators of new communities and social needs.

But innovation is not merely good. Striving for new ideas and products has costs, both direct and indirect. The direct costs are obvious: similar to the 'race for monopoly' described above, the 'race for the next big thing' produces a multiplicity of efforts, most of which do not create the big hit each firm is hoping to latch on to. When pushing for novelty, the older products become obsolete, as do working methods and sometimes workers. Expanding our view beyond the specific markets of antitrust, innovation is an engine of production, bringing with it externalities such as pollution and enhanced consumerism, which some may view as a social bad.[11] Even the 'internet revolution' lauded for the promulgation of information and enhanced opportunities for countless users, can be viewed as bad due to enhanced social alienation and a possible increase of social inequality

[11] See discussion below in n 62 and in ch 3 n 69 and accompanying text.

(not to speak of how much easier it makes life for purveyors of child pornography and terrorist communication).

This is not to say that innovation is bad, should serve as a reminder that even regarding innovation, society might prefer optimization to maximization. This question lies well beyond the realm of conventional antitrust, but given that competition policy is often justified on the basis of inducing innovation, one might wonder if this is always a good thing. When a merger is allowed or blocked to its effect on innovation, the state takes a stand in the matter, assuming that more is always better. Maximization of innovation is thus in effect part of competition policy.[12] Of course, competition agencies and courts are probably not the best determiners of social policy regarding innovation, rendering the question moot under current circumstances. Yet since this book focuses both on optimal policy and philosophical justifications thereof, we shall return to the issue when assessing the balancing test antitrust must internalize and the good it is assumed to produce. The basic intuition regarding innovation as a good may stem from the advantages outweighing the disadvantages, but may stem from a different perspective altogether, of the *process* of innovation being what society wants, rather than its material outcomes. In other words, measuring the good and the bad arising from innovation may cause us to miss the point entirely—that society benefits from the process of change regardless of its outcomes. The appropriate frame for the discussion of innovation is thus in its connection to competition as a social process rather its efficiency results. To this perspective I shall return shortly, when section II turns to competition as an independent goal, beyond being a proxy for efficiency. For now, though, let us assume that competition (or more precisely, the type of competition enforceable by the state) enhances innovative efficiency, and that this is a good thing.

The basic innovation-related argument in favour of antitrust, is that competitors look to innovation as their way of 'getting ahead' while an established monopolist is more likely to be content to 'keep things as they are', thus will not invest as much in innovation. Furthermore, monopolists have an incentive to strategically prevent innovation by their competitors (if they have that option), as new products or marketing techniques may upset their current superiority. If this is true, antitrust enhances innovation by protecting competition. Of course, an opposite claim may also be made. Monopolists favour profits just as any other, thus cost-reducing or demand-enhancing innovation is in their interest as well. Furthermore, innovation oftentimes requires 'deep pockets' and the ability to plan for the long term. Monopolists are well situated to explore research opportunities since they can plan on reaping the rewards that investment sows. Large firms, which are dominant in their industries, are not necessarily low on innovation, as

[12] This is not to say that this policy is *achieved*. Indeed, the relationship between antitrust and innovation is complex and the former does not always promote the latter. See I Segal and MD Whinston, 'Antitrust in Innovative Industries' (2007) 97 *American Economic Review* 1703; J Vickers, 'Competition Policy and Property Rights' (2010) 120 *The Economic Journal* 375.

Microsoft, Bell Labs and others have shown. Of course, the Schumpeterian version is that innovation requires monopoly, both as financial basis and as incentive in the 'race for the market'. According to this version, monopoly is the reward sought and reducing its potential reduces incentives to innovate.[13] Of course, there is no need to commit ourselves to one extreme or the other. Innovation is carried out at multiple levels, by both competitive and monopolistic firms, making context and case-specific circumstances matter.[14]

i. Predatory Innovation: Vaporware and Voluntary Network Effects

While generally efficiency is considered a social good, two types of innovation stand out as problematic and require specific mention. The first is predatory innovation, aimed at deterring entry or limiting competitors. Predatory innovation is possible where one firm possesses comparative advantage in innovation due to lower R&D costs, larger patent pools, or simply better access to capital or relevant inputs. In such cases, it might seek to force competitors to 'match suit' in introducing new products or add-ons, thus raising their costs relative to its own.[15] An established monopolist might likewise use innovation to deter entry, since the extra costs would preclude all but those with matching characteristics from entering, effectively posing as entry barriers.

High-tech industries added 'spice' and body to the literature on predatory innovation, including a new method of predation previously unknown—'vaporware'. Vaporware is the practice of misleadingly announcing a new development with

[13] See below, n 21 and accompanying text. Some take this point further in order to argue that the antitrust laws themselves retard innovation and growth, see, eg, RB McKenzie and DR Lee, *In Defense of Monopoly: How Market Power Fosters Creative Production* (Ann Arbor: University of Michigan Press, 2008).

[14] See, eg, JB Baker, 'Fringe Firms and Incentives to Innovate' (1995) 63 *Antitrust Law Journal* 621, reviewing the conflicting economic theories, as well as empirical data supporting each side; RJ Gilbert and SC Sunshine, 'Incorporating Dynamic Efficiency Concerns in Merger Analysis: The Use of Innovation Markets' (1995) 63 *Antitrust Law Journal* 569, text at fn 65, where they include R&D assessment in merger analysis, while arguing that initially dominated industries are more prone to innovation concerns than mergers creating market power.

[15] Here we see an interaction between predatory innovation and raising rivals' costs, which has been argued to be a feasible anti-competitive strategy for some firms. For a general test of predation that offers insights to innovation as well, see JA Ordover and RD Willig, 'An Economic Definition of Predation: Pricing and Product Innovation' (1981) 91 *Yale Law Journal* 8. But see JG Sidak, 'Debunking Predatory Innovation' (1983) 83 *Columbia Law Review* 1121 arguing that Ordover and Willig offer little to correct what was wrong with previous predation literature, and the subject should be dropped altogether. On the other hand, the same author relied on the concept of raising rivals' costs in assessing the role of governmental regulation setting more stringent standards for incumbents than for entrants, essentially preferring the latecomers. See JG Sidak and DF Spulber, *Deregulatory Takings and the Regulatory Contract* (Cambridge: Cambridge University Press, 1998). For a general discussion of the concepts involved, see TG Krattenmaker and SC Salop, 'Anticompetitive Exclusion: Raising Rivals' Costs to Achieve Power over Price' (1986) 96 *Yale Law Journal* 209, 268–72 and SC Salop and DT Scheffman, 'Raising Rivals' Costs' (1983) 73 *American Economic Review* 267.

no intent of marketing it at the specified time, if at all.[16] This occurs mainly in the software industry (hence its name), and the deceit is aimed at preempting developments by competitors. It works by convincing consumers to delay acquisitions of other products, expected to be made obsolete (or at least outdated) by the pre-announced development. Developers delay production of applications based on existing products, in order to conform to the new product they believe will come out soon.[17] Competitors hold off their own developments, or forgo specific investments they believe stand little chance of success against the pre-announced product, especially if the announcing firm is a dominant one in the market and in consumer perception.[18]

On one hand, pre-announcements of software products are both common practice and beneficial to all involved. The relevant players may plan their actions with a touch more certainty than is usual in this constantly changing market. On the other hand, pre-announcements allow for manipulation of expectations. A pre-announcement that turns out to be overly optimistic is neither rare nor necessarily malfeasant, but it does allow the announcer a strong strategic technique curtailing competition before it has begun. Recognizing a specific pre-announcement as misleading is difficult at best, but ex post enforcement may harness previously unavailable information while curtailing ex ante incentives.[19]

Where network effects are strong, lock-in effects can be expected, whereby initial advantages in a developing market translate to a strong hold on consumers. This is relevant both where a basic product is used as platform for later add-ons, and where the product facilitates exchange among its users, thus early adopters lock-in

[16] See R Prentice, 'Vaporware: Imaginary High-Tech Products and Real Antitrust Liability in a Post-Chicago World' (1996) 57 *Ohio State Law Journal* 1163. Empirical analysis revealed some firms use vaporware as a signal to dissuade others from developing their own competing products, see BL Bayus, S Jain and AG Rao, 'Truth or Consequences: An Analysis of Vaporware and New Product Announcements' (2001) 38 *Journal of Marketing Research* 3.

[17] Here the focus is on vertical relations, one product using another as an input or platform, where the application is to be compatible with the pre-announced product. The same analysis holds true when the applications do not depend on the product, but their compatibility grants them some externalized benefits, due to network characteristics.

[18] The same effect may be created by capital markets being fooled by the pre-announcement. Outside investors may be unwilling to support a competitor (or developer) when they hear of a new and better product being 'in the making'. One possibility recently examined, is that of vaporware being a signalling effect of low development costs, thus lowering competitor incentive to enter. Vaporware thus facilitates a partial separating equilibrium, allowing firms with actual low development costs to reap longer interim monopoly profits, while firms with high development costs find vaporware unprofitable in the long-run. See Bayus, Jain and Rao (n 16).

[19] Overall welfare effects of vaporware are difficult to discern; see MA Haan, 'Vaporware as a Means of Entry Deterrence' (2003) 51 *Journal of Industrial Economics* 345. Some have argued that vaporware is more a theoretical worry than a real one, since reputation effects loom large and firms can rarely fool customers more than once; see SM Levy, 'Should Vaporware Be an Antitrust Concern?' (1997) 42 *Antitrust Bulletin* 33. Others argue that life is more complicated, and announcements can fall in between the extremes of 'true' and 'false', and even false statements cannot be discerned from hopeful projections. See Prentice (n 16).

a technological standard that is inferior to later (but less successful) versions.[20] Innovation in network markets has been characterized as 'winner takes all' and is precisely the type of 'creative destruction' that Schumpeter expounded. [21]

Beyond utilization of existing network effects, firms may strategically invest in *creating* network effects as well. Innovative add-ons may introduce network effects to previously standard products, or strengthen latent network effects to monopoly-inducing levels. Under this formulation, technological network effects are not merely *present*, but actively *planned*. An example might be the introduction of an add-on component facilitating communication among users of a product, when its cost exceeds direct benefit. A firm might nonetheless invest due to the network effect strengthening residual demand, ie, driving consumers to its product at the expense of others. This is precisely the type of rent-seeking assessed above in section I.A, and just as wasteful.

Pricing may also be used to introduce or strengthen network effects, in what has become to be known as PMNE—price mediated network effects. As an example, consider on-net versus off-net pricing in mobile phone contracts. Where firms charge higher prices for calls made to customers of other networks, a network effect is created that creates an incentive to join the large network, where chances are higher that more calls will be made on-net. This creates competition between the firms to become known as the larger firm (perceptions guiding consumer behaviour more than actual size), introducing tipping into this market as well. While most of the literature on network effects has traditionally viewed them as exogenously determined (such as the benefit from collaboration among users of the same software), strategic introduction of network effects merits special antitrust concern. What may be innovative practices increasing consumer satisfaction, may also be the source of voluntary network effects created for monopolistic purposes.[22] Antitrust agencies thus have their hands full in trying to determine where innovation is a social good, and where it is a forbidden business practice, detrimental to aggregate efficiency.

The discussion so far has shown that innovation, once considered to be ultimately beneficial and at risk in monopolistic markets, in fact demands closer attention and more complex analysis in order to determine society's interests in it.

[20] The basis for the analysis of network effects was laid by Jeffrey Rohlfs; J Rohlfs, 'A Theory of Interdependent Demand for a Communications Service' (1974) 5 *Bell Journal of Economics* 16. For a general easy-to-read survey, see ML Katz and C Shapiro, 'Systems Competition and Network Effects' (1994) 8 *Journal of Economic Perspectives* 93. For an extensive survey, see J Farrell and P Klemperer, 'Coordination and Lock-In: Competition with Switching Costs and Network Effects' in M Armstrong and RH Porter (eds), *Handbook of Industrial Organization*, vol 3 (North-Holland: Elsevier, 2007) 1967–2072.

[21] For an extensive review of the underlying dynamics, see Farrell and Klemperer (n 20). The hypothesis that extensive innovation is conducted by monopolies eager to protect their dominant position (and by would-be entrants hoping to supplant them) is famously associated with Schumpeter, *Capitalism, Socialism and Democracy* (n 7). For an application of this dynamic to 'new economy' network-effect models, see R Schmalensee, 'Antitrust Issues in Schumpeterian Industries' (2000) 90 *American Economic Review* 192.

[22] See A Ayal, 'Monopolization via Voluntary Network Effects' (2010) 76 *Antitrust Law Journal* 799.

This section aimed not at solving such disputes, but rather using them to highlight the fact that, even if efficiency is accepted as a justifiable goal of competition policy, this is far from sufficient to lead courts and regulators to clear-cut prescriptions separating good practices from bad. In this, as in all things antitrust, context matters and case-specific implementation is required.

D. Expecting the Impossible: When Collusion is Efficient

Horizontal collusion has long been regarded as the most clearly inefficient of interactions between firms, with 'plain-vanilla' cartels vilified by all. Indeed, the one case where the per se rule in antitrust is unquestioningly accepted, is with respect to anticompetitive horizontal agreements. The deadweight loss of horizontal price fixing is (when perfectly conducted) equal to that of a single firm monopoly. Of course, collusion is never perfectly conducted, exacerbating costs even further.[23] Still, arguments against antitrust enforcement have been made even in this clear-cut case.

The simplest qualification is that of hard core believers in market efficiency—that the market itself will correct by inducing cartel members to 'cheat' or by attracting new entrants. A cheating cartel member expands production beyond his quota, or lowers price, enjoying the protective 'umbrella' of cartel pricing while maximizing his own profit just below it. Since cheating is undeniably lucrative, a cartel is inherently unstable, and thus will defeat itself over time. In the case of monopoly, excessive pricing attracts entrants, and unless entry barriers are both high and permanent, cartels and monopoly inherently induce entry, creating their own downfall. The theory of contestable markets intended to generalize this argument, so that from market conditions alone we would be able to identify when enforcement is necessary and when time will heal anticompetitive ailments.[24]

Beyond the instability of long-term cartel behaviour, a far more thought provoking argument is that the solution is not in eventual competition, but that collusion itself is to be tolerated, if not applauded. Donald Dewey described collusion as potentially welfare enhancing, due to its potential in lowering information

[23] Total welfare loss from horizontal collusion may be even greater than from a single monopoly, though. Assume a cartel perfectly restricting output to monopoly level—while deadweight loss is equal, transaction costs and productive inefficiencies due to multi-firm coordination may add costs while adding no monopoly profit. See WJ Baumol, 'Horizontal Collusion and Innovation' (1992) 102 *The Economic Journal* 129. Note, though, his argument that such collusion may enhance innovation along the way.

[24] Potential competition can be as effective at policing monopolistic practices as actual competition. Where a firm expects that raising prices will induce entry, prices will remain low even prior to entry occurring. Thus, we could observe markets where monopoly persists in fact, but competitive pricing is in effect. See generally, WJ Baumol, JC Panzar and RD Willig, *Contestable Markets and the Theory of Industry Structure* (New York: Harcourt Brace Jovanovich, 1982).

costs and variance as to future rates of return.[25] This in turn leads to fewer price changes, lower inventories and higher producer investment due to the lower uncertainty regarding returns. The result is expanded production leading to higher total welfare—with no antitrust enforcement and little competition.

Dewey himself conceded that barriers to entry limited application of his model, but since horizontal price fixing remains per se illegal in most legal systems, the application of his model is still relevant. If antitrust enforcement does not require proof of entry barriers or actual resulting inefficiency, it may very well be socially detrimental in cases where the effects that Dewey pointed out exist. One important qualification may be the separation of price fixing and the information exchange usually associated with it.[26] While information exchange is beneficial to planning and thus expanded output, as Dewey argued, price coordination is not necessarily required for this result. Allowing information exchange among competitors while retaining the demand for unilateral pricing may significantly reduce the costs of collusion while retaining most of its benefits. Implementation is tricky. While most regimes allow for theoretical separation of these, information exchange is often the factual evidence used for price-fixing convictions. Furthermore, enforcing agreements among firms is often tricky as well. Since each firm retains its own profit, fear of 'cheating' persists, and often price coordination is the only realistic way for firms to achieve the incentive effects they aim for. In other words, since cooperation depends on profitability and enforcement, without the clarity of agreements on price, firms might fail to achieve the efficiencies described.

Obviously, price coordination is not always (or even mostly) good. Difficulty of implementation, though, should not automatically constrain either the development of an alternative theory or questioning the appropriateness of current policy. If price-fixing aims at enhancing efficiency, we should balance costs and benefits of alternative suggested regimes. If costs of current policies are ignored, perhaps the aim of antitrust is not truly efficiency, but another goal. Dewey himself concluded that antitrust is actually aimed at decentralization—with efficiency *reduction* as its cost (see section II.A below).[27] Were it really only efficiency that mattered, it is far from obvious that current policies would be justified, or so broadly accepted.

One effect deserves special mention: if collusion is neither *absolutely* prevented, nor absolutely allowed, then some industries will collude while others will not. This is the case where specific exemptions are granted from antitrust enforcement, such as agriculture or labour unions. In such cases, we should expect larger inefficiencies resulting from misallocation among the different industries due to 'second-best' considerations. Aiming at abolition of monopolistic practices is

[25] D Dewey, 'Information, Entry and Welfare: The Case for Collusion' (1979) 69 *American Economic Review* 587.

[26] K Bullock and SJ La Croix, 'Welfare and Collusion: Comment' (1982) 72 *American Economic Review* 256.

[27] D Dewey, 'Welfare and Collusion—Reply' (1982) 72 *American Economic Review* 276.

one thing, while reducing them in one market only to allow them in another, is something else altogether. We have very little to rely on that will show that even in theory this will enhance aggregate welfare, much less when the imperfections and costs of actual implementation are taken into consideration.[28]

Dewey's argument may be supported by a similar argument, more broadly applied to monopoly power as such. Reduced output may be caused not only by efforts to drive prices up, but by *dynamic uncertainty*.[29] Instability in demand causes firms to correct with intertemporal arbitrage: adjusting production and inventory to meet with expected fluctuations in sales. Since a large inventory incurs costs, and most goods diminish in value over time stored, variance in demand and prices may lead to under-stocking and under-production. Introduce risk aversion and the effect is compounded, as the risk associated with forgone sales might be lower than the risk of destroyed stock.[30] Stabilizing prices is thus not just in the producers' interest, but is often efficiency enhancing as well. Perfect competition optimizes short-term considerations, driving prices to marginal cost. Monopoly, on the other hand, may stabilize prices over time, correcting for instability. Thus, even if higher pricing occurs, other social benefits are achieved. Dennis Carlton applied a similar analysis to conditions of uncertainty in demand, concluding that 'compared to the social optimum, a competitive equilibrium will usually not devote sufficient resources to production of the good that is subject to shortages'.[31] He concludes that firms would pay premiums for inducing loyalty and large orders by customers, which seems economically very reasonable, but is sometimes legally construed as monopolization or a 'facilitating practice' for the purpose of proving illegal collusion.[32] Another application of similar dynamics can be observed with respect to employment, where fluctuating demand may lead

[28] See RG Lipsey and RK Lancaster, 'The General Theory of Second Best' (1975) 24 *Review of Economic Studies* 11; RS Markovits, 'Second-Best Theory and the Standard Analysis of Monopoly Rent Seeking: A Generalizable Critique, a Sociological Account, and Some Illustrative Stories' (1993) 78 *Iowa Law Review* 327 and generally Symposium: 'Second-Best Theory and Law & Economics' (1998) 73 *Chicago-Kent Law Review* 1.

[29] SY Wu, 'An Essay on Monopoly Power and Stable Price Policy' (1979) 69 *American Economic Review* 60.

[30] Without going into absolute numbers of units forgone, as these are very case dependent, note that a unit not sold due to under-stocking incurs loss of marginal profit (price less marginal cost), while a unit wasted due to deterioration incurs loss of its marginal cost of production. While circumstances vary, it is reasonable to assume that the latter is often much higher than the former, especially under the P=MC assumption of competitive markets.

[31] DW Carlton, 'Market Behavior with Demand Uncertainty and Price Inflexibility' (1978) 68 *American Economic Review* 571, 580. These dynamics often create incentives for vertical integration or the creation of supplier networks that can internalize these effects, smoothing consumption and enhancing planning. See RE Kranton and DF Minehart, 'Networks versus Vertical Integration' (2000) 31 *Rand Journal of Economics* 570.

[32] Indeed 'loyalty programmes' are rampant in the marketplace, and vigorous debate ensues as to their increasing switching costs, reducing entry and facilitating tacit collusion. For various perspectives on the issue, see R Caminal and A Claici, 'Are Loyalty-rewarding Pricing Schemes Anti-competitive?' (2007) 4 *International Journal of Industrial Organization* 647; D Reitman and P Greenlee, 'Distinguishing Competitive and Exclusionary Uses of Loyalty Discounts' (2005) 50 *Antitrust Bulletin* 441; Yuk-Fai Fong and Qihong Liu, 'Loyalty Rewards Facilitate Tacit Collusion' (2011) 20 *Journal of*

firms to fire and hire workers periodically. A stabilizing agreement might reduce transaction costs as well as the need for training, thus count as efficiency enhancing despite its collusive nature.[33]

The need for care and strict scrutiny regarding common assumptions regarding the inefficiency of monopoly and collusion is thus very clear. Common wisdom regarding the need for and justification of antitrust may be mistaken, or at least, overstated.[34]

E. When Antitrust Fails: Costs of Enforcement and Strategic Manipulation

Up to this point, antitrust was assessed as to its efficiency-related benefits, whether in outlining the results sought, or in explaining why hopes therefore might be overly optimistic. A serious commitment to efficiency, though, requires not only attention to the benefits of antitrust (and limitations thereof), but also to the flip side—the costs of actively enforcing competition rules. As we are still within the efficiency model of antitrust, the relevant costs are those measured (or at least approximated) in terms of aggregate social wealth. Other 'costs' exist as well, those which are imposed on specific parties for the (presumed) benefit of society at large, and those will be assessed in chapter four regarding the rights of (and harm to) monopolists.

Costs of antitrust fall into two general categories—direct and indirect. Direct costs are the most obvious, including enforcement costs as well as costs borne by firms in defending themselves from antitrust suits (both criminal and civil) or preparing briefs for merger review. Indirect costs include social costs from overdeterrence (firms forgoing competitive acts for fear that they will be challenged by agencies or competitors) as well as investment in lobbying for legal change and seeking more 'consideration' from enforcement agencies. This section aims not for measurement of costs—but pointing out their prevalence. Since the efficiency case *for* antitrust is clear and intuitive, I focus on the relevant costs to ensure that they receive their deserved consideration in the balancing test to be developed in chapters five, six and seven. I shall outline the direct costs, and go into more detail regarding the indirect ones—as these are often overlooked in the intuitive case for antitrust.

Economics & Management Strategy 739; G Faella, 'The Antitrust Assessment of Loyalty Discounts and Rebates' (2008) 4 *Journal of Competition Law and Economics* 375.

33 L Kjolbye, 'The New Commission Guidelines on the Application of Article 81(3): An Economic Approach to Article 81' (2004) *European Competition Law Review* 570; G Monti, *EC Competition Law* (Cambridge: Cambridge University Press, 2007) 121–22.

34 See also FM Scherer, 'Antitrust, Efficiency, and Progress' (1987) 62 *New York University Law Review* 998, suggesting care in implementing any form of general argument to answer specific cases, precisely because so many questions remain open with conflicting theoretical conjectures.

Direct costs of antitrust include the funds necessary to handle the day-to-day activities of antitrust enforcers as well as costs of legislation, including public deliberation and implementation of standards by courts. The most obvious starting point is the budget required for antitrust enforcement agencies. Legislative committees, administrative task forces, specialists' testimony and the entire technical and secretarial staff labouring behind the scenes come at a price. When evaluating how much antitrust contributes to aggregate efficiency, all these and more must be considered. Furthermore, many private interest groups affected by antitrust rules hire their own specialists and advisers, again expending resources that could have been employed elsewhere. Add to that the specific expenditures necessitated by each case brought (legal, accounting and other fees, time wasted, etc) and we reach sizeable proportions.[35] This is not to say that the costs justify non-intervention (indeed, this might lead to worse results altogether), but that both sides must be studied before an efficiency-based conclusion is warranted. Regardless of how large the benefits may be, net societal gain cannot be assessed without subtracting costs.[36]

Indirect costs include over-deterrence, which can be seen as an unavoidable cost even of an optimal policy, and one which would be very difficult to measure. How many efficient business practices were forbidden by over zealous agencies or overly suspicious attitudes towards misunderstood attempts of playing hardball competition? How many times did businesses forgo *in advance* a policy which might have been socially beneficial, perhaps even authorized by agencies or courts—but the relevant managers (or lawyers) thought it too dangerous to try or too costly to address?

Frank Easterbrook wrote of unavoidable mistakes in antirust policy (indeed, in every realistic policy), separating mistaken over-enforcement from mistaken under-enforcement.[37] The former he referred to as 'false positives' and the latter

[35] Indeed, some see the increased sophistication of 'post-Chicago' economics as increasing costs even further, as complex case-by-case analysis is necessary. The same can be said regarding rule-of-reason analysis more generally—perhaps more precise, but definitely more costly and less predictable. See MS Jacobs, 'The New Sophistication in Antitrust' (1994) 79 *Minnesota Law Review* 1. See also DA Crane, 'Rules versus Standards in Antitrust Adjudication' (2007) 64 *Washington and Lee Law Review* 49 relying on similar arguments (and others) to prefer clear-cut rules which would reduce adjudication costs.

[36] Eg, Gregory Werden, Senior Economic Counsel at the Department of Justice, wrote extensively regarding the benefits of antitrust enforcement without once raising the issue of costs, despite the title he chose: GJ Werden, 'Assessing the Effects of Antitrust Enforcement in the US' (2008) 156 *De Economist* 433. For a review of different perspectives regarding cost-benefit-assessment of antitrust, compare J Baker, 'The Case for Antitrust Enforcement' (2003) 17 *Journal of Economic Perspectives* 27 with RW Crandall and C Winston, 'Does Antitrust Policy Improve Consumer Welfare? Assessing the Evidence' (2003) 17 *Journal of Economic Perspectives* 3.

[37] See his papers on the subject: F Easterbrook, 'The Limits of Antitrust' (1984) 63 *Texas Law Review* 1 and 'Allocating Antitrust Decision-making Tasks' (1987) 76 *Georgetown Law Journal* 305 generated extensive scholarship and the application of the 'positive versus negative mistakes' model has become *sine qua non* in antitrust and beyond. For a recent discussion of these issues from multiple perspectives, see Special Issue: 'The Limits of Antitrust Revisited' (2010) 6 *Journal of Competition Law and Economics*.

as 'false negatives'. The main difference between them (as far as costs go) is that under-enforcement allows a monopolistic practice to continue unhindered, though still checked by the power of markets. For example, a merger mistakenly allowed which increased the merging firms' market power creates monopoly pricing and allocative inefficiency. Fringe firms will be drawn in by the high prices, benefiting from the market leader's 'price umbrella'. In effect, monopoly pricing attracts competitors, who drive prices down. Thus, false negatives bear their own correction through market mechanisms. False positives, on the other hand, forbid an efficient practice, and (unless enforcement is very weak, making the point moot) the market will not correct the issue until another court steps in and repeals the inefficient precedent. Minimizing mistakes is obviously best but, taking into account realities of imperfect foresight and enforcement, this distinction leads us to be more wary of excessive levels of deterrence than improperly low ones.

i. Empirical Evidence: Questions Raised

Empirical evidence has ambivalent qualities. On one hand it speaks of objective facts witnessed in reality, deserving of more credibility than theoretical conjectures. On the other hand, it is forever the anecdotal description those facts collected, susceptible to conflicting interpretations as to normative implications and governed by implicit assumptions as to 'rest of the world' influences. This section brings but a few central examples of studies showing results that would question the one-sided, unambiguous nature of the classic model's anti-monopoly implications. Again, a caveat is in order. Choice of studies remains a researcher's bias, and the argument here is not that 'no good comes of antitrust'; it is merely the *dominance* of the view that monopoly is bad and antitrust good which leads me to raise alternative viewpoints, to balance what seems to be a biased world view leaning too heavily in one direction. My argument is for the need for care in normative judgments and for balancing competing interests, rather than any eventual result of such balancing. The fact is that most people, most of the time, embrace the anti-monopoly rhetoric as gospel—this is what makes contrary considerations so necessary.

An illustrating example is one of the first cases to bring about the per se condemnation of horizontal collusion: *US v Addyston Pipe & Steel Co.*[38] The Court applied the per se standard, though stressing that the price fixed was itself unreasonable. A study conducted almost a century later showed that market characteristics were such that pricing was unstable and competitive equilibrium could not exist, thus the automatic aversion to collusive behaviour was not appropriate.[39] In any case, after the horizontal agreement was deemed illegal, the firms merged

[38] *US v Addyston Pipe & Steel Co*, 175 US 211 (1899).

[39] Absent market conditions allowing for competitive equilibrium in the first place, there is no way to generalize that collusion raised actual price levels. See G Bittlingmayer, 'Decreasing Average Cost and Competition: A New Look at the Addyston Pipe Case' (1982) 25 *Journal of Law and Economics* 201.

instead into 'US Cast Iron Pipe and Foundry', exemplifying the necessity for antitrust policy to cover all aspects of possible commercial behaviour or none at all. Indeed, the lack of merger control in the Sherman Act led firms unable to contract for collusion, to merge instead. The Supreme Court reacted with the *Northern Securities* case, subjecting mergers to antitrust analysis as well, but in the few years until that loophole was closed, hundreds of mergers were carried out, arguably in order to escape antitrust enforcement.[40] In 1914, the Clayton and Federal Trade Commission Acts were enacted, specifically targeting mergers and requiring firms to seek approval prior to merger consummation.

Economic analysis of specific cases is often conducted on an academic level. This allows us to review not only the knowledge available to the courts, but sometimes to benefit from the passing of time and new economic learning. Paul Rubin assessed a large number of such articles as to their conclusions: were the cases reviewed decided correctly, and did implementation enhance efficiency?[41] Such a study has obvious benefits in our context. If antitrust is to enhance efficiency, implementation should be successful. If final analysis shows implementation to be inefficient, then even substantiated theory need not lead to legal policy.

Two interesting points follow from Rubin's assessment. First, while a majority of the cases were judged to be justified, ie, brought against parties truly involved in anticompetitive behaviour, this was by a very small margin—53 to 47 per cent, or 61 to 39 per cent, depending on the method of analysis chosen.[42] Second, actual implementation is even more disheartening, both as to the 'right' party winning litigation, and especially as to actual effect of the decision on subsequent competitiveness. A 'correct' *legal* result occurred in barely half the cases sampled.[43] Analysis of ex post implementation of decrees showed some to be absolutely irrelevant, while those judged *effective* were divided evenly between effective in *promoting efficiency* and effective in *deterring it*. Rubin's final note is that 'factors other than a search for efficiency must be driving antitrust policy'.[44] If this were a conscious decision to pay in aggregate efficiency a price for attaining other social values, we might find it acceptable.[45] If, on the other hand, this result follows from either inappropriate antitrust doctrine or incompetent implementation thereof, serious reconsideration is warranted.

[40] See G Bittlingmayer, 'Did Antitrust Policy Cause the Great Merger Wave?' (1985) 28 *Journal of Law and Economics* 77.

[41] PH Rubin, 'What Do Economists Think about Antitrust? A Random Walk Down Pennsylvania Avenue' in FS McChesney and WF Shughart (eds), *The Causes and Consequences of Antitrust* (Chicago: University of Chicago Press, 1995).

[42] See ibid, Tables 3.3 and 3.4, p 60.

[43] A 'correct' result is a plaintiff winning a justified case, or defendant winning an unjustified one (cumulatively 48 to 54%, depending on method of analysis), while an 'incorrect' result is the 'wrong' party winning (conversely, 46 to 52% of the cases).

[44] Ibid, 61.

[45] This is not meant tongue-in-cheek. Below I shall assess non-efficiency reasons supporting antitrust intervention and insofar as these are convincing, paying an economic price for attaining non-economic benefits can be justified as social policy. Of course, the comparative extent of price and benefits matters, which is precisely where the balancing test proposed below, is headed.

An interesting study in this context was conducted by Michael Sproul who examined 25 antitrust cases filed for price-fixing, in order to deduce the effect on prices charged. While the commonly assumed (and hoped-for) effect of antitrust enforcement is lowering prices, Sproul's study showed that prices *rose* after indictments for price-fixing by an average of 7 per cent over the four years following the indictment.[46] The fact that prices tended to rise after an indictment for price-fixing runs contrary to expectations, and raises serious concerns that enforcement causes more harm than good. It is important to note that the social costs assessed are *independent of enforcement costs*, ignored in his study. Thus, even if antitrust was costless (which it is not) doubts as to the desirability of antitrust enforcement are compounded.

Beyond the general effect of rising prices, some immediate drops in prices have been recorded as well. The problem is that the largest of these have been in cases where the defendants were finally acquitted! This finding strengthens our suspicion of antitrust enforcement as a tool for reducing the social costs of monopoly. If practices considered illegal are targeted and the result is a rise in prices on one hand, and prosecuting practices ultimately found to be legal reduce prices on the other, perhaps the contention that aggregate welfare is enhanced by antitrust fails the tests of reality. The one result of Sproul's study that supported the conventional wisdom of antitrust enforcement is that 'prices subsequent to the indictment are negatively correlated with the severity of penalties'.[47] Thus, the harsher the penalties imposed, the less price rose subsequently, though it must be stressed that prices *still rose* post-indictment and only the extent lessened.

What are we to deduce from this study? An extreme answer would desist from prosecuting price-fixing offences altogether. Another possibility would be raising penalties even further and prosecuting only the most flagrant offenders.[48] In any case, it is enough for us to express concern about antitrust enforcement achieving its stated aims, and the need for more research, or at least care before wholeheartedly accepting the premises of antitrust.[49]

[46] MF Sproul, 'Antitrust and Prices' (1993) 101 *The Journal of Political Economy* 741. Note that price changes were relative to otherwise assumed market conditions, ie, expected price without enforcement. For criticism of the methodology employed, see JM Connor, 'Price-fixing Overcharges: Legal and Economic Evidence' in RO Zerbe and JB Kirkwood (eds), *Research in Law and Economics: A Journal of Policy* (Bingley: Emerald Group Publishing, 2007).

[47] Sproul (n 46) 751. See also Figure 4 on p 752 for detail of changes in pricing after indictment before and after 1976, when penalties were raised.

[48] This option is favoured by Sproul (n 46) 753.

[49] Other studies have raised questions as to basic assumptions common to antitrust as well. See, eg, P Asch and JJ Seneca, 'Is Collusion Profitable?' (1976) 58 *Review of Economics and Statistics* 1, finding collusion and profitability negatively correlated though rejecting an outright causal explanation; WF Long, R Schramm and RD Tollison, 'The Economic Determinants of Antitrust Activity' (1973) 16 *Journal of Law and Economics* 351, finding that enforcement activities of the DOJ are more related to industry sales than potential for economic loss or excess profits; Bittlingmayer, 'Did Antitrust Policy Cause the Great Merger Wave?' (n 40), finding strong positive correlation between increased antitrust activity and mergers among enforcement targets, incurring direct and indirect costs while thwarting enforcement efforts. A different form of study assessed the effect of the mere filing of private antitrust suits on the share value of the firms involved. Statistically, plaintiffs' share value rose, while defendants'

While most commentators on antitrust focus on firm-specific and industry-specific efficiencies, one study has tested the influence of enforcement on employment.[50] Antitrust enforcement in specific industries may detrimentally affect the relevant labour markets (the assumption is that such industries suffer from downsizing, causing employees to shift towards other industries). Macroeconomic effects, on the other hand, depend more on the *predictability* of enforcement activities, since markets should clear taking these into account *ex ante*. The problem, thus, is in sudden shifts of antitrust activity, since changes frustrate planning and employment coordination among various labour markets. When unpredictability is introduced, unemployment is caused by fluctuations in enforcement. Shughart and Tollison conclude that the pass-through level is 15 per cent, ie, a 1 per cent increase in enforcement expenditures on part of the Antitrust Division of the US Department of Justice led to a 0.15 per cent rise in the unemployment rate. Antitrust activity thus incurs macroeconomic costs, usually unaddressed by proponents of increased enforcement. When combined with the previously discussed question of antitrust's efficacy at actually achieving the results hoped for, the case that aggregate efficiency is enhanced by antitrust law is further crippled.

The above examples should not be misconstrued as an argument that antitrust is inefficient as such. My focus here is on evidence raising *doubt* as to antitrust's contribution to efficiency, and thus the sample is biased. Economic acceptance of antitrust as efficiency enhancing is prevalent, and one should not confuse the 'devil's advocate' role taken here with a wholehearted condemnation of the antitrust enterprise.[51]

ii. Strategic Manipulation of Antitrust: The Public Choice Perspective

When empirical analysis shows that antitrust-originated directives benefit some actors but not total welfare (or even when benefits are skewed towards some and away from others), one could blame imperfect implementation of a good idea. Public choice theorists, on the other hand, examine the results achieved as the target, rather than unwanted side effect, and then deduce which interest groups benefited in order to examine their influence on the implementation of antitrust.

share value fell. What is interesting though, is that there remained a difference between the two, so that altogether a significant wealth loss was ascertained. See JM Bizjak and JL Coles, 'The Effect of Private Antitrust Litigation on the Stock-Market Valuation of the Firm' (1995) 85 *American Economic Review* 436.

[50] WF Shughart and RD Tollison, 'The Employment Consequences of the Sherman and Clayton Acts' (1991) 147 *Journal of Institutional and Theoretical Economics* 38.

[51] As an interesting example of a paper favouring antitrust intervention (one among many), see F Warzynski, 'Did Tough Antitrust Policy Lead to Lower Mark-Ups in the US Manufacturing Industry?' (2001) 70 *Economics Letters* 139. Warzynski answers affirmatively, finding negative correlation between stringent antitrust enforcement and price-cost mark-ups. What makes this study interesting, is its methodology allowing for analysis of an aggregation of American manufacturing industries (approximately 450 industries), rather than specific case studies.

It is important here to distinguish between two strands of the public choice literature in antitrust: one dealing with critique of the legislature's intent when *enacting* antitrust laws and the other dealing with strategic *implementation* of antitrust.

The second issue, of strategic *use* of antitrust law towards uncompetitive aims, is more relevant to our discussion. Here, we focus not on the appropriateness of antitrust legislation and enforcement in and of themselves, but on their manipulation so that even 'good' laws might be used in ways aggregately harmful. When deciding whether antitrust as a whole, or particular antitrust policies, create more benefit than harm, the potential for misuse must be considered in order to allow for realistic expectations. Furthermore, where it is possible to distinguish in advance which types of rules allow for more misuse, the appropriate makeup of antitrust should be to adapted circumvent (or minimize) this danger.

Some scholars, for example, focus on the treble damages rule enacted by the Clayton Act as especially problematic, since it creates an especially strong incentive for strategic use of antitrust. The common justification for the treble damages rule is that it allows for counteracting the generally low probability of detection and enforcement. Thus, if a firm is to be deterred from profitable (but illegal) monopolistic activity, merely paying the damages caused is insufficient, and a multiplier (here, of three) is necessary. Furthermore, in order to incentivize private enforcement, the potential plaintiff must reap sufficiently large rewards. This is similar to the same argument used in class action jurisprudence, justifying compensation for the representative plaintiffs in order to increase incentives for beneficial suits which deter malfeasance and compensate victims.

Plaintiffs foresee large expenditures on litigation, as well as unknown probabilities of success, thus multiplying their (uncertain) rewards increases their willingness to file suit—essentially a public service assisting many others who would be potentially harmed by monopolistic activity. One must bear in mind that such deterrence is beneficial not just to those harmed by the specific monopolistic activity adjucated in the private suit, but all other activities which potential monopolists forgo due to their fear of civil litigation incentivized by treble damages. The rule is broad in its domain, and some would argue overly so.

Baumol and Ordover argued that where rent-seeking is common, aggregate efficiency may be enhanced by reducing the factor by which private damages are multiplied—in some cases even to less than 1.[52] This would entail limiting the successful plaintiff's rewards to *less than* actual damages, precisely the opposite of the Clayton Act's trebling rule, and a strange result in a court system premised

[52] WJ Baumol and JA Ordover, 'The Use of Antitrust to Subvert Competition' (1985) 28 *Journal of Law and Economics* 247. Lowering the multiplier below 1 means that even a successful plaintiff (thus assumed to be a victim, and justified in her claim) would not recover full damages. Acceptance of this result would rely on assumption of aggregate effects as more important than individual fairness considerations. See also LA Graglia, 'Is Antitrust Obsolete?' (1999) 23 *Harvard Journal of Law & Public Policy* 11; text at fn 36, arguing more generally that antitrust has been transformed into a tool for protecting weak competitors rather than protecting competition or consumers.

on the victim's right to compensation for wrongs suffered. Baumol and Ordover justify their unintuitive claim by pointing out that the harm caused by excessive antitrust enforcement includes not only the direct costs of litigation, but the leading firm's apprehension about engaging in pro-competitive actions that might be subsequently deemed antitrust offences. Innovation and price reductions could be judged to be predatory, cooperation in R&D might be deemed a guise for collusion and novel structures of business hierarchies or pricing schemes risk being deemed attempted monopolization. Given the broad reach and ambiguous definitions of competition law, firms 'playing it safe' might jeopardize both their own profits and aggregate efficiency. Since real-world implementation is by its nature imperfect, taking into account the fear of 'false positives' might thus justify a policy aimed at under-enforcement, especially where the price of positive mistakes outweighs the price of negative ones.[53]

Strategic use of antitrust enforcement may occur in different contexts as well. Once the machinery for litigation is in place, firms and individuals wishing to extort a leading firm may use it, regardless of the nature and context of their true aim.[54] Furthermore, the breadth of antitrust together with its important commercial ramifications, make it a lucrative source of favours to be distributed, or traded, by relevant politicians. Some politicians may owe their commission to specific private-interest groups, or geographically homogeneous voters (where most worry about employment in the local plant more than aggregate welfare, especially where the latter accrues to spreadout consumers rather than localized producers). Allowing such private interests to influence antitrust enforcement becomes then especially troublesome.

In one example, a group of researchers empirically tested the hypothesis that the FTC was influenced by private interests of the politicians controlling the agency's budget, who in turn are indebted to their local jurisdictions. Agency decisions to pursue or drop cases against firms with headquarters in relevant locations were found to be predicted by the states from which the specific elected officials on the budgeting committee originated.[55] Perhaps even more interesting is their analysis

[53] See Easterbrook (n 37) and accompanying text.

[54] Eg, managers may use antitrust litigation to stop a hostile takeover that they oppose. See F Easterbrook and D Fischel, 'Antitrust Suits by Targets of Tender Offers' (1982) 80 *Michigan Law Review* 1155. Of course, the same is true of other venues of litigation as well, eg, health regulation, regulated industries, etc. See JC Miller, 'Comments on Baumol and Ordover' (1985) 28 *Journal of Law and Economics* 267.

[55] See RL Faith, DR Leavens and RD Tollison, 'Antitrust Pork Barrel' (1982) 25 *Journal of Law and Economics* 329. Contrary observations (though lacking in empirical support) are made by FTC 'insiders' WJ Baer and DA Balto, 'The Politics of Federal Antitrust Enforcement' (1999) 23 *Harvard Journal of Law & Public Policy* 111. They argue for the advantage of a professional agency that insulates at least some of the political pressure that would otherwise guide state intervention. It must be stressed, though, that this argument is relevant only if antitrust as a whole is assumed to be justified, as they focus on method of enforcement only—and not the law's initial basis. See also FS McChesney, 'Economics versus Politics in Antitrust' (1999) 23 *Harvard Journal of Law & Public Policy* 133, text at fns 26–28, arguing that judges appointed for life are less at risk of succumbing to political pressure than enforcement agency officials.

of the FTC reforms of the early 1970s. Rather than minimize such protectionism, the reforms had the effect of reducing the number of formal actions instigated by the FTC, while *strengthening* individual committee members and their private-interest influence.

The group most often said to benefit from antitrust intervention is that of small business owners. Aside from limiting monopolistic practices (benefiting both fringe firms and aggregate efficiency), antitrust limits efficient business practices that push smaller and less efficient businesses out of the market. One study approaching this subject from a novel perspective analyzes the relation between antitrust enforcement and foreign competition.[56] There, foreign competition is assumed to be a substitute for antitrust, since entry (actual or potential) creates competitive pressure on dominant firms, thus alleviating fears of monopolistic practices. Empirical study showed that antitrust budgets are significantly higher following periods of increased import penetration, allowing for more enforcement that would insulate the smaller firms from the 'perils' of international competition. The effect created is a wealth transfer away from the larger and dominant firms towards the smaller firms—a result in accordance with some of the historical arguments that antitrust laws were passed at the bequest of small businesses.[57]

Of course, other studies show counter-examples, contrary to a public choice interpretation.[58] The point made here is not that antitrust is *always* aimed at private-interest goals, but that the opposite view—of antitrust as benefiting society at large—is not without its limits as well. As we proceed and examine the different viewpoints from which antitrust can (and should) be assessed, it is important to bear in mind the limitations from which each suffers. Such care is all the more important when examining the basic efficiency goal treatment of antitrust, as here intuitive judgment combines with historical dominance to cause most students of the subject to assume a priori that monopolistic practices must be bad and state-sponsored antitrust good. Our focus here was on caveats to this

[56] WF Shughart, JD Silverman and RD Tollison, 'Antitrust Enforcement and Foreign Competition' in FS McChesney and WF Shughart (eds), *The Causes and Consequences of Antitrust* (Chicago: University of Chicago Press, 1995).

[57] As stated above, we need not delve into the historical arguments here. For examples of relevant analysis, See DJ Boudreaux, TJ DiLorenzo and S Parker, 'Antitrust Before the Sherman Act' in FS McChesney and WF Shughart (eds), *The Causes and Consequences of Antitrust* (Chicago: University of Chicago Press, 1995), showing statistically significant correlation between legislation and local agricultural interests harmed by technological developments rendering local farmers inefficient by comparison. See also RB Ekelund, MJ McDonald and RD Tollison, 'Business Restraints and the Clayton Act of 1914: Public- or Private-Interest Legislation?' in FS McChesney and WF Shughart (eds), *The Causes and Consequences of Antitrust* (Chicago: University of Chicago Press, 1995), showing the Clayton Act favoured established firms (both small and large) over growing firms attempting entry into interstate commerce.

[58] See, eg, V Ghosal and J Gallo, 'The Cyclical Behavior of the Department of Justice's Antitrust Enforcement Activity' (2001) 19 *International Journal of Industrial Organization* 27 showing evidence that the DOJ brings more antitrust suits in periods of economic downturn (counter-cyclical activity), fitting with hypotheses of targeting collusion rather than producer protection.

view, first with respect to the economic case for competition as such, and then with respect to the specific issue of state intervention. The backing of the state is a powerful thing; it allows for superior force to be brought to bear through the court system, transforming the economically powerful monopolist to a legally challenged defendant. Furthermore, state action has an expressive effect, making illegal activity not just unprofitable (due to enforcement), but also socially frowned upon—creating ripple effects tainting the reputations of those involved in such practices. These issues will be further developed below, when discussing the relative right-based arguments of the parties involved and the effect of state intervention on behalf of one side and against the other. After reviewing the dominant paradigm of antitrust as efficiency oriented (and qualifying some of its arguments), let us move on to other social goods antitrust may contribute to, beyond mere economic efficiency.[59]

II. COMPETITION BEYOND EFFICIENCY: BETWEEN PROXY AND INDEPENDENT GOAL

Most bodies of law dealing with these issues refer to 'competition' as the general object of protection. Naturally, this begs the question—what is competition good for and why is it protected? Oliver Black lists five competing definitions of competition, from the process of rivalry to Bork's consequentialist view that competition exists where legal intervention would yield no enhancement of welfare.[60] Law and economics are not alone in their ambiguity as to what competition entails, as the natural sciences fare no better in providing a clear definition of the term, regardless of its importance in explaining much of observed animal behaviour.[61]

[59] The more common debate within antitrust scholarship deals with its emphasis on 'consumer welfare' versus 'total welfare'; see ch 1, n 47 and accompanying text. Regardless of the term used, those focusing on consumers rather than aggregate effect are not advocating efficiency, but a distributional concern relying on an implicit assumption that consumers *deserve* the benefits of trade, precisely what I set out to examine here. For views on the prevalent (and confusing!) uses of the terms, see, BY Orbach, 'The Antitrust Consumer Welfare Paradox' (2011) 7 *Journal of Competition Law and Economics* 133, arguing that 'consumer welfare' long had a standard definition in economics, which was consumer surplus; JB Kirkwood, 'Consumers, Economics and Antitrust' in JB Kirkwood (ed), *Antitrust Law and Economics*, vol 21 (Bingley: Emerald Group Publishing, 2004) arguing that 'consumer welfare' is used in economics to refer to total surplus. Practical implementation has focused on merger enforcement; see, eg, D Besanko and DS Spulber, 'Contested Mergers and Equilibrium Antitrust Policy' (1993) 9 *Journal of Law, Economics and Organization* 1; J Farrell and ML Katz, 'The Economics of Welfare Standards in Antitrust' (2006) 2 *Competition Policy International* 3; S-O Fridolfsson, 'A Consumer Surplus Defense in Merger Control' in V Ghosal and J Stennek (eds), *The Political Economy of Antitrust* (Amsterdam: Elsevier, 2007); K Heyer, 'Welfare Standards and Merger Analysis: Why Not the Best?' (2006) 2 *Competition Policy International* 29; Neven and Röller (n 5); R Pittman, 'Consumer Surplus as the Appropriate Standard for Antitrust Enforcement' (2007) 3 *Competition Policy International* 205; RH Lande, 'A Traditional and Textualist Analysis of the Goals of Antitrust: Efficiency, Preventing Theft from Consumers, and Consumer Choice' (2013) 81 *Fordham Law Review* 2349.

[60] O Black, *Conceptual Foundations of Antitrust* (Cambridge: Cambridge University Press, 2005) 6.

[61] See, LC Birch, 'The Meaning of Competition' (1957) 91 *American Naturalist* 5.

The previous section outlined the efficiency-enhancing role of free trade, and the economics literature is replete with models showing how competition ensures goods will be used in the best manner possible, maximizing societal resources. But beyond efficiency, competition is often associated with freedom, entrepreneurship and social mobility. Indeed, some see democracy itself as rooted in the existence of competition.[62]

Modern antitrust scholarship focuses on economics, and almost exclusively on efficiency. But one must question the confluence of competition and efficiency, as these occasionally contradict, and then society must choose between them. As long as 'normal' conditions apply, where competition enhances efficiency, we may view the two as synonymous and use competition policy as a proxy for attaining efficiency. As seen above, when circumstances include economies of scale and scope, network effects, uncertain demand and excessive costly innovation, competition is not necessarily efficient. In such cases, society must choose between competition and efficiency as two potentially conflicting values. Those viewing competition as a proxy for efficiency should naturally expect the latter to govern, allowing concentration to rise or competitors to collude where such conduct is efficient. Those viewing competition as an independent value, should be willing to forgo efficient combinations in order to enjoy competition as a socially beneficial process. It is such cases where values collide that I shall stress below, as they allow for a true examination of commonly held beliefs and social values. The more common case, where competition is also efficient, is perhaps preferable, but allows for a confluence of factors which masks important distinctions between them.

Competition is not always good. In some markets, where economies of scale or economies of scope are significant, a single monopolistic provider might be able to manufacture at a much lower cost, and even taking into account monopoly markup, prices may still be lower. In other cases, where learning-by-doing is important, monopoly might allow more experience and knowledge to be gained, reducing mistakes later on. Sometimes stability over time is paramount, and a monopolistic firm will end up providing better service to society, even if prices are higher in the short run. And sometimes the existence of network effects makes competition less attractive, as consumers will naturally flock to the dominant platform in order to enjoy the company of other consumers.

These are but economic effects. However, when assessing competition, we must also consider the element of fairness. Manifestations of fairness include the protection of rights, the freedom to innovate and express oneself in the marketplace and one's autonomy and right to make a profit through exchange of goods and services. Here also, competition has its downfalls. Competition may create

[62] See, eg, M Stucke, 'Should Competition Policy Promote Happiness?' (2013) 81 *Fordham Law Review* 2575, text at fn 42. See also O Andriychuk, 'Can We Protect Competition without Protecting Consumers?' (2010) 6 *Competition Law Review* 77, arguing for a clear separation between competition as deontological value in itself and its welfare consequences, which may, or may not, merit teleological protection.

opportunities, but also take others away. A worker who is disabled is less successful at competing with others, and is protected in a variety of (uncompetitive) ways. Competition can wreak havoc on local communities through the decimation of small locally-owned businesses or widespread outsourcing aimed at cutting costs. Public discourse on this issue might bring up names such as Walmart, Microsoft or other fiercely powerful (and efficient?) competitors bringing national or international economies of scale and scope to bear on fledgling 'mom and pop stores' (as well as dominance in local labour markets threatening underprivileged workers). Similarly, markets such as telecommunication, aviation, or regulated industries might be central to the debate. In late nineteenth-century America, it would have been monopolies such as Standard Oil that bore the blame for economic conditions of less privileged market participants. Antitrust law in the US was formed in the context of small businesses being deemed worthy of preservation, sometimes to the detriment of aggregate efficiency or innovative practices. Later on, it became clear that it is 'competition, not competitors' that antitrust set out to protect, supposedly making policy more coherent due to its unitary focus. But what competition exists without protecting competitors? While individual competitors are not protected, at some point competition policy may determine that allowing existing businesses to fail will leave only one large provider, thus making competition suffer.

When competition is treated as a proxy for efficiency, it is not an independent goal. When it is treated as a proxy for protection of consumer choice, small businesses, or other groups, it relies on a conception of fairness towards members of such groups—to be investigated in chapter three below. Here, we focus on competition as an independent goal, of value to society as a whole, beyond economics. Competition is thus viewed as a protected process rather than a method for achieving specific results.[63] It is my contention that this view of competition permeates society and is so prevalent as to make competition policy a component of social morality, not merely economic wealth maximization.[64] In other words, competition is important enough that even where it is *efficiency-reducing*, most Western societies would choose to uphold it, paying its economic cost in order to achieve its non-economic benefits.[65]

[63] See, eg, GJ Werden, 'Competition, Consumer Welfare, and the Sherman Act' (2008) 9 *The Sedona Conference Journal* 87, 89–90, focusing on the competitive process rather than its results. But see also L Kaplow and C Shapiro, 'Antitrust' in AM Polinsky and Shavell (eds), *Handbook of Law and Economics*, vol 2 (North-Holland: Elsevier, 2007) 1073, distinguishing between competition and its economic effects and stating that economics is an appropriate tool for assessing efficiency, but not the value of competition itself.

[64] Indeed, some reject the goal of welfare-maximization for antitrust altogether. Black states: 'Neither the economic approach nor the philosophical approach to the maximization of welfare supports the welfare-based argument for competition and antitrust. The current orthodoxy should therefore be abandoned'; see Black (n 60) 61.

[65] Of course, some would argue that 'economic things matter only insofar as they make people happier', treating efficiency as a proxy itself. See AJ Oswald, 'Happiness and Economic Performance' (1997) 107 *Economic Journal* 1815. This view has merit, as money and material things are worthwhile for what they allow people to do, means rather than ends. The context competition policy's goals

A. Competition as a Democratic Process: Individual Choice and the Problem of Bigness

> If we will not endure a king as a political power, we should not endure a king over the production, transportation, and sale of any of the necessaries of life.
> (Senator John Sherman, arguing for enactment of the Sherman Act)[66]

> Competition … is first and foremost a system of decentralized economic power.[67]

There is something inherently democratic about the process of competition. At its best, competition is a process allowing the best product to attract the most consumers, inducing manufacturers to cut costs, entrepreneurs to innovate and assess consumer preferences and participants in the market to apply themselves towards success using their own best judgement. As a democratic process, competition has two main prongs. First, it allows for individual initiative and keeps the government out of the economic exchange between producers and consumers. As such, free choice is facilitated, both in consumption and in occupation. Each individual can choose for him or herself how best to plan their economic endeavours, in a manner respecting personal autonomy and maintaining non-intervention as state policy.[68] The second prong is that competition facilitates democracy by preventing the entrenchment of firms, whose economic power might translate into political prowess.[69] As long as competition ensues, the state remains neutral between contenders, maintaining a distinction between the economic and the political spheres of public life; or so one would hope.

Viewing competition as a democratic value promotes the process regardless of its outcome, thus justifying competition policy even where economically costly.[70] Of course, no value is absolute, thus in some cases potential efficiencies may

does not require delving into that debate, as the focus is on values *other than* economic efficiency concomitantly being pursued. Why we strive for efficiency requires less explanation here than when we are willing to forgo it. For a more general discussion of the interplay between economic outcomes and personal satisfaction, including the difficulties in deducing welfare from efficiency, see BS Frey and A Stutzer, 'What can Economists learn from Happiness Research?' (2002) 40 *Journal of Economic Literature* 402. For direct application to competition policy, see Stucke, 'Should Competition Policy Promote Happiness?' (n 62).

66 21 Congressional Record 2457 (1890).

67 W Adams and JW Brock, *The Bigness Complex: Industry, Labor, and Government in the American Economy* (Stanford, CA: Stanford University Press, 2004) 98.

68 See, eg, W Kerber, 'Competition, Innovation, and Maintaining Diversity through Competition Law' in J Drexl et al (eds), *Competition Policy and the Economic Approach: Foundations and Limitations* (Cheltenham: Edward Elgar, 2011); O Andriychuk, 'Rediscovering the Spirit of Competition: On the Normative Value of the Competitive Process' (2010) 6 *European Competition Journal* 575.

69 Most famously espoused by Justice Brandeis, 'The Curse of Bigness' was described as a major plague on democratic society and justifying antitrust intervention. See LD Brandeis, *Other People's Money and How the Bankers Use It* (New York: Stokes, 1914) ch 8.

70 Some offer a similar perspective, though framed as short-term costs to allow the long-term gains of discovery and innovation. See, eg, FA von Hayek, 'Competition as a Discovery Procedure' (2002) 5 *Quarterly Journal of Austrian Economics* 9; IM Kirzner, 'Entrepreneurial Discovery and the Competitive Market Process' (1997) 35 *Journal of Economic Literature* 60.

outweigh democratic costs, but these are outliers justified by extreme circumstances. Such concerns with clashes between protected values will be assessed in chapters five and seven below, as part of the general discussion of the balancing test antitrust must satisfy.

The issue of 'bigness' is one which dominated early antitrust scholarship and has been downplayed considerably as many have come to accept economic efficiency as antitrust's most important (only?) goal. Since economies of scale and scope are often considerable, large firms enjoy advantages in the marketplace. When such advantages allow them to eliminate competitive pressure, we are presented with a welfare trade-off of the type made famous by Oliver Williamson and prominent in the discussion of efficiencies within merger policy.[71] Yet before assessing the role of bigness in competition policy, the concept must be defined. What makes a firm 'big' for antitrust purposes? Market share cannot be the answer, as this is addressed directly when assessing market power, regardless of firm size or effects beyond the specific narrowly-construed product market. Firm size is a probable contender, but then again we must choose between proxies for size such as annual sales, market capitalization, assets owned, or even such parameters as number of employees, percentage of local employment and more. The operational definition for size depends on the values to be protected; thus we must first assess the fear competition policy addresses before ascribing to one definition or another. This section addresses the fear of large firms achieving power over political processes, ie, bigness as threatening the democratic institutions of the state. The next section will then address bigness with respect to participation in market processes, ie, as contrary to a society of entrepreneurs or small businesses.[72]

Democratic rule of law depends on the state being stronger than any of the parties which it regulates. Size and physical force are far from sufficient, as large firms may hold sway over political processes through the use of campaign donations, investment in lobbying activities and the like.[73] Similarly to merger policy, ex ante

[71] OE Williamson, 'Efficiencies as an Antitrust Defense: The Welfare Tradeoffs' (1968) 58 *American Economic Review* 18.

[72] The view that antitrust should target economic power and not just market power has fallen from favour in antitrust circles. Some go to the extreme of referring to economic power concerns as 'an irrational fear of corporate consolidation', eg, B Orbach and G Campbell Rebling, 'The Antitrust Curse of Bigness' (2012) 85 *Southern California Law Review* 605 and ES Rockefeller, *The Antitrust Religion* (Washington DC: Cato Institute, 2007) 8. Others sidestep the issue and focus on allocative concerns within specific markets more conducive to empirical investigation. I have delved into this issue elsewhere, and refer the interested reader there for more detail. See A Ayal, 'The Market for Bigness: Economic Power and Competition Agencies' Duty to Curtail It' (2013) 2 *Journal of Antitrust Enforcement* 1.

[73] See W Adams and JW Brock, 'Antitrust and Efficiency: A Comment' (1987) 62 *New York University Law Review* 1116, text at fns 27–32, as well as the discussion of 'public choice', section E.ii. This focus on economic power and political influence was prevalent in early antitrust jurisprudence; see, eg, RJ Peritz, 'A Counter-History of Antitrust Law' (1990) *Duke Law Journal* 263; AJ Meese, 'Liberty and Antitrust in the Formative Era' (1999) 79 *Boston University Law Review* 1; E Foner, *Give Me Liberty! An American History* (New York: WW Norton & Company, 2006) ch 17; TB Nachbar, 'Monopoly, Mercantilism and the Politics of Regulation' (2005) 91 *Virginia Law Review* 1313.

prevention of commercial firms' political influence is paramount, as limiting it ex post is unlikely to succeed.

The means for imposing private will on state action are available to firms and individuals with large amounts of cash on hand, but not only to them. If governmental actions have a strong influence on economic benefits, those aspiring to receive those benefits will find sources of capital to fund any endeavour promising a positive net present value (benefits exceeding losses). As stated by Luigi Zingales: 'the most powerful argument in favor of antitrust, is one that is rarely made: antitrust law reduces the political power of firms'.[74]

It is not economic size, then, that should be targeted, as where there are sufficient incentives, the means will be found by the relevant individuals, firms or organizations.[75] This leads us to focus on the extent of economic interests for governmental influence, rather than the size of the firm itself, or the extent of its economic resources. Limitation of agglomeration of power within the media is well known and usually accepted as necessary for protection of the democratic process, but here our argument goes further, to ask where general commercial relations might give rise to similar concerns.[76]

Large conglomerates, with interests ranging over diverse and unconnected industries might be argued to be more problematic than large firms as such. A conglomerate might be so involved in various markets, that almost every governmental action would influence its welfare.[77] Thus, it would enjoy economies of scale in rent-seeking, since once it attains influence over state officials (especially those with wide-ranging power), it could use this influence every time one of its diverse

[74] L Zingales, A Capitalism for the People: Recapturing the Lost Genius of American Prosperity (New York: Basic Books, 2012) 38.

[75] This assumes, of course, the efficiency of capital markets. An argument to the contrary should not only disprove this assumption, but also show why large firms have a liquidity advantage over other types of firms and institutions. See also T Calvani, 'What is the Objective of Antitrust?' in T Calvani and J Siegfried (eds), *Economic Analysis and Antitrust Law*, 2nd edn (Boston: Little, Brown & Co, 1988) 11.

[76] Media concentration is generally seen as increasing over time, but reality is more complex; see EM Noam, *Media Ownership and Concentration in America* (Oxford: Oxford University Press, 2009). Some see the problem of media concentration as requiring direct action, see, eg, ME Stucke and AP Grunes, 'Toward A Better Competition Policy For The Media' (2009) 42 *Connecticut Law Review* 101, explicating the importance of the media in the marketplace of ideas, and calling on Congress to formulate a national media policy taking this into account; K Conrad, 'Media Mergers: First Step in a New Shift of Antitrust Analysis?' (1997) 49 *Federal Communications Law Journal* 675, arguing in favour of stringent antitrust intervention in media markets. But see HA Shelanski, 'Antitrust Law as Mass Media Regulation: Can Merger Standards Protect the Public Interest?' (2006) 94 *California Law Review* 371, delineating a democracy argument and an efficiency argument in media regulation, and arguing that antitrust alone is unlikely to protect the democracy interest. In order to overcome the antitrust deficiency, ME Stucke and AP Grunes, 'Antitrust and the Marketplace of Ideas' (2001) 69 *Antitrust Law Journal* 249 argue that antitrust analysis should focus on competition in editorial content, rather than traditional financial indicators. J Temple Lang, 'Media, multimedia, and European Community antitrust law' (1997) 21 *Fordham International Law Journal* 1296 discusses the European perspective, arguing that these issues will continue to arise in Member State litigation, as their core difficulties have yet to be worked out.

[77] R Morck, D Wolfenzon and B Yeung, 'Corporate Governance, Economic Entrenchment, and Growth' (2005) 43 *Journal of Economic Literature* 655.

interests were affected. An opposite claim could also be made, that conglomerates by definition have diversified interests, thus actions benefiting or harming one industry would be dampened by different effects on another industry.[78] Thus, a conglomerate has less incentive to invest in attaining industry-specific benefits. One exception suggests itself: the type of intervention large conglomerates *would* be very much interested in, is *redistributional* efforts. The level of corporate taxation, for example, is of great concern to *all divisions* within a conglomerate. It is here that the incentives for gaining influence over decision-makers are the greatest, and where fears of non-democratic influence the most substantiated. Similarly, firms involved in regulated industries, or conglomerates with holdings in multiple industries subject to even partial regulation (as most industries are), may be especially prone to seek political influence. It seems then, that if competition policy is to protect democracy by insulating political institutions from undue influence, preventing the accumulation of power large firms or conglomerates achieve requires context-dependent enforcement that takes into account firm incentives and standards differing by industry and market structure.

While our discussion is normative rather than positive, it is illuminating to note that the current state of affairs in antitrust enforcement rejects the notion that bigness is a problem. In an address by Joel Klein, then the head official of the US Department of Justice Antitrust Division, he referred to such merger control as a trend of the 1960s and 1970s past, unjustified then and now: '[c]hallenging a deal simply because it is big is now unthinkable. I think, the 'big is bad' notion clearly was a mistake'.[79] It bears mention, though, that the policies he referred to targeted bigness as *overly efficient*, attempting to protect small 'mom-and-pop stores' from the perils of competition. Our current discussion of bigness as an issue from a democratic perspective is very different. In addition, one must take into account the lessons learned from recent financial crises, and the aggregate problems caused when important industries are dominated by a few interconnected players.[80]

[78] Of course, if we do decide to target conglomerates, their specific efficiencies should also be taken into account. If capital markets are inefficient, eg, conglomerate organization may be an appropriate correction of market failure. See OE Williamson, *Antitrust Economics: Mergers, Contracting, and Strategic Behavior* (Cambridge: Basil Blackwell, 1987) 49–50. This view is not shared by all. See HM Blake, 'Conglomerate Mergers and the Antirust Laws' (1973) 73 *Columbia Law Review* 555, 562–63, arguing that conglomerate mergers are beneficial only in terms of enhancing the market for corporate control. For a general review of large business groups, stressing their efficiencies and stability-enhancing characteristics, see RW Masulis, P Kien Pham and J Zein, 'Family Business Groups around the World: Financing Advantages, Control Motivations, and Organizational Choices' (2011) 24 *Review of Financial Studies* 3556. For a contrary view, stressing the collusive and strategic implications of interdependencies between large and diversified conglomerates, see G Spagnolo, 'On Interdependent Supergames: Multimarket Contact, Concavity, and Collusion' (1999) 89 *Journal of Economic Theory* 127.

[79] JI Klein, 'Antitrust Enforcement in the Twenty-First Century' (2000) 32 *Connecticut Law Review* 1065, 1068.

[80] The economic downturn following the financial meltdown of 2008 produced a plethora of condemnations regarding bigness and concentration, albeit in more specific circumstances than those antitrust routinely deals with. For an argument that the focus on efficiency and economies of scale and scope produced problematic results and an application to antitrust, see JW Markham, 'Lessons for Competition Law from the Economic Crises: The Prospect for Antitrust Responses to the

The use of antitrust to prevent over-concentration need not be committed preference of small over large businesses, which will be discussed in the next section.[81] De-concentration can be attained while allowing firms to reach comparatively large size, emphasizing benefits a small business economy cannot offer and avoiding some of its efficiency drawbacks.

Government is supposed to be independent of wealthy corporations' pressure, so that equal regard is given to all citizens. But government today is constantly bombarded with lobbying efforts from all directions, many of them successful. To say that we need to shield our government from external private interest influences expresses exaggerated optimism as to the current state of affairs. The 'Public Choice' literature abounds with laws and regulations passed under the influence of pressure groups of all varieties, within and beyond antitrust. To be sure, large corporations are part of this tendency, but they are not alone. To limit the size of corporations, then, may not achieve the effect wished for, other than to change somewhat the focus and means used to subvert 'democracy' as we envision it should be. The antitrust laws themselves have been characterized as the result of precisely this sort of undue influence—preferring the interests of a strong lobby of small business owners to the interests of other parts of society.[82]

Antitrust might be argued to be overly broad as a tool for combating economic power, as it applies to *all* monopolistic practices, from a small firm (indeed, even individual) monopolizing a distinct market, to a combination of small businesses seeking to cooperate in order to survive in the competitive war against large and efficient firms (think Walmart)—and discovering that a cartel is illegal even when it helps the small against the large. The focus on narrowly-delineated markets common in today's antitrust jurisprudence posits the large with the small, the politically connected with the purely commercial. Using antitrust to combat political influence by preventing concentration of economic power thus requires a shift in focus.

"Too-Big-To-Fail" Phenomenon' (2011) 16 *Fordham Journal of Corporate and Financial Law* 261. For a contrary view, see A Devlin, 'Antitrust in an Era of Market Failure' (2010) 33 *Harvard Journal of Law and Public Policy* 557, arguing that the problem had to do with specificities of the financial market, and regulation, rather than antitrust is implicated. On the other hand, there are those arguing that any large firm, financial or otherwise, invites governmental intervention and ex post bailout, due to the political ramifications of large-firm collapse; see JR Macey and JP Holdcroft, 'Failure is an Option: An Ersatz-Antitrust Approach to Financial Regulation' (2010) 120 *Yale Law Journal* 1368.

81 See R Pitofski, 'The Political Content of Antitrust' (1979) 127 *University of Pennsylvania Law Review* 1051, 1053; LB Schwartz, 'Justice and other Non-Economic Goals of Antitrust' (1979) 127 *University of Pennsylvania Law Review* 1076, 1078. Indeed, while Pitofski argued for 'political' goals of antitrust, including this democratic argument, he expressly argued *against* protection of small businesses. See also LA Sullivan and W Fikentscher, 'On the Growth of the Antitrust Idea' (1998) 16 *Berkeley Journal of International Law* 197, arguing that this view is distinctly American, and one that German antitrust tradition is less concerned with.

82 See Baer and Balto (n 55) fn 15.

The economic power argument for antitrust mirrors the political separation of powers.[83] In a democracy, we do not allow one despot to reign with absolute power, but divide state powers between several independent institutions. This 'separation of powers' has been incorporated into every form of democracy we know, due to a basic distrust of individual self restraint. 'Power tends to corrupt', it is said, 'and absolute power—corrupts absolutely'.[84] Thus, if we find limiting political power acceptable, should we not limit economic power as well?

III. ANTITRUST AS FACILITATING A SOCIETY OF ENTREPRENEURS

By now faintly anachronistic, the view that antitrust is aimed at fostering a better society through protecting the ability of small business people to compete in the market has strong historical roots. In early American politics, Thomas Jefferson and Alexander Hamilton debated this issue vigorously regarding the type of society they were founding. Jefferson propounded the idea that a society comprised of entrepreneurs would be better for all involved, while Hamilton was focused on a viable industrial policy for the state as a whole. One might say that the Jeffersonian ideal was an individualist society, where a man could work for himself, taking orders from no one, while the Hamiltonian view accepted a need for centralist institutions coordinating individual action.[85] In Europe, the Ordoliberals set the groundwork for similar ideals in their strict separation between spheres of influence and emphasis on individual choice.[86] The argument for facilitating a society of small businesses and entrepreneurs is different from the 'competition as democracy' view expounded above. There, the focus was on maintaining a competitive process, one where incumbents must constantly fear entry and battle other providers vying for market share. Here, we go one step further to ask whether society has an interest in maintaining small firm size in order to maximize independence. The 'entrepreneurial society' is one where not only are there multiple competitors in every market, but self-owned businesses are the norm. The distinction is starkest in markets where small businesses are less efficient, and larger firms could be accommodated without alleviating competitive

[83] J Baker, 'Economics and Politics: Perspectives on the Goals and Future of Antitrust' (2013) 81 *Fordham Law Review* 2175 presents this as one of the future directions of antitrust, portraying it as a centrist-leftist concern. See also H Vedder, 'Of jurisdiction and Justification; Why Competition is Good for 'Non-economic' Goals, but may need to be Restricted' (2009) 6 *The Competition Law Review* 51, arguing that antitrust is best suited to the task of preventing regulatory capture.

[84] Lord Acton, *Letter to Bishop Mandell Creighton* (5 April 1887), quoted in J Bartlett, *Familiar Quotations*, 16th edn (Boston: Little, Brown & Co, 1992).

[85] See MD Peterson, *The Jefferson Image in the American Mind* (New York: Oxford University Press, 1962) 79–81; F McDonald, *The Presidency of Thomas Jefferson* (Lawrence: University Press of Kansas, 1976) 18–21. The Sherman Act itself was described as a compromise between the two world views; see SM Elkins and EL McKitrick, *The Age of Federalism* (New York: Oxford University Press, 1993) 18–29.

[86] Though the Ordoliberal view might be seen as aiming at a combination between the two, forming the institutional infrastructure that will best support individual action. See ch 1, nn 16–29.

pressure. In such cases, efficiency is reduced by precluding economies of scale, not just in production, but in corporate structure as well.

To what extent is this issue relevant to current antitrust debate? The history of competition policy shows that case law and scholarship have moved away from such issues, at least explicitly. Efficiency is now key, and even raising the issue of competition policy as betterment of society seems out of place. Despite this, both intellectual rigour and open-mindedness demand we approach the issue with respect. My purpose here is to *explore* the justifications for antitrust, rather than assuming a priori that some are relevant and basing analysis on them alone. I thus seek to learn from all perspectives and focus on the balancing test required to facilitate achieving all goals desired, to the greatest possible extent.

It should be stressed that our discussion here is of *societal goals*, thus the frame will be what society as a whole gains from the existence of entrepreneurs and small businesses, rather than what *they themselves* might be entitled to. The second issue, of individual (usually small) businesses vying for a state-protected *right* to participate in the marketplace will be addressed in the next chapter, regarding the fairness claims that monopoly's victims might raise.[87]

The question of whether society would be better off when most of the economic arena is dominated by small rather than large businesses relies on individual value judgements.[88] Given the nature of today's economy, an argument that large businesses are detrimental to society seems almost anachronistic. Corporations have grown to immense proportions, some owning more assets than most states, and this is far from a new development.[89] Early antitrust jurisprudence was guided by precisely this sentiment, and in some ways it is returning to past splendour today with popular resistance to large corporations, and the rise of movements such as '99 per cent', 'occupy Wall Street' and the like.[90]

[87] The distinction between the two is most striking in cases where antitrust law would forbid acquisition of small businesses by larger firms. While society may benefit from maintaining independence of small businesses and the resulting competitive pressure, their owners may very well *prefer* the profit accruing from such a sale. Thus, society's interests in small businesses may sometimes act to the detriment of the small business people themselves.

[88] It is interesting to note that it was once competition that was considered immoral: 'The competitive system tends to develop what is worst in the character of all ... the qualities which it discourages are the noblest and most generous that men have, and the qualities which it rewards are ... selfish and sordid instincts'. See E Bellamy, *Plutocracy or Nationalism—Which?* (1889) 2 [quoted in MJ Horowitz, *The Transformation of American Law* (New York: Oxford University Press, 1992) 82].

[89] Henn's book on corporate law discussed this as an obvious problem four decades ago. See HG Henn, *Corporations* (St Paul, MN: West Publishing Co, 1974) 27–51 and citations therein.

[90] Recent writings in corporate scholarship, as well as popular debate, are reminiscent of this view that society suffers when large corporate actors dominate the economic arena. See, eg, J Bakan, *The Corporation: The Pathological Pursuit of Profit and Power* (US: Free Press, 2004), explaining the corporation as a vehicle for assimilating the work of many fine individuals into one psychopathic behemoth. Kent Greenfield examined corporate law in greater depth to assess similar claims; see K Greenfield, *The Failure of Corporate Law* (Chicago: University of Chicago Press, 2006). While interesting and thought provoking, these ideas are relevant to corporations in general, rather than monopolistic ones—our focus here. Monopolistic firms are sometimes large, though not always, with the converse true as well. We shall thus return to these and similar issues in our discussion of the rights or corporate actors as such, within the fairness goals discussed in ch 4.

The fact that as a society we have moved towards ever-increasing firm size does not necessarily mean that this trend is inevitable, or morally superior to its alternatives. This section thus attempts to draft out the main arguments for the policy of consciously facilitating a society of small businesses and entrepreneurs, followed by references to drawbacks, costs and finally, the question if antitrust policy as we know it is suited to the task.

The early argument in favour small businesses was that a person who owns their own business is more involved, leading to higher productivity and a greater sense of belonging—within society and state.[91] Furthermore, one might fear corporations growing sufficiently strong to overpower the state, thus threatening democracy. Thus, individual independence was considered both economically efficient and politically facilitating a 'government of the people'.[92] As stated in one of the earliest examples of antitrust jurisprudence:

> [I]t is not for the real prosperity of any country that such changes should occur which result in transferring an independent business man, the head of his establishment, small though it might be, into a mere servant or agent of a corporation for selling the commodities which he once manufactured or dealt in, having no voice in shaping the business policy for the company and bound to obey orders issued by others.[93]

In the United States, Franklin Delano Roosevelt saw antitrust as relating to the concentration of economic interests which increase social inequality, allowing the wealthy to become even wealthier and enlarge the gap between them and those labouring within the large, impersonal firms.[94] Furthermore, allowing firms to grow creates opportunities for them to economic power, thus requiring regulatory oversight so that this power is not abused (either commercially or politically). Such regulation is wasteful, a pure cost to society of allowing private power to grow to the point of requiring limitation. It is better, so the argument goes, to maintain a competitive marketplace of small businesses ex ante, than to expend resources and effort in regulation after the fact.

In a nutshell, a small business society was said to achieve four main benefits (aside from limiting economic despotism, discussed in section II.A above):

1. Facilitating individual choice and freedom that would otherwise be limited in larger corporations.

[91] See SF Ross, *Principles of Antitrust Law* (Westbury, New York: The Foundation Press, 1993) 6, fn 12. For perceived effects on the effect of market structure on personal character, see R Hofstadter, 'What Happened to the Antitrust Movement?' in *The Paranoid Style in American Politics and Other Essays* (New York: Vintage Books, 1965) 207–09. It is interesting to note the similarity of these views to the Marxist critique of capitalism as creating a separation between the worker and his work, and concentrating production in large firms (factories) as detrimental to human dignity.

[92] See Note, Mr Justice Brandeis, 'Competition and Smallness: A Dilemma Re-examined' (1956) 66 *Yale Law Journal* 69, 74–75.

[93] *US v Trans-Missouri Freight Association*, 166 US 290, 324 (1897) (Justice Peckham).

[94] The Public Papers and Addresses of Franklin D Roosevelt (New York: Russell & Russell, 1938) 305–32.

2. Ensuring economic efficiency through higher individual incentive to innovate and vigorously compete.
3. Limiting social inequality that a corporate economy would otherwise create.
4. Economizing on resources otherwise needed to regulate monopolies.

Our next step is to examine these aims, first as to their coherence and applicability today, and then as to the appropriateness of antitrust law (rather than other social and legal norms) in attaining them.

A. Competition as Facilitating Individual Choice

Is it true that smaller businesses allow more individual choice? On the one hand, an owner of a business is independent to decide the field of investment, the type of work she does herself and the type she subcontracts to others, her hours of labour and such. On the other hand, an independent businesswoman is independent only of a formal employer. The market, the demand for her product or service, the physical constraints of production and similar concerns are constraints she must accommodate or perish. The realistic pressure of running a business requires that those wishing for 'independence' should define their aims more clearly. Many working men and women seek jobs in large institutions precisely because they wish for a more relaxed way of doing business, externalizing the stress of maintaining profit margins on to management or shareholders. For many, working in their chosen vocation is possible *only* within larger corporations, where division of labour is such that they may concentrate on what interests them. On a personal note, it would be difficult to concentrate on research (or even teaching) if academics were constantly busy with 'running the business' which generates these opportunities, and securing the funds with which to do them. The concept of the 'small businessperson's independence' is thus overly idealized, with many of those with real world experience of it, smirking at the concept. A popular adage says 'working for a salary, you have one boss, running a business—you have many'.

Granted, some value the joy of creation, independently bringing an idea from dream to reality, as more important than all other considerations. But a regime in which most people would be constrained to managing their own business is not necessarily beneficial to their freedom of choice. That this argument historically generated so much agreement may be ascribed to two sources. First, the argument was raised and propagated at a time when family farming was a major source of income for many, and businesses were usually local. In such a society, the move from independent owner to corporate pawn could be traumatic. Second, the argument relies on emotion stirred more by fantasy than reality. The wish for independence is instilled in us by the very Western, democratic society in which we were raised. A call for self-determination is thus attractive, though not necessarily remaining so when the physical reality of the *costs* associated with such individual entrepreneurship are considered.[95]

Finally, I should stress that this is not an argument against the legitimacy of small, self-owned businesses as such. They are, of course, a legitimate form of business, beneficial to many. It is only that individual choice includes the choice whether to take on their benefits with their costs, or prefer what may be a tamer role within a large corporation (or a subtle variation between the two extremes). If individual choice is the true object, both types of possibilities should exist with the state careful in granting one a preference over the other.

B. Facilitating Economic Efficiency

The fact that this goal is mentioned is to be attributed to the history from which the argument as a whole was drawn. During the eighteenth and nineteenth centuries, it may have been reasonable to assume that when an individual's livelihood was at stake, his incentive was greater and thus he would be more efficient. The economies of scale and scope of larger corporations, coupled with technological innovations, management efficiencies and capital-raising techniques possible *only* within a hierarchic organization, are today clear and require no repeating here.[96] Economic efficiency may indeed be a worthy social goal, but limiting firm size is hardly an appropriate means to that end.

C. Limiting Social Inequality

The goal itself may be respected, but has it really anything to do with small versus large businesses? With the technology of today, one cannot necessarily associate personal wealth with the size of the business; it is enough to mention the sizable sums young entrepreneurs have received for their technological innovations. Start-up companies can lead to riches or ruin, while corporate employment can facilitate social mobility, relying on others' capital to make one's own. Again, what perhaps was true in the late nineteenth century is no longer true today (if indeed it ever was). In a world of social inequality and inherited wealth, it is difficult to

[95] As a side note, the benefits of choice are often overrated as well. While striving for enhanced choice sets we often reduce our own ability to understand the different options, and worsen the results. For a discussion of the psychological literature on the subject, and an implementation in modern commerce (including anticompetitive tactics based on such human frailty), see A Ayal, 'On Consumers' Freedom of Choice: Lessons from the Cellular Market' (2011) 74 *Law and Contemporary Problems* 91.

[96] See, eg, P Areeda and L Kaplow, *Antitrust Analysis*, 4th edn (Boston: Little, Brown & Co, 1988) 31–33 and citations therein.

tie inequitable distribution to the size of firms. Social inequality existed (indeed, in a much more severe form) well prior to the invention of the corporation and the opening up of capital markets. It is not clear how aiming for small businesses would solve this age old problem.

D. Economizing on Monopoly Regulation

This argument needs to be considered on two levels. First, is this an aim coherent with the stated means of maintaining a small business society? Second, is it not a presumption of that which is to be proven? I begin with the second.

The view that the creation of antitrust law and maintaining a small business economy economizes on monopoly regulation is akin to putting the cart before the horse. Economizing on monopoly regulation cannot be used as an explanation for the creation of antitrust law, since the regulation itself is not yet proven to be needed. Only an external argument can justify the regulation of monopoly, and only once that question is settled, can we turn to the means of regulation—whether by ex ante or ex post intervention. Since our aim here is to justify the primary contention of the need for antitrust to begin with, this argument is not helpful. The question of preference of ex post or ex ante intervention is indeed an important one, but one to be considered after clarifying the aims sought for, not in expounding the initial justifications for competition policy as such.

The first question, though, will not go unanswered. Were we to accept the 'economizing' argument, would aiming for a small business society be an appropriate means? I think not. If the need for some sort of regulation is taken for granted, ex ante intervention might be easier to accomplish and cheaper to administer than ex post, but why aim for small businesses? It might be easier to aim at market share, entry barriers, or any other traditional antitrust characteristic. Small businesses as such may still collude and cause the exact harm we seek to avoid. If small businesses are an appropriate aim, it must be independently proven, and the 'economizing' argument is neither theoretically nor practically helpful in this matter.

In the end, the small business society may be preferred if the empirical questions set out above were answered in a satisfactory manner. Independence and creativity are legitimate social values, and a society wishing to protect them may choose small businesses as appropriate means. This, though, depends on unproven assumptions regarding the types of firms where these values are achievable, and seems to enshrine traditional rhetoric over contemporary analysis. Choice, efficiency and equality are laudable values, but their protection is not served by limiting firm size and maintaining a small business economy. Choice entails allowing for diverse market structures and opportunities and efficiency requires scale and scope unachievable in most small businesses. Economic equality, if posed as a social good, could be better attained through non-antitrust means (and no serious notion of posing it as a social good was entertained herein). Political equality is equivalent to the 'bigness' and protection of democracy argument assessed above, but requires a more nuanced approach than the 'big is bad' rhetoric associated with traditional arguments in favour of the entrepreneur society. Antitrust can (and should!) be used to protect social goods such as democracy and preventing excess political influence, but the focus should be more specific and more accepting of the need for large firms alongside the small.

3

Monopoly's Victims

After the previous chapter's focus on society's aggregate concerns with the benefits (and costs) of preserving competition, this chapter analyzes *fairness* arguments justifying antitrust intervention. Fairness arguments as such are focused on a distinct individual or category of persons claiming a right to be protected. State action could take the form of forming a legal claim enforceable in civil litigation, criminal proceedings initiated by the state against those infringing upon a protected right or administrative proceedings whereby state agencies act to foster an economic environment that the claiming party could participate in. While the *means* for the protection of these rights may differ, our focus will be on the question of the rights' *existence*, and to what extent a justifiable claim for state action could be made on their behalf. Later on, after assessing similar claims made by monopolists (broadly defined), we shall examine the balancing test required to assess situations where the rights of different parties conflict and contextual application requires some give and take between them. Only then will it be possible to assess the different means used within competition policy and form opinions regarding circumstances where one type of enforcement is preferable to the other. This chapter will focus on those who might argue for state-fostered competition policy, while the next will focus on the other side of the debate—monopolists, both real and potential, who might argue against state intervention.

Insofar as personal rights exist in our context, claimants can expect a just social order to take their interests into account, even at positive cost borne by society at large. This essentially means that even if efficiency analysis or protection of the other public values assessed in chapter two fail to justify a proposed antitrust rule, claimants of rights-based protection would still be entitled to (at least some) relief. All the more so, if society as a whole *gains* from antitrust, as then both aggregate and individual concerns could be met in one coherent framework. Indeed, as discussed in chapter two, the almost unanimous support for antitrust assumes (implicitly) that prohibiting monopolistic practices is both efficient *and* fair, preventing the deadweight-loss triangle and the wealth-transfer rectangle alike.

One might hope for achieving both types of goal with one stroke, but this is not always possible. A classic juxtaposition between the two runs along the lines of the following: 'it might increase aggregate efficiency to allow business practice such-and-such (for example, an efficient merger increasing market power), but the harm caused to *X* would then go uncorrected—and that would unfairly infringe upon his/her/their rights'. *X*, of course, may be consumers, workers, competitors, or any other group whose interests are harmed by monopolistic practices, *as long as these interests are deemed worthy of state protection.*[1]

Efficiency and fairness considerations are juxtaposed in this way, not because they inherently collide (indeed, as shown above, they many times lead to similar conclusions), but because this is usually the great dividing line between those arguing for antitrust intervention and those arguing against it. Efficiency analysis has been dubbed 'the right side of antitrust', relying on a 'Chicago School' preference for non-intervention and trust in market forces, while fairness considerations are sometimes said to pose 'the left side', stressing the state's position in protecting the weak.[2]

Fairness arguments are typically made on behalf of representative groups which are likely to be harmed by monopolistic practices, with consumers being the paradigmatic victims, but workers, competitors and local communities alluded to as well. I shall analyze each of these in turn, assessing the rights claimed by each group, and how these are protected by the enforcement of competition law. It must be stressed that this chapter is necessarily one-sided (as will be the next one, though in the opposite direction) and conclusions as to justifiable intervention may be reached only after both are assessed and balanced accordingly. I begin with the basic 'wealth transfer' argument and then move on to more sophisticated analysis of property rights underlying it, as well as procedural justice analysis

[1] By focusing on infringed upon rights, we move away from the prevalent view of antitrust as economics oriented and efficiency justified. Indeed, the efficiency view of antitrust has become so broadly accepted that some writers find it almost unnecessary to discuss fairness issues, eg, 'I am going to be brief in discussing the noneconomic objections to monopolization because ... the courts and the scholars alike are now pretty uniformly committed to the economic approach'; R Posner, *Antitrust Law*, 2nd edn (Chicago: University of Chicago Press, 2001) 23. Needless to say, I disagree. As shown in ch 1, popular support for antitrust stems more from its contribution to perceived fairness than the economic benefits ascribed to it. Nonetheless, the economic arguments lend antitrust an air of objective neutrality—at least as long as efficiency supports policies also perceived to be fair. See also EL Robertson, 'A Corrective Justice Theory of Antitrust Regulation' (1999–2000) 49 *Catholic University Law Review* 741; A Kunzler, 'Economic Content of Competition Law: The Point of Regulating Preferences' in D Zimmer (ed), *The Goals of Competition Law* (Cheltenham: Edward Elgar, 2012).

[2] The terms are drawn from EJ Hughes, 'The Left Side of Antitrust: What Fairness means and Why it Matters' (1994) 77 *Marquette Law Review* 265. The examples of fairness/efficiency juxtaposition are too numerous to adequately review, thus I refer interested readers only to the most prominent writings and their development over time: Symposium, 'The Goals of Antitrust: A Dialogue on Policy' (1965) 65 *Columbia Law Review* 363, including articles by RH Bork, WS Bowman, HM Blake and WK Jones; Symposium: 'Antitrust Law and Economics' (1979) 127 *University of Pennsylvania Law Review* 917, including articles by RA Posner, RR Nelson, OE Williamson, R Schmalensee, R Pitofsky, LB Schwartz, P Areeda, D Turner and LW Weiss; Symposium, 'The Antitrust Alternative' (1987) 62 *New York University Law Review* 931 and 76 *Georgetown Law Journal* 237 (1987) (the papers delivered at the symposium were divided between the two journals for publication), including articles by EM Fox, R Pitofski, LA Sullivan, R Abrams, FM Scherer, JF Brodley, H First, WF Mueller, W Adams, JW Brock, JJ Flynn, JF Ponsoldt, WS Comanor, TG Krattenmaker, RH Lande, SC Salop, OE Williamson, FH Easterbrook, E Correia and SD Susman. For a general survey of the contrasting views, see W Page, 'Ideological Conflict and the Origins of Antitrust Policy' (1991) 66 *Tulane Law Review* 1 and R Pitofsky (ed), *How the Chicago School Overshot the Mark: The Effect of Conservative Economic Analysis on US Antitrust* (Oxford: Oxford University Press, 2008).

which might justify consumer protection on other grounds. Deeper conceptual issues regarding the nature of property, such as an argument that the right to property is limited by a caveat that it be used only in a pro-competitive fashion are important to our analysis, and may be relevant to several of the groups assessed below. The chapter will thus begin with consumers, examining who they are and in what way competition analysis protects them. Concepts borrowed from moral and political philosophy will then be used to ask a deeper question, namely: what justifies the special treatment consumers receive and whether a just society would enact the rules of antitrust as we know them today? The same general themes will then be applied to other potential claimants, such as workers, competitors and local communities. The next chapter will make use of the same philosophical modelling to examine whether monopolists might make similar claims as well.

One issue stands out, and that is that most 'monopolists' limited by competition law are firms, while 'consumers' are usually taken to be human beings, natural persons for whom the state operates. This issue will be tackled in chapter four, raising both practical issues (most antitrust litigation is brought on behalf of firms, and most benefits accrue to firms, not natural persons) as well as conceptual ones (as whether firms' rights differ from those of natural persons). While almost a non-issue in antitrust, this distinction will prove central in investigating the divide between intuition and practice in competition policy, allowing us to ask in what ways modern economic modelling has moved antitrust away from its origins, and what has been lost in the process.

I. CONSUMERS AND THEIR CENTRALITY IN THE FAIRNESS DISCUSSION

The protection of consumers is undoubtedly the most often cited justification for antitrust law. Both popular accounts and scholarly writings stress consumers' centrality, seeing them as the most obvious victims of monopolistic practices.[3]

[3] In the 'popular accounts' category we include newspaper and general interest journals, but also the rhetoric of political debate. Politicians—either due to aiming at wide audiences, or due to their own limitations—generally use arguments of a more colourful nature and focus less on comprehensive analysis. For a review of 'popular revolt' terminology used against monopolies in the mid-nineteenth to early twentieth century, see SL Piott, *The Anti-Monopoly Persuasion* (Westport, CT: Greenwood Press, 1985); for a comparative view, see DM Raybould and A Firth, *Law of Monopolies: Competition Law and Practice in the USA, EEC, Germany and the UK* (London: Graham & Trotman, 1991) 3–7. Scholarly focus on consumers as the prime recipients of antitrust benefits is too pervasive to survey, but see, eg, W Adams and JW Brock, 'Antitrust, Ideology, and the Arabesques of Economic Theory' (1995) 66 *University of Colorado Law Review* 257, arguing against the trend focusing on economic arguments at all, due to their inherent ideological content; P Areeda and L Kaplow, *Antitrust Analysis*, 4th edn (Boston: Little, Brown & Co, 1988) 56–57; DT Armentano, *Antitrust Policy: The Case for Repeal* (Washington DC: The Cato Institute, 1986) 9–10; JF Brodley, 'The Economic Goals of Antitrust: Efficiency, Consumer Welfare, and technological Progress' (1987) 62 *New York University Law Review* 1020 (citing consumer surplus as a constraint on efficiency and the driving force behind antitrust). See also EM Fox, 'Antitrust Welfare—The Bodley Synthesis' (2010) 90 *Boston University Law Review*

The different arguments raised on consumers' behalf will be assessed, but first we must consider a more basic question: who are the consumers?

A. Is Every Buyer a Consumer or Merely the End User?

Since consumers are so central to fairness arguments, this distinction is extremely relevant. If every buyer is considered a 'consumer', antitrust protection is afforded at multiple levels of production and trade. Imagine for example a monopolist, *A*, selling a good that serves as an input to the buyer, *B*, who subsequently sells the finished product to *C*. If the consumer to be protected is *C* alone (the end user), *B* has no independent claim for protection from *A*'s monopoly. Of course, if the monopoly surcharge is passed on to *C*, *C*'s claim for protection may in turn benefit *B* as well.[4] But do we really think of antitrust law as limited in this way? The question becomes relevant when realistic market imperfections make *C* indifferent to the good's price.[5] While often simple producer–consumer (or seller–buyer) models are used for explanatory purposes, the manufacture of even a simple good passes through a long vertical chain from primary inputs, through processing, assembly, packaging, shipping, distributing and retailing—at the very least. Indeed, one of Milton Friedman's famous demonstrations was holding up a pencil and arguing that no one producer knows how to make this simple product. Wood, plastic, rubber, paint, metal—all come together through various manufacturers and intermediaries to make one end product: the pencil. Add in marketing, advertising and so on, and the proportions are staggering. Thus, for a monopoly surcharge to reach the end user, either the monopoly must be located at a stage

1375, characterizing Brodley's insights as prescient and the focus on rivalry central to antitrust. An interesting contrast is between DW Barnes, 'Non-efficiency Goals in the Antitrust Law of Mergers' (1989) 30 *William and Mary Law Review* 787, arguing consumer interests dominate economic ones, and JA Hausman and GK Leonard, 'Efficiencies from the Consumer Viewpoint' (1999) 7 *George Mason Law Review* 707, arguing for an opposite perspective, showing merger efficiencies to be specifically in the *consumer's* interest. Of course, this reminds one of the historical impetuses of enactment of the antitrust laws in America, argued by some to focus on consumers' *right* to be free of wealth transfers. See RH Lande, 'Wealth Transfers as the Original and Primary Concern of Antitrust: The Efficiency Interpretation Challenged' (1982) 34 *Hastings Law Journal* 65 (see also accompanying text to ch 1, n 39 and ch 2, n 4).

[4] This may not be so. If *A* is truly a monopolist while *B* is in a competitive market, the monopoly surcharge is equal for all of *B*'s competitors as well. Thus this part of production costs is higher for all, and will be passed on to *C* in inverse proportion to demand elasticity. *B* may benefit from reduction in the input's price, lowering his costs and thus raising quantity demanded for *his* product (assuming a downward-sloping demand schedule), but slight imperfections in his product market may change things considerably, eg, if *B*'s manufacturing process uses the good less intensively than his competitors, lowering the good's price will actually lower competitor costs relative to his, thus harming *B*.

[5] An example of such a case can be found in *Brooke Group Ltd v Brown & Williamson Tobacco Corporation*, 61 USLW 4699 (1993). While the case focused on other aspects, the discounts and rebates offered by cigarette manufacturers to wholesalers were rarely passed on to retailers, let alone individual buyers. See WB Burnett, 'Predation by a Non-dominant Firm: The Ligget Case' in JE Kwoka and LJ White (eds), *The Antitrust Revolution*, 3rd edn (New York: Oxford University Press, 1999).

very near the end user, or markets through which the good and its inputs pass must be perfectly competitive. Taking into account that 'perfectly competitive' entails not only lack of market power, but also perfectly available information, zero transaction costs, etc, this is a tall order indeed, and rarely realistic.

Limiting consumer status to end users alone would limit the application of competition law quite severely. As will be shown, the main consumer-oriented arguments pertain to wealth transfers, a phenomenon arguably present in all direct purchases from a monopolistic seller.[6] The buyer may enter the transaction for personal consumption or for material gain through subsequent trade or manufacture—the harm suffered is the same. A caveat might be if we distinguish between end users and intermediate buyers (purchasing inputs for later resale after modification) due to the former being natural persons and the latter (usually) being firms, though this issue will be tackled below.

As a matter of positive law in the US, the *Illinois Brick* doctrine barred indirect purchasers from claiming antitrust injury, while *Hanover Shoe* held that defendants cannot argue that monopoly overcharge was passed on to downstream consumers.[7] Thus, *C* in our example would have no claim against *A*, leaving *B* alone with a right of action, and barring *A* from claiming that *B* suffered no injury due to his passing on the monopoly surcharge to *C*. These cases have been described as inseparable twins, and analyzed as procedural safeguards against overly complex demands made on the litigation process.[8] While it may be counterintuitive to deny end consumers standing in antitrust, powerful procedural considerations support this result. Streamlining the antitrust process and reducing litigation costs creates aggregate benefits, as well as generating incentives for direct purchasers to initiate proceedings that would deter antitrust injury ex ante. End consumers are thus protected, though by indirect means.

In 2007, the US Antitrust Modernization Commission (AMC) proposed repealing *Illinois Brick*, and replacing it with a more complex (and realistic) method for allocating antitrust standing between those affected, though this proposal has yet to be accepted.[9] It is interesting to note that due to the federal system of American law, individual states have the freedom to diverge on this matter, and numerous

[6] See, eg, NW Averitt and RH Lande, 'Consumer Sovereignty: A Unified Theory of Antitrust and Consumer Protection Law' (1997) 65 *Antitrust Law Journal* 713, fn 12.

[7] *Illinois Brick Co v Illinois*, 431 US 720 (1977); *Hanover Shoe Inc v United Machinery Corp*, 329 US 481 (1968). The *Hanover Shoe* doctrine rejecting the pass-on defence includes a few caveats allowing for cases where it might be allowed, though the Court itself stated that these are 'normally insurmountable'. See ibid, 493–94. These exceptions have been narrowly construed by the Court, even as to 'cost-plus' contract expressly mentioned in *Illinois Brick* which supposedly allows for a simple calculation of passed-on overcharges. See *Kansas v UtiliCorp United*, 497 US 199 (1990).

[8] See WM Landes and RA Posner, 'Should Indirect Purchasers Have Standing to Sue under the Antitrust Laws? An Economic Analysis of the Rule of Illinois Brick' (1979) 46 *The University of Chicago Law Review* 602.

[9] See *AMC Report and Recommendations* (2007), ch III.B: govinfo.library.unt.edu/amc/report_recommendation/amc_final_report.pdf. The *Illinois Brick* doctrine continues to be applied by American courts, often barring end-user consumer litigation. See, eg, *Kansas v UtiliCorp United* (n 7); *Kloth v Microsoft Corp*, 444 F 3d 312 (2006).

states have done so.[10] Thus, federal antitrust law continues to bar indirect purchasers, maintaining that 'consumers' for litigation purposes are only those in direct contact with monopolistic providers. AMC recommendations and state exceptions exhibit a movement away from this doctrine.[11] As our concern is with normative analysis rather than positive law, it is interesting to view these developments as telling of the public sentiment underlying them. The 'indirect purchaser' doctrine serves to avoid complication of antitrust proceedings and burdening the courts with analysis of the elasticities determining pass-on capabilities, though simultaneously removing end user consumers from legal consideration. This may be useful and efficient in legal application perhaps, but problematic when much of the rhetoric underlying competition law relies on precisely these consumers' centrality.

In the European Union, private enforcement of competition law plays a much more limited role, relative to public enforcement via administrative proceedings.[12] Private suits are generally allowed, and the European Commission has stated its support for increasing their prevalence in practice.[13] Nonetheless, private enforcement is limited in the EU both for lack of such a tradition and due to the fact that while public enforcement is initiated by the Directorate General—Competition and based on Articles 101 and 102 of the TFEU, private suits must be brought within Member States and under national law.[14] The question of direct versus indirect purchasers has yet to receive a final union wide answer from the European Court of Justice, as while indirect parties were allowed to sue, the extent of causation between the suspect practice and any harm suffered was left for national courts to determine.[15]

[10] See *Antitrust Law Developments*, 7th edn (Chicago, IL: American Bar Association, 2012) 772.

[11] On the other hand, AMC recommendations might be less important than its credentials imply, as in practice such commissions are routinely ignored. See S Calkins, 'Antitrust Modernization: Looking Backwards' (2006) 31 *Journal of Corporate Law* 421.

[12] See DJ Gerber, 'Private Enforcement of Competition Law: A Comparative Perspective' in T Mollers and A Heinemann (eds), *The Enforcement of Competition Law in Europe* (Cambridge: Cambridge University Press, 2007).

[13] See Council Regulation (EC) No 1/2003 (16 December 2002), on the Implementation of the Rules on Competition Laid Down in Articles 81 and 82 of the Treaty, [2003] OJ L1/1. Some have argued against this, as private litigation has the potential to flood the courts and bias application due to the interests of plaintiffs being sometimes misaligned with public interest underlying the competition laws. See WPJ Wils, 'Should Private Antitrust Enforcement be Encouraged in Europe?' (2003) 26 *World Competition* 473.

[14] See G Berrisch, E Jordan and R Salvador, 'EU Competition and Private Actions for Damages' (2003–04) 24 *Northwestern Journal of International Law and Business* 585.

[15] Case 295/04, *Vincenzo Manfredi v Lloyd Adriatico Assicurazioni SpA* [2006] ECR I-6619. Some argue that the lack of a single legal forum determining these issues EU-wide prevents both successful fostering of private enforcement and ensures a legal quagmire threatening what private suits will emerge. See F Cengiz, 'Passing-On Defense and Indirect Purchaser Standing in Actions for Damages Against the Violations of Competition Law: What Can the EC Learn from the US?' (2007) CCP Working Paper No 07-21: ssrn.com/abstract=1038521.

Even assuming indirect purchasers are granted standing and a partial passing on defence is allowed, the private enforcement of competition laws is heavily weighted towards direct purchasers who have both the relevant information and the stronger incentive to litigate. While one might expect that end consumers benefit from this arrangement, this depends on the extent such benefits pass through multiple levels of supply. Economic analysis suggests we should be sceptical of ambitious claims in this context, since market imperfections exist at every level, and it is plausible in many cases to assume benefits will be accrued by firms within the supply chain, with end consumers affected slightly if at all. Of course, to the extent that private enforcement deters uncompetitive practices, the aims of antitrust may still be served—though again, this would probably benefit producing and distributing firms more than end consumers.

Taking into account how central the term 'consumers' is to the justification of competition policy, it is important to keep in mind that its implementation differs greatly from the intuitive picture conjured by the rhetoric used. This is not to say that the indirect purchaser rule negates consumer benefit, or even that its repeal would necessarily benefit consumers, especially taking into account litigation imperfections mentioned above. Given that 'consumers' is a key term, calling to mind weak individuals exploited by powerful monopolies, it is worthwhile to note that application in the real world differs to a large extent.

In most of competition policy, consumer-centric rhetoric is thus justified to the extent that consumers benefit from enforcement. Whether this truly serves the goals of fairness, ie, whether consumers truly merit such protection even when at the expense of other less protected groups, is the subject of our investigation below. Reminding ourselves about who 'consumers' are in private litigation serves as an introduction to a more general point: how general rules of competition policy are applied in ways incongruent with their professed aim. Thus, favouring consumers and placing them on an intuitive pedestal might be rhetorically pleasing, as long as we are unaware that the sentiment is often used to protect firms rather than individuals, and large economically powerful firms at that.

B. The Interests and Rights of Consumers

Assessing the claims consumers make for antitrust based protection requires two intellectual steps. First, we must analyze what *interests* they have, ie, what are the benefits they seek from antitrust law? After assessing their interests, we shall turn to the question of justifiability of protection, ie, do they have a *right* to protect these interests? Without an applicable right, consumers' interests are no more than a wish, to be sympathized with perhaps, but not to be acted upon by anyone other than themselves.

What are the consumer interests, then, that antitrust might protect? The harm most often referred to is the 'wealth transfer'—the higher price which monopoly almost invariably leads to.[16] The need to pay a higher price to secure a monopolized good diminishes the consumer's finite resources, thereby creating an antitrust relevant cost that is always positive, though its size depends on each individual consumer's personal circumstances. Another harm potentially caused to the consumer is the loss of variety that may follow from successful monopolization (though this is not always the case).[17] A third interest lies in the accelerated innovation that is said to accompany the competitive process, and that monopolies might inhibit.[18] Let us then turn to assessing each of these interests.

i. Consumers' Interest in Avoiding Wealth Transfers

In basic economic terms, wealth is transferred in every transaction where a good is sold for a price above its cost of production. Literally, the wealth of the consumer acquiring the product is being transferred to the producer selling it, but the focus is on the added value, or total welfare created. The consumer values the product at *X* (his subjective expected utility from the product's use), the producer values the same product at *Y* (the marginal cost of its production[19]) and total welfare created by trade is the amount of *X-Y*, the surplus value. This surplus may be enjoyed by the consumer (paying a price lower than his expected utility), the producer (receiving a price above the cost incurred), or divided between them.[20] Any surplus enjoyed by the producer may be said to have been 'transferred away' from the consumer, but the opposite is true as well.

[16] See, eg, SF Ross, *Principles of Antitrust Law* (Westbury, New York: The Foundation Press, 1993) 5–11; Areeda and Kaplow (n 3) 56–58 (most of those arguing for non-efficiency goals place preventing wealth transfers as one of the main justifications for antitrust, see generally nn 2–3 above and n 24 below).

[17] It may be that a profit-maximizing monopolist will unilaterally keep a multitude of brands in the market, since consumers are willing to pay a premium on variety, and this premium exceeds the cost-savings associated with homogeneous manufacturing lines. Furthermore, monopolization may often be the result of acquisition of control over rivals' plants (either through sale of assets, stock, or merger), thus a implementing a decision to cease marketing certain brands may be more problematic and costly than maintaining the current status quo. In markets with high product differentiation, maintaining several differentiated brands may prove especially profitable, as they allow for price discrimination between different types of consumers. See also n 22 below.

[18] This is related, but not identical, to the discussion of innovative efficiency in ch 2. There, the focus was on aggregate benefits from competition, while here we will limit ourselves to potential claims of individuals, or distinct groups, of innovation as a protected right for *them* rather than for society at large.

[19] This is true when considering any single unit of product. If we take into account the product as one of the indistinguishable units produced, average variable cost should be the criterion. If the analysis is *ex ante*, before sunk costs are incurred, average total cost is relevant. The difference between these is especially important where infrastructure is expensive, leading to economies of scale and declining average costs. There, selling a product at marginal cost is a losing proposition and without some sort of monopoly power the market itself is at risk.

[20] It must be remembered here, that even in models of perfect competition, most products are sold at a price above their marginal cost of production, since price is set by MC of the *last* unit sold. Thus, assuming marginal cost to be rising with quantity produced (after economies of scale have been exhausted), all previous transactions create surplus, transferred at least in part to the producer.

The more common use of the term 'wealth transfer', one carrying with it a negative connotation, is specific to firms enjoying market power. This definition of the term refers to monopoly profit, meaning the amount of surplus that a monopolistic firm is able to divert away from consumers (relative to the competitive benchmark) by raising price. The higher price may mean that quantity demanded will fall, but those units sold will be at a price closer to the consumers' average willingness to pay, thus more profitable for the seller. In economic terms, the producer surplus is enhanced at the expense of the consumer surplus (in addition to the deadweight loss created, as explained in the previous chapter). It is this 'excess profit' which is the crux of the wealth transfer argument.

Any rational monopolist (or other business owner for that matter) places profit as a primary objective. While profits may be accumulated through conduct benefiting all those involved in trade, wealth transfers can be an important source of a producer's profit. Undoubtedly, preventing wealth transfers would benefit the consumer at the expense of the monopolist. The question posed here, though, is whether preventing wealth transfers by producers should represent an independent justification for antitrust.[21]

Efficiency analysis is usually opposed to wealth transfers, since it involves raising prices, which in turn lowers quantity produced, thus creating a deadweight loss for society. Examining this as a *fairness* consideration, though, demands the separation of these effects. If wealth transfers are in and of themselves unfair and represent an evil to be corrected, they should be forbidden regardless of their effect on allocative efficiency.[22]

Regarding wealth transfers as illegitimate presupposes a preference of consumers over producers.[23] If this were not so, we might be happy for the producers, or generally oblivious to any one group's outcome. Of course, realism regarding prevalent attitudes favouring consumers over producing firms requires we take into account popular conceptions of individuals versus firms, and a natural tendency

[21] There are also cases where antitrust intervention would *harm* the consumers, by lowering their surplus. See, eg, SJ Davis, KM Murphy and RH Topel, 'Entry, Pricing and Product Design in an Initially Monopolized Market' (2004) 112 *Journal of Political Economy* 188. There, a model is proposed according to which consumers would prefer perfect monopoly pricing to the differentiating effects that would occur with new entry.

[22] Eg, perfect price discrimination, where wealth transfers need not be accompanied by a reduction of output. Other cases (more plausibly expected) are where other efficiency considerations cancel out the deadweight loss, eg, achieving certain economies of scale may contribute to aggregate efficiency more that the deadweight loss diminishes it. The classic formulation is in the context of mergers simultaneously increasing market power and productive efficiency achieved by the merging firms. See OE Williamson, 'Efficiencies as an Antitrust Defense: The Welfare Tradeoffs' (1968) 58 *American Economic Review* 18.

[23] See Lande, (n 3); Williamson (n 22). A clear example of this sentiment is found in JB Kirkwood, 'The Goals of Essence of Antitrust: Protecting Consumers and Small Suppliers from Anticompetitive Conduct' (2013) 81 *Fordham Law Review* 2425: 'Everyone is a consumer, and the most egregious form of anticompetitive behavior—hardcore price fixing—harms consumers without justification. It raises the prices they pay, transfers their wealth to the conspirators, and rarely, if ever, has redeeming virtues'.

to favour the underdog over the economically privileged. We must remember that monopolistic firms can be small (operating in segregated markets), consumers can be large (direct purchasers rather than end users) and both are usually firms employing workers and operate at the behest of stockholders (allowing for public investment and involvement at all levels).[24] Our analysis must therefore explain the reasons for an automatic preference for one side, or consider both groups a priori equal, and balance harms to each according to some external standard.

There is one more option. It is possible to be averse to wealth transfers not because of preference for the *consumers* bearing the price, but as part of a general aversion to one party using its economic strength to extract the other's property. If this is the case, we may categorize wealth transfers as merely a sophisticated form of robbery, to be banned and prohibited by law.

In order for this argument to succeed and the 'property' of consumers to be acknowledged, a vested *right* to be protected, and not merely an interest, must be indentified. A right is a much stronger claim than an interest. While interests justify an individual's effort to achieve that in which he is interested, it is not a justification for *others* to spring into action. Rights exist to provide protection from outside interference, and in some cases, demand positive action to be taken by others. Rights, however, 'trump' interests. Thus, if one party claims a protected right, the fact that another party has conflicting interests is no longer relevant.[25] It is only if the other can 'raise' his claim to a status of right (ie, argue for the rights underlying the protection of his stated interest), that the two will be on the same level.

Assessing economic rights requires delineation, and two main sources present themselves: the right to property and the right to freedom of contract.[26] Each shall therefore be assessed and implemented: first, as to consumers' claims and subsequently to other relevant groups. I shall begin by treating property generally, and then move on to more nuanced understandings of what this right entails. The general formulation treats property as a coherent concept, asking whether (and how) it applies. The more nuanced version deconstructs the concept of property to its underlying values, and then asks whether one of these values is competition itself, thus limiting the possibility of claiming a property right to forestall competition or profit from its deficiency.

It may also be argued that consumers (and subsequently others as well) have a right to protection, stemming not from an individual rights perspective, but from that of social rights. According to this view, certain levels of welfare should

[24] See T Calvani, 'What is the Objective of Antitrust?' in T Calvani and J Siegfried (eds), *Economic Analysis and Antitrust Law*, 2nd edn (Boston: Little, Brown & Co, 1988).

[25] Terminology and general analysis here draws on the 'rights as trumps' argument made by RM Dworkin, *Taking Rights Seriously* (Cambridge, MA: Harvard University Press, 1977).

[26] This is not to say that other rights cannot be argued to be relevant as well. The focus on property and contract allows for exposing the main aspects associated with antitrust intervention, as well as the central issues discussed when assessing the need for (and justification of) state intervention in what would otherwise be seen as a matter of private transactions. It should be stressed that my focus here is on economic rights, rather than political or personal rights which may require different modes of analysis. See JP Day, *Liberty and Justice* (London: Croom Helm, 1987) 205–06.

be guaranteed by society, regardless of an individual's ability to secure his own position. The social rights theory demands social protection of consumers due to their diminished economic power relative to monopolists. Thus, this theory will also be examined as to the relevant groups protected, and as to the appropriateness of using antitrust law for such protection.

ii. Do Wealth Transfers Infringe upon Consumers' Property Rights?

The existence of the right to property is undoubtedly one of the most basic propositions made with regard to human rights, outside the realm of the individual's physical body or belief system. In our context we do not need to argue for the *existence* of this right, but we may need to argue about its *domain*. The right to property is commonly presumed to encompass not only the fact of ownership, but also the ability to utilize the property in a beneficial way and profit thereof.[27] This right is of course not omnipotent. The right to property and its utilization are often interfered with by the state in situations such as takings, taxation, planning laws and many more.[28]

In order to justify an antitrust claim based on property rights, it is important to identify what property of the consumers has been unjustly appropriated by the monopolist. Where wealth transfers are concerned, the basic argument posits that competitive markets would have bestowed a certain consumer surplus upon the buyer, and this surplus was unjustly taken by the monopolist and added to their own (producer) surplus. Since the starkest case of a wealth transfer is exemplified by monopoly pricing visibly seen in the wealth-transfer rectangle shown in Figure 1 in chapter two above, that case will serve as a focal point here. The extreme case is instructive in its simplicity, though the argument also applies in modified form to more complex forms of monopolization, mergers and collusion cases. All these practices are limited to some extent in order to protect consumers from the higher prices stemming from wealth transfers.

Consumers undoubtedly have a right to the property they accumulate, including the money they use to pay for a monopolized product. If a monopolist manages to 'transfer away' some of these funds, the consumer deserves protection. But

[27] See J Narveson, 'Democracy and Economic Rights' in EF Paul, FD Miller and J Paul (eds), *Economic Rights* (Cambridge: Cambridge University Press, 1992); R Epstein, 'Private Property and the Public Domain: The Case of Antitrust' in JR Pennock and JW Chapman (eds), *Ethics, Economics and the Law, Nomos XXIV* (New York: New York University Press, 1982) 57.

[28] Takings form the most blunt of state interventions in property, since the property itself is confiscated by the state (either with or without compensation) regardless of the owner's consent. Taxation is usually seen as acceptable and unavoidable in the modern state, yet any tax places a demand on the private property of individuals. Progressive taxes, such as income tax, interfere even more directly with the right to profit, since the higher the profit attained, the higher the 'price' an individual must pay to society. While planning laws do not interfere with ownership directly, they do dictate the uses allowed or forbidden of certain assets. The most common example is, of course, the limitations placed on construction in certain zones (limiting the use of real estate), but even noise laws restrict the use an owner of a stereo set (or air hammer for that matter) may enjoy of his property.

here we may ask, is demanding a high price in order to part with a specific good akin to stealing (or otherwise removing without consent) the buyer's money?

In order for such a claim to be sustained, it must be shown that the consumer either (a) has a specific positive right to buy at some determined price which the monopolist unduly deprived him of, or (b) has indeed suffered diminished funds without giving consent. The first claim supposes a form of property right the consumer has in the consumer surplus (thus justifying that the price set should retain that surplus), while the second is contractual in nature: that while his physical action of payment was not forced (since those cases lie beyond monopolistic practices, and are dealt with by other bodies of law), full contractual agreement was not achieved either.

This section deals with the property implications of (a) and the next shall deal with the contractual elements of (b). One thing bears remembering as we delve into these points: consumers' claims have been central not just within competition policy, but seem to enjoy strong popular and academic support in other contexts as well. Intellectual honesty and rigour thus demand that we take care to avoid automatically accepting such claims and undervaluing competing ones made by those we are used to seeing as 'the bad guys' in the antitrust debate, namely monopolists of all sorts and creeds. Analysis will therefore proceed from a preference-neutral perspective, taking both groups, and all claims made, to task.

iii. Can a Non-Existent Surplus be the Object of a Property Right?

What property is it that consumers claim to have a right to? It cannot be the product which is the subject of the trade, since the product belonged to the monopolist until the transaction was consummated. If consumers had a property right to the product, they could claim a right to have it produced, or that it belonged (in some way) to them prior to the sale itself. It cannot be the money with which they intend to pay for the specific good, since that is theirs to begin with and has nothing to do with the monopolist with whom they are contracting. Thus, the only viable object of a property right in this context is the consumer surplus made possible by the trade itself.

While granting consumers a property right to consumer surplus seems intuitively correct, one must note that despite its name, this surplus is *created* by the trade itself and does not exist prior to the transaction. Can property created only by interaction between two autonomous parties be said to belong to any one of them prior to its existence? Can a party argue that he has a *right* to that property, or to a distinct part thereof? If we answer affirmatively, the property right of the consumer must correspond with the producer's duty to respect and preserve the consumer's surplus during trade. But this gives rise to the argument that the producer has a corresponding duty *to produce and to trade*, so that the consumer surplus is realized and the consumer's property right protected; such a duty would commit the producer to labour for the consumers' benefit.

Placing on the producer such a duty of forced labour is undoubtedly well beyond the intuitive meaning granted by even the most ardent supporters of preventing wealth transfers. But intuitive meanings are not of much importance in philosophical or jurisprudential debates. The question is not if this is what most supporters of antitrust *intend*, but if it follows from their stated arguments.[29]

The 'forced labour' conclusion, however, is not the only possible end result from the argument that consumers bear a property right to consumer surplus. Only a view which holds the consumer surplus to be an *absolute right* is committed to the 'forced labour' result. A weaker, and more convincing, claim posits that consumers bear a right to normal consumer surplus created by trade, but that right is contingent upon the trade occurring consensually. Thus, forced labour on the part of producers is avoided while protecting the consumer's right to the share of the surplus. Where, then, would such a contingent right stem from?

In order to assess these issues, a broader perspective is necessary, one drawing on the origins of these rights and showing how to determine their content, developing them to our context. The next section will thus assess competitive price as a procedural requirement, explaining what about the *competitive process* generates justifiable claims on behalf of consumers for state protection. It should be noted that our focus here is on property rights and freedom of contract alone, putting the individual consumer(s) centre stage. This is contrary to the related discussion in chapter two above, regarding the competitive process as an aggregate social interest due to its influences on democracy and contribution to the attainment of other social goods, economic and otherwise. In chapter six we will return to the issue from a different perspective, of *competitive price* as a criterion for fairness, ie, when the resulting distribution of surplus is inherently fair or unfair regardless of the process leading up to it.

iv. Competitive Price as a Procedural Requirement

The idea of a right not to a predetermined price, but to a *process* determining price, is much more palatable to those unwilling to endorse state determined prices in every market and at every level. The argument goes as follows: no party has a right to any *specific* price being offered, other than his own right to refuse trade when the price seems unattractive. But, the prices offered must not be the result of arbitrary choice on part of the seller, but the result of an external process

[29] This argument is reminiscent of a similar 'forced labour' argument made in the debate as to the justification of unequal taxation. Robert Nozick argued that horizontal equity (fairness considerations that demand equal treatment of people in equal, or 'horizontal', positions) demands that if unequal taxation is justified on redistribution grounds, so that those with less opportunity be compensated, then those with opportunity but preferring leisure to increased income should be forced to work more—so that they may be taxed as well. While most refused to accept such a result and searched for ways to avoid it, some accepted the argument and justified such 'forced labour' as unavoidable. See R Nozick, *Anarchy, State, and Utopia* (New York: Basic Books, 1974) 169–70; see also RJ Arneson, 'Property Rights in Persons' in EF Paul, FD Miller and J Paul (eds), *Economic Rights* (Cambridge: Cambridge University Press, 1992) 204–06 for acceptance of the 'forced labour' argument.

limiting the discretion of both seller and buyer. One such process is unfettered competition, attractive both because of competition being a 'democratic' process (in the sense examined in chapter two) and because of its efficiency in the allocation of goods within society.

The seller in a competitive market will know that any price in excess of the competitive one will simply be met by consumers shopping elsewhere. The buyer, likewise, may wish for a substantially lower price, but will find no seller willing to accommodate her. In a perfectly competitive market, we are taught that price will be set at the marginal cost of the last unit produced. Realistic, imperfectly competitive markets will approximate that result. Does this mean that we are to regulate prices according to the marginal costs of production? Not at all; the argument for antitrust law is that where competition exists (even the imperfect type), the market will self-regulate so that prices approximate marginal costs. Thus, what is necessary and justified, is maintaining the process of competition alone. Antitrust law should thus preclude actions that limit competitive markets, so that the pricing mechanisms are allowed to operate freely.

Put simply, this consumers' rights argument does not claim the right to a certain price, but the right to buy at $P = MC$, as economic textbooks promise. Any price significantly above MC is considered harmful to consumers' rights. While $P > MC$ is not in itself an actionable claim in competition law, it is the theoretical underpinning justifying most state intervention in the matter. A softer version of this claim maintains that where an individual attempts to influence market dynamics so as to lessen competition, this interferes with consumers' rights to the process, and the state should intervene. Note that the softer version stresses interference with the process alone, while the first version focuses on its result—marginal cost pricing.

There is, though, a flaw in this argument, both versions thereof. They rely on a conception of competition protecting consumers, relying on a juxtaposition of the competitive ideal with the textbook monopoly model. What is missing is the effect of supply and demand elasticities. The standard graph denoting consumer and producer surplus (such as in Figure 1 in chapter two above) shows a sizable and symmetrical (though not necessarily equal) portion for each. We are led to believe that, left alone, the market would 'take care' of all players, so that restoration of market conditions (or their simulation) is enough to protect consumers. This, though, is true only in limited circumstances. Even where competition is perfect, elasticity of demand determines the consumers' portion of total welfare created, and this can be large or small. Competitive price, then, does not promise any level of surplus, to either consumer or producer.

Consumers' elasticity of demand thus affects their surplus in the same way that monopolistic pricing does. The difference is that in the latter case it is the producer who controls the situation. It may be said that the voluntary nature of monopolistic pricing is exactly what makes it so repulsive. We do not control destructive acts of nature, but we do our best to control human behaviour when it harms others. On the other hand, the basic question has not been answered: what is the *origin* of this supposed right to consumer surplus? Why is competition a satisfying procedural standard, other than it being intuitively appealing due to our having grown accustomed to the idea? I shall assess in turn two claimed arguments for such a right. The first claim relies on just rules of conduct (including competition) leading to just results (*the procedural justice argument*), while the second relies on a presumed a priori agreement of producers to forgo potential monopoly power in order to secure a competitive framework (*the implicit agreement argument*).

a. Procedural Justice

Procedural justice seeks to assess what is just without resorting to substantive principles stemming from one ideological standpoint or another. Pure procedural justice can be defined as where 'the outcome is ... fair, whatever it is, provided that the procedure has been properly followed'.[30] Where competition is accepted as the procedure determining fairness, it follows that subversion of competition is by definition unfair, and those suffering from it may justifiably claim a right to state protection.

Two weaknesses are immediately apparent with the application of procedural justice to competition. First, what is it about competition that inherently makes it a determinant of fairness? In the famous Rawlsian account, pure procedural justice depends not only on the existence of a procedure which can be impartially applied, but also on *the lack of any substantive principle of justice* simultaneously relevant.[31] Is this true of commercial activities in general? If competition is merely a procedure for which no primary justification obtains, why not choose any other procedure, ranging from state-governed manufacture and distribution to total lack of intervention, leaving producers and consumers to fend for themselves in the marketplace? Besides, are we really convinced that no other substantive principle of justice applies?

The second apparent weakness is the term 'competition' itself and its definition. True, many use the term with conviction, but is there really one accepted meaning therefore? Competition could be defined as any series of consensual transactions, where consumers choose with whom to interact from an existing pool of producers (however large or small that pool may be). Competition may alternatively be defined as allowing every person to engage in unilateral production or consumption, as long as collusion with others is avoided. At the extreme, this anti-collusion focus would preclude the existence of conglomerates, vertically integrated firms, cartels and even firms in general, thus returning to markets alone as allocative

[30] J Rawls, *A Theory of Justice*, rev edn (Cambridge, MA: Belknap Press, 1999) 75; see also FA von Hayek, *Law, Legislation, and Liberty*, vol 2 (Chicago, IL: University of Chicago Press, 1976) 126–28. There, Hayek describes such 'abstract rules of just conduct' as affecting chances of success alone, with no claim for specific results being justified.

[31] See Rawls, *A Theory of Justice*, rev edn (n 30) 75: 'pure procedural justice obtains when there is no independent criterion for the right result'.

institutions with business hierarchies deemed anticompetitive altogether. While seeming absurd to the modern economically-oriented mind, there is nothing in the term 'competition' to preclude such a result when assessing it from the ground up. Furthermore, those familiar with the law of 'unfair competition' will immediately recognize that many prevalent business tactics are questionable at best. Thus, relying on competition as a *determinant* of fairness requires much thought and elaboration as to the specific meaning the general term should bear.[32] In short, competition as procedural justice leaves much to be defined. Of course, this is precisely where we are heading—explicating the values and standards that would guide judges and regulators in determining the forms of competition required by a commitment to fairness.

The common economic definition of a competitive market maintains that all buyers and sellers of each commodity operate as 'price takers' with no one holding sufficient economic power to unilaterally affect market price or quantity. But if this is our goal, should we not forbid monopolies altogether, despite the consequences of limiting growth and economies of scale? Or if monopoly *is* created through the competitive process, is it not inherently fair due to its resulting from the set out procedure, thereby rendering intervention inappropriate?[33] US antitrust doctrine leans precisely towards such non-intervention, especially after the Supreme Court's acceptance of monopoly pricing as not only legal, but part of the competitive process itself.[34] As outlined in chapter one, the US and EU doctrines regarding monopolization are very different in this regard, as the latter directly intervenes in 'unfair pricing' by dominant concerns, while the former all but lauds monopolistic pricing as competition enhancing. Both jurisdictions allow monopoly and regulate monopolistic firms differently from competitive ones, limiting any action protecting or enhancing market power. It seems, then,

[32] Consider, eg, negative advertising, 'bait and switch' strategies, exploiting consumers' bounded rationality, disclosing warranty limitations in small type, etc. These and more are ubiquitous in today's marketplace, though questionable as to their fairness.

[33] A monopoly may be created through the competitive process due to the 'superior business acumen' of the monopolist, luck, timing, or many other factors. Some would argue that in a truly competitive world such a monopoly would not last for long, drawing entry. But see ch 2 for arguments to the contrary.

[34] The Court stated this issue in very strong terms in *Verizon Communications Inc v Law Offices of Curtis V Trinko LLP*, 3540 US 398, 407 (2004): 'The mere possession of monopoly power, and the concomitant charging of monopoly prices, is not only not unlawful; it is an important element of the free-market system. The opportunity to charge monopoly prices—at least for a short period—is what attracts "'business acumen" in the first place; it induces risk taking that produces innovation and economic growth. To safeguard the incentive to innovate, the possession of monopoly power will not be found unlawful unless it is accompanied by an element of anticompetitive *conduct*'. Note that it is charging monopoly *prices* which the Court condoned, and in no small part due to its positive effect on *competition*. The fact that monopoly subjects its holder to different (stricter) *conduct* rules was never disputed or overruled. As shown in ch 1, European competition law takes a very different direction, more favourable to regulation of monopoly pricing. Elhauge argued that this distinctly European strand of competition law, regulating prices and not merely facilitating competition, can be seen as a requirement that those who profited from illegal monopolization disgorge their profits, thus bringing the American and European paradigms one step closer. See E Elhauge, 'Disgorgement as an Antitrust Remedy' (2009) 76 *Antitrust Law Journal* 501.

that current competition policy views end results at least as important as the process leading up to them.

Pure procedural justice, therefore, leaves us begging the question once again. First, the 'right' procedure (ie, the exact definition of 'fair' competition) is difficult to ascertain. Even if a 'correct' definition could be found, the mere fact that it is not universally agreed upon negates the belief that common intuitions regarding the evils of monopoly are truly based on procedure rather than substance. If substantive rights *are* relevant, their source should be explored, in order to more deeply understand and critique current conceptions.

b. A Just Procedure: What would Rawls do?

Exploring the underlying justifications of antitrust a priori is difficult given that we grew up with the current doctrines and might take for granted their implicit assumptions. The dominant world view regarding antitrust assumes it to be both morally 'right' and economically efficient, enjoying an almost complete consensus among the relevant professional communities (both scholars and practitioners) as wellas the general populace (and the lawmakers representing them).[35] Of course, there are exceptions, but these are few and far between regarding the basic perception of antitrust.[36] *Within* the current framework there are many debates and schools of thought regarding details of its application or scope, but as mentioned above, these usually focus either on the fairness versus efficiency debate (assuming a priori that fairness favours consumers) or on whether specific practices are (or are not) truly efficient.[37]

It is difficult, to say the least, to extract ourselves from this web of agreement in order to truly reassess the position of antitrust in our society and the implicit assumptions upon which it relies.[38] Human beings think in metaphors and

[35] Robert Lande and others documented the popular support for antitrust in its incipiency (see ch 1, n 39) and Richard Hofstadter asked where popular debate regarding the subject disappeared, as far back as 1966. He ascribed this lack of public interest to a change in the way Americans viewed big business: from fear and distrust in the early twentieth century, to a reliance on business interests to promote economic growth in post-war years. See R Hofstadter, 'What Happened to the Antitrust Movement?' in *The Paranoid Style in America Politics* (London: Jonathan Cape, 1966). Dan Crane documented the relative lack of public and political attention to antitrust in recent decades, and concluded that a professionally-run scientific application of antitrust rules is less politically enthralling than emotional appeals regarding size and economic control which characterized the early days of antitrust. See DA Crane, 'Technocracy and Antitrust' (2008) 86 *Texas Law Review* 1159. All of the above document an American acceptance of antitrust as a consensual matter. Herbert Hovenkamp states this unequivocally in the first line of his latest book: 'After decades of debate, today we enjoy more consensuses about the goals of the antitrust laws than at any time in the last half century'; see H Hovenkamp, *The Antitrust Enterprise: Principle and Execution* (Cambridge, MA: Harvard University Press, 2005) 1.

[36] See, eg, Armentano (n 3); RB McKenzie and DR Lee, *In Defense of Monopoly: How Market Power Fosters Creative Production* (Ann Arbor: University of Michigan Press, 2008); G Hull (ed), *The Abolition of Antitrust* (New Brunswick, NJ: Transaction, 2005).

[37] See ch 1, n 39 and accompanying text.

[38] This problem is discussed more generally (and interestingly so) in J Hanson and D Yosifon, 'The Situation: An Introduction to the Situational Character, Critical Realism, Power Economics, and Deep Capture' (2003) 152 *University of Pennsylvania Law Review* 129.

categories, and once these are cemented into our common experience, everything we see is coloured by the prism through which we observe it.[39] Under these circumstances, an appealing framework is John Rawls' 'thought experiment' of imagining ourselves in an 'original position' behind a veil of ignorance.[40]

The idea is both subtle and simple, essentially placing ourselves in a hypothetical situation where any knowledge of our personal circumstances is erased, while all worldly knowledge of general matters and scientific understanding are retained. At its core, the thought experiment proceeds as follows: imagine yourself, together with all members of the relevant society (all citizens or world inhabitants, depending on the generality sought), magically transformed to a contemplative state, looking on our world from above. Here, members of society need to deliberate rules which will govern life 'down there' once deliberation ends. None of the deliberating individuals knows which body 'down there' is theirs, thus all are uncertain as to which social situation they will be transported into once the game-rules are agreed upon. Of course, each proposed rule can benefit or harm (or both!) different individuals according to their social position and particular needs. This 'blind deliberation' forces us to assimilate all effects and take into consideration all affected persons—as each one of them might be us.

Rawls uses this 'veil of ignorance' (as to our particular circumstances) to determine the values that should govern our society in real life. The assumption is that the rules agreed upon in such a state approximate true justice, as they reflect our true conceptions, free from personal bias. The driving force of this analysis is that when choosing core values and instrumental applications, we divest ourselves from their influence on our own well-being. Thus, we take into account all possibilities: we may be the highest or lowest in the social pecking order, healthy or sick, rich or poor, industrialist or employee.[41]

How can antitrust benefit from the Rawlsian framework? If we seek to truly assess our core assumptions, envisioning ourselves behind a veil of ignorance allows for stepping away from biases generated by living in a world dominated by current doctrine. The significant question for our analysis here is which antitrust

[39] As aptly put by Mary Douglas: 'whatever we perceive is organized into patterns for which we the perceivers are largely responsible ... As time goes on and experience builds up, we make greater investment in our systems of labels. So a conservative bias is built in. It gives us confidence'; M Douglas, *Purity and Danger: An Analysis of Concepts of Pollution and Taboo* (London: Routledge and Kegan Paul, 1966) 41. For a fascinating modern implementation and a suggested framework for motivating organizational change, see CF Kurtz and DJ Snowden, 'The New Dynamics of Strategy: Sense-making in a Complex and Complicated World' (2003) 42 *IBM Systems Journal* 462. While applications loom far and wide, within antitrust we can discern the axiomatic attitude towards 'monopoly as bad' and consumers as deserving 'their fair share' of the wealth created by trade. What this fair share is, and how we determine the relevant criteria, is precisely the aim of our discussion here. See ch 6 for a different model attempting to shed light on this issue by abstracting away from commonly-held intuitions.

[40] J Rawls, *A Theory of Justice*, 2nd edn (Oxford: Oxford University Press, 1999).

[41] A similar sentiment was expressed by one of Rawls' most notable intellectual opponents, Friedrich Hayek: 'we should regard as the most desirable order of society one which we would choose if we knew that our initial position in it would be decided purely by chance (such as the fact of our being born into a particular family)'; see Hayek (n 30) 132.

principles would be agreed upon. Specifically, what would be the main focus of an antitrust regime enacted behind the veil of ignorance? Many details of application could be assessed, but the core value I hope to convince readers of is both stark and simple: in such a state we would require a balancing test to compare the benefits and harms accruing to the different parties influenced by intervention (or lack of it), and that without such context-specific balancing the state errs in infringing upon protected rights. The balancing issue is best dealt with after assessing what (if any) standing those limited by competition law should have in the matter, thus shall be returned to after chapter four presents and defends the argument that monopolists should be heard. The context specificity I argue for relies on a claim that behind the veil of ignorance not all antitrust is alike. The principles justifying intervention in the paradigmatic case of powerful monopolist versus disenfranchised consumers do not necessarily apply to other scenarios which are no less realistic and probably much more prevalent.

Generally, the veil of ignorance framework allows us to ask which rules would be chosen to govern the marketplace and under what circumstances we would want the government to step in. One could go back to first principles to critically assess existing conceptions of property (as Rawls does), but given our specific focus I shall assume private property and freedom of contract as an agreed upon baseline.[42] Focusing on application within competition policy, I focus upon one main question: would those behind the veil of ignorance choose a Universalist antitrust regime, applying identically in very different circumstances? In other words, would enhancing economic efficiency, or protecting consumers, always be considered an improvement, regardless of the effect on those subject to limitation, the monopolists?

Antitrust as practised today operates according to general rules. We seek to separate per se offences from rule of reason analysis, and we apply the rule of reason according to the efficiency criterion or the effect of the suspected practice on consumers. Current antitrust doctrines do not differentiate between various types of goods, classes of consumers, or other affected parties. Thus, markets for luxury items and those for basic goods receive identical treatment in antitrust, wealthy consumers are protected no less than poor ones, and small locally-owned

[42] Of course, one might argue that private property and free markets would not be chosen at all. Rawls posited that property and trade would be allowed, in order to achieve Pareto optimality in societal use of resources, albeit subject to a maximin principle. Human beings, he assumed, are generally risk-averse (especially as to basic needs), thus would be willing to sacrifice some efficiency and some benefit in better-than-average states of the world, in order to protect themselves from the downfalls of worse states of the world, see Rawls, *A Theory of Justice*, 2nd edn (n 40) 144. Given that behind the veil of ignorance we do not know which state of the world will apply to *us*, Rawls argued we would choose to maximize the well-being of those worse off in society, which he called the 'maximin principle' (similar to the game-theoretic concept). Equality is not mandated due to its limiting effect on attaining efficiency (thus private property is allowed), but distributive concerns dominate productive ones near the low end of the social-benefit spectrum. For critique of Rawls' assumptions regarding the possibility of achieving equal liberty for all while allowing unequal economic (and thus social) positions, see N Daniels, 'Equal Liberty and Unequal Worth' in N Daniels (ed), *Reading Rawls* (Stanford, CT: Stanford University Press, 1989).

firms with market power are regulated according to the same rules governing international conglomerates. The *rules* of antitrust are context free.[43]

This context freeness is justified by a belief that antitrust operates objectively, devoid of value judgements as to the product in question, allowing for scientific analysis employing quantitative economic tools.[44] The value of objectivity requires no elaboration, and the fact that different markets are treated identically aims to achieve predictability which allows for streamlining business planning, enhancing efficiency and reducing litigation costs. It seems, then, that this scientific view of antitrust has much to commend it, and decision-makers in the original position would value it highly.

Two main objections can be raised to this account. First, that antitrust is not value neutral as it intervenes on behalf of consumers to the detriment of monopolists, choosing sides in the process. Second, that this focus on objective criteria is more attractive to antitrust specialists than it is to other members of society. The first objection could be answered by stressing that we are all consumers, thus this is not a choice benefiting one group at the expense of another. This issue was addressed above, and will be returned to below in chapter four. I will add, though, that the original position does not *equalize* social positions, but merely makes us blind to our own. It is thus possible that even behind the veil of ignorance one would choose to risk the unequal distribution of benefits generated by monopolistic phenomena, in the hope that luck posits us in the favourable position of power once the veil is lifted.[45] Furthermore, 'protection of consumers' seems like a good general proposition, but once differentiated into its disparate effects within distinct markets and contexts, it loses some of its seemingly obvious appeal. Not all consumers are alike, and not all markets would necessarily be viewed as equally important in justifying legal intervention.[46]

[43] The only caveat being that national enforcement agencies enjoy discretion as to how they expend their limited budgets, ie, which market to investigate and when to litigate. The *rules* themselves, are identical, as are the possibilities for private enforcement, which operates free of any 'public good' constraint.

[44] Observe, for example, the *Ligget* case, discussed in n 5, where not once did the courts consider that the market for cigarettes induces social harm, thus perhaps monopolistic practices raising price and reducing demand are beneficial for society at large or even for affected consumers reducing intake of poisonous materials. See DA Crane, 'Harmful Output in the Antitrust Domain: Lessons from the Tobacco Industry' (2005) 39 *Georgia Law Review* 321. Some exceptions exist, such as the special attention given to media markets (due to their centrality in affecting democratic discourse), but even then it is not antitrust which adapts, but other fields of law which interject. See, eg, HA Shelanski, 'Antitrust Law as Mass Media Regulation: Can Merger Standards Protect the Public Interest?' (2006) 94 *California Law Review* 371.

[45] This is similar, but not identical to the 'monopoly as investment incentive' rhetoric in the *Verizon* decision (n 34). The difference is the focus on aggregate benefits of 'competition for the market' reminiscent of Schumpeterian analysis discussed in ch 2. There, the focus was on the aggregate, while here at issue is a risky choice on part of individuals. Rawls famously posited that people would be risk-averse in the original position, but this assumption can be challenged as well.

[46] See W Kerber, 'Should Competition Law Promote Efficiency? Some Reflections of an Economist on the Normative Foundations of Competition Law' in J Drexl et al (eds), *Economic Theory and Competition Law* (Cheltenham: Edward Elgar, 2009) 14 using a similar framework to argue that: 'the normative asymmetry which holds that competition law is only about the protection of the

Moving to the second objection: is an 'objective and scientific' antitrust policy indeed more attractive to specialists than to the general populace? As an antirust aficionado myself, trained in mathematical economics, I confess to preferring quantitative analysis as a basis for debate, as this creates common language and allows for coherence over multiple implementations.[47] Yet imagining what would be chosen behind the veil of ignorance raises additional concerns. Current antitrust doctrine employs micro-market analysis, whether through traditional market definition or through more adaptable econometric techniques of assessing associated demand functions to focus analysis.[48] Such analysis focuses on effects within a relevant market, but ignores questions of cross-market economic power, such as the influence of large firms on political debate, questions of individual autonomy (as discussed above in chapter two) and effect on local communities of big-box retailers and large factories exploiting economies of scale. In short, the focus on objective quantifiable analysis leads to context freeness that would not necessarily be viewed favourably by individuals in the original position who might prefer taking into account the way in which this strive for economic efficiency influences their day-to-day lives.

It is difficult to presume knowledge of the way residents of the original position would vote. Given the hypothetical nature of the examination, different people might have different predictions, thus any assessment offered is both subjective and imperfect. The mere fact that, in the real world, monopolistic behaviour was sufficiently hated to vilify it in constitutional documents and criminalize it worldwide,[49] shows that something is at work beyond economics alone, values beyond efficiency. Simply stated, the moral intuition shared by those supporting state limitation of monopolistic practices is that large monopolistic firms preventing would-be competitors from participating in the market is unfair both to those whose creative efforts are stymied, and to consumers who would enjoy their wares.

The main question of interest is whether these sentiments would be similarly crafted behind a veil of ignorance if we were to transfer from a historical exploration to a hypothetical one. Since we have yet to substantiate that monopolists

consumers' interests and that the interests of all other firms on the upstream markets are irrelevant, is hard to justify from a constitutional economics perspective'.

[47] For an account of antitrust as shifting more and more in this direction, see DA Crane, 'Rules versus Standards in Antitrust Adjudication' (2007) 64 *Washington and Lee Law Review* 49.

[48] See L Kaplow, 'Why (Ever) Define Markets' (2010) 124 *Harvard Law Review* 437 and citations therein. Kaplow's suggestion to do away with standard market definition has created a backlash of opposing views, focusing mostly on administrative concerns and commending market definition as a threshold requirement; see, eg, KN Hylton, '*Brown Shoe* Versus the Horizontal Merger Guidelines' (2011) 39 *Review of Industrial Organization* 95; GJ Werden, 'Why (Ever) Define Markets? An Answer to Professor Kaplow' (13 February 2012): ssrn.com/abstract=2004655.

[49] See ch 1. While European doctrine is aimed more at administrative controls than criminalization, the different jurisdictions share a common sentiment condemning the use of monopoly power, even where they differ in the means used. See discussion of criminalization and its underpinnings in WPJ Wils, *Efficiency and Justice in European Antitrust Enforcement* (Oxford: Hart Publishing, 2008).

deserve a role in the moral debate, and the contextual balancing test is yet to be developed (see chapters four and five respectively for these), the stage shall be set outlining and critically assessing my personal biases in the matter, lest they implicitly affect analysis.

I believe competition law would be enacted behind the veil of ignorance, though in a form closer to the historical than current practice. I believe that in the original position we would agree to competition in the marketplace as our guiding economic framework, and we would agree also to government protection and intervention where market failures are concerned. At the same time we would be wary of governmental intervention, given that government is as imperfect as markets are and mistakes are unavoidable, thus we would forgo intervention except in the most pressing cases.[50] I believe further that, when taking into account that state action constrains individual rights (a view more easily seen behind the veil of ignorance where we avoid personal bias stemming from our own position as consumers), intervention would be more acceptable in some markets than others. The current micro-market analysis which posits monopoly as always harmful (sufficiently so that attempting to achieve it is criminalized in the US) regardless of context, does not hold up to this standard.

An antitrust policy accepted in the original position, would probably distinguish between markets for essential goods and markets for luxury items, focusing on harm to the process of competition rather than on static analysis of wealth transfers. In other words, competition as producing innovation and product variety would be favoured, as would the freedom to trade claimed by competitors, while consumers' property right to a certain share of the surplus (implicit in the wealth transfer argument) would be far from obvious. From the history of competition policy we see that public support centred on cases where economic effects were large and affected all of society, and especially where economic size led to political influence. *Economic power, rather than market power*, would have been the main issue of an antitrust policy chosen to protect democratic society—especially when the former interacted with political or regulatory power.[51]

Furthermore, intervention which constrains personal freedoms (such as with whom to do business, under which terms to sell, how to bundle products, etc) might have been agreed upon as a general matter, but subjected to contextual analysis taking into account the specific benefits and costs accruing to specific affected parties. In short—a balancing test would be required in order to show that the harm prevented outweighs the harm caused by each intervention sought. Which balancing test would be used is less clear, but the lexical ordering employed today positing *any* consumer harm as decisive regardless of the extent of producer benefit would be rejected once we see ourselves as potential monopolists

[50] This is obviously reminiscent of Easterbrook's type of mistake analysis, see ch 2, n 37.

[51] A telling example is antitrust scrutiny of the media market. Big media is especially problematic from a democratic point of view due to the role of the media in forming public opinion and presenting information which allows for formation of critical views. See ch 2, n 76.

as well as consumers and consider state action as an exception to be justified on a case-by-case basis.

Governmental and private enforcement differ greatly, although identical antitrust standards govern both. When state agencies choose whether to intervene, they are likely to consider context and effect on the general populace, as enforcement resources are limited and enforcement must be optimized. Private enforcement, on the other hand, depends on the interests of those choosing to bring suit, thus expected to depend less on public interest than personal gain. Private enforcement may thus be deemed more problematic, and is in turn more justifiably constrained than state action. That current substantive doctrine applies to both private and public antitrust litigation stems from a strong assumption regarding antitrust as always justified and that pursuing economic efficiency or consumer welfare are sufficient reasons for court relief.[52] Going back to the original position and taking into account the rights of monopolists (alongside consumers and others) requires reassessment of these assumptions, or at least a more inquisitive look for exceptions to the rule. This will be our focus in developing a balancing test, after chapter four explicates the potential claims monopolists might make, and why they are relevant to debate. Therefore, once the grounds for debate are set, we shall return to Rawls' original position as a criterion to be used within the balancing test. Before moving on, though, we must consider additional arguments on behalf of consumers, as well as other affected parties who benefit from antitrust intervention and whose legitimate claims should be included in the debate.

v. *Wealth Transfers as Infringing upon Contractual Rights*

Preventing wealth transfers is considered a central aim of competition policy, though we saw above that questions remain as to its justification. If property rights seem less than convincing as a source for consumers' claims, perhaps it is possible to substantiate them with a claim that contractual freedom is impaired when consumers are forced into deals with monopolistic providers. On the other hand, the transaction between producer and consumer is (almost always) a voluntary one, conducted within the boundaries of the market (albeit an imperfect one). Any claim made on behalf of a party to the transaction must therefore overcome a counterclaim that he has agreed to the conditions of trade and is bound by them. Contractual freedom is thus intuitively supportive of non-intervention, since the consumer has allegedly agreed to the terms of trade, including monopoly price.

[52] Indeed, Dan Crane sees this as a reason courts constrained the application of general antitrust principles, as they were trying to curb the increase in private litigation. See DA Crane, *The Institutional Structure of Antitrust Enforcement* (Oxford: Oxford University Press, 2011) 63. If so, antitrust's substance was limited not due to internal fault, but due to the lack of a procedural solution to a growing problem. The fact that the state and individuals are subject to the same rules and apply the same substantive laws is thus a severe disadvantage, as they differ greatly regarding the agency problem characterizing private-interest litigation while applying public-interest legal rules.

An exception may be relevant. Market transactions are legally and morally binding due to the parties' exercising free will in entering them. But not all transactions involve free will. If one party was compelled to accept the contract, free will was not exercised and the compelled party has every right to be excused from performance.[53] Can we not assume transactions in a monopolized market to be thus compelled?

Here the context of our argument is key. If 'monopolized transactions' are automatically defined as compelled and thus void (or subject to special treatment to protect the compelled party's interests),[54] then this must hold true for *all* transactions within a similar monopoly context. Is the existence of monopoly enough for this result? Two issues are at the forefront here: the role of demand elasticity and the types of goods involved.

a. Elasticity of Demand

Contractual compulsion entails that, under the circumstances, the consumer had no alternative other than to sign the contract. Even if 'no alternative' is too strong a statement, any form of compulsion entails a lack of *viable* alternatives—otherwise an invitation to trade is merely that, an invitation, uncompelled. Of course, viability is relative and depends on timing, geographical location, costs of possible alternatives, switching costs and potential lock-in and a multitude of variables changing from one consumer to the next.[55] While dealing with each consumer specifically is impossible, a general principle allowing for intervention based on the extent of consumers' freedom to forgo the transaction might inform competition law and justify state intervention.

In the context of monopolized markets, the tool for measuring alternatives which *consumers* deem viable is their elasticity of demand. If demand is elastic, a monopolistic producer raising price will simply find herself facing a large reduction of quantity demanded and thus the wealth transfer effects may be negligible (not to mention the whole endeavour unprofitable). On the other hand, elasticity

[53] See EA Farnsworth, *Contracts*, 3rd edn (New York: Aspen Law and Business, 1999) 264.

[54] While contract law is quite specific as to such contracts being void, we need not commit ourselves to that result. The claim made here is for a special type of intervention which might be justified even where contractual tests of compulsion have not been satisfied. Thus, 'monopolistic compulsion' may be of a weaker sort, not excusing performance in contract law, but justifying intervention through competition law.

[55] There is a difference between compulsion in contract (duress), and unconscionable contracts. Compulsion exists where one party acted to create circumstances so that the other will have no alternative, generating his 'agreement' to the proposed terms. The most obvious example is a party signing the contract 'with a gun to his head'. Unconscionable contracts, on the other hand, are those where one party takes advantage of the other's dire circumstances—but those which *he did not create*, eg, Shylock's demanding 'a pound of flesh' as part of a loan agreement in Shakespeare's *The Merchant of Venice*. Though the two differ significantly, we need not address the differences here. It is enough to say that monopolist/consumer agreements are usually more similar to the unconscionable type than the compulsion type, since even if the monopolist did create the market structure (which is often untrue), she is not responsible for the consumer's need for the product itself or the decision to acquire it. In both cases intervention might be warranted, though its extent differs. See Farnsworth (n 53) 307–09.

may vary among consumers, so that raising price causes the marginal consumers (whose demand is elastic at the relevant price) to reduce consumption, but harms remaining consumers for whom the same alternatives are less attractive. The result is context-specific—both as to some consumers being 'compelled' but not others, and as to compulsion being present in some markets but not others.

b. Types of Goods

Even with relatively inelastic demand, the compulsion argument is not necessarily relevant to all types of goods competition law traditionally covers. Let us imagine, for example, the market for luxury cars. To keep things simple, assume that differentiation is such that this constitutes an independent antitrust market and that luxury cars are monopolized by a single manufacturer selling directly to end users. It stands to reason that the relevant consumers are wealthy individuals, and that large firms are seeking to appeal to their senior employees' preferences. Assume further that demand at competitive level prices is inelastic, and the manufacturer raises prices to maximize monopoly profit. The compulsion argument, if based on elasticity alone, would be applicable as there are no relevant alternatives, thus consumers are compelled to buy from this producer alone—justifying intervention. Somehow, posing the argument in this context reduces its appeal.

The reason we hesitate to acknowledge compulsion in acquiring a luxury car is that this type of consumer, purchasing this type of good, is not what we readily conceive of as requiring external protection. Most would be more prone to reply: 'if a luxury automobile is what you want, make your own choices and pay the price'. The argument for consumer protection, then, depends not only on elasticity of demand, but on the product itself being of a type deemed so necessary that a consumer 'must have it' and could be 'compelled' in the process.[56]

An alternative conception views the competitive market not as a primary right, but as a means to achieve satisfaction of preferences. The market as a means has no inherent value, with the determination of protection deserved depending on parties' rights to acquire the goods involved. According to this view, if monopolistic practices deprive consumers of the ability to protect their own economic interests due to lack of viable alternatives, and therefore markets fail their objective, intervention is justified.[57] The premise for market protection is thus that individuals are the most knowledgeable and best equipped to protect their own interests through consensual trade. When monopoly compromises this premise, state intervention is warranted.

The problem with this view is that it begs the question: what is the *source* of consumers' rights? Protecting weak consumers from strong monopolists

[56] Of course, the arguments for intervention in the name of *efficiency* might still apply, but those were addressed in ch 2 and our enquiry here is whether there are also independent *fairness* justifications relying on consumers' contractual freedom. The question of the consumers' entitlement is key—both as to the product in question and as to the price at which such a product must be provided.

[57] See Day (n 26) 215–16.

sounds attractive (even romantic), but without differentiating between types of consumers and goods, we cannot ascertain that this is truly occurring within antitrust. Some would argue that 'freedom is diminished to achieve fairness',[58] but the fairness claim itself must first be determined, and this argument fails as to the broad scope that markets competition law encompasses.

A more limited argument, as to protecting consumers' basic needs, might be made, but that would justify not general antitrust law, but only specific protective measures, better dealt with by tools more precise than antitrust. This argument will be addressed directly below in the more general context of social justice.

c. Implicit Agreement

Implicit agreement is often used to argue that contracts include more than the terms specified in them, or that a party assumed upon himself more than explicitly acknowledged. The basic idea is that in some cases a person's action shows he accepted a premise, implicitly agreeing to it, even if the issue was never discussed. In our context it might be employed to argue monopolists accepted the 'game-rules' of competition when deciding to participate in the market. Competition works at times to their advantage (creating the market and allowing their participation in it) and in other times to their detriment (constraining business practices), but they are not allowed to alter the governing mechanism through monopolization of any kind. This argument is similar to the 'social contract' theories in political philosophy. There, implied agreement is used to justify limitations placed on citizens in order for the state, which limits all for the benefit of all, to exist.[59] Here, the same type of argument is used to justify a state-protected market, so that competitive riches may be bestowed on all participants—namely the existence and viability of trade and the efficient manufacture of goods. The price for such a public good to exist includes both the arbitrariness of the competitive process (its results depending on luck and not just merit) and the limitations on those who seek more power than competition allows.

If we can conclude that monopolists have implicitly agreed to the current competitive framework, they are enjoined from arguing against it. Obviously, most

[58] Ibid, 216. Note that Day at no point defines what exactly is unfair about a certain good's price being higher than otherwise possible—other than a general reference to an aim 'that neither producers nor consumers are *exploited*, ie taken unfair advantage of' (italics in original). On the other hand, some argue that consent of the governed is only rarely a justification for constitutional orders, as the implicit agreement argument requires *unanimous* consent, as those opposing the rule cannot justifiably be forced to comply with it. See R Barnett, *Restoring the Lost Constitution: The Presumption of Liberty* (Princeton, NJ: Princeton University Press, 2004). While this argument has merit, one might combine the implicit agreement with the Rawlsian framework presented above to argue that the populace would accept *majority rule* as a procedural safeguard against excessive compulsion on the one hand, and restrictive statism on the other. This combination posits universal implicit agreement, of the unanimous type argued for by Barnett.

[59] Eg, Thomas Hobbes, *Leviathan* (Schlager Publishing, 1651); Jean-Jacques Rousseau, *The Social Contract* (1762). The theory of justice promoted by Rawls uses the same type of implied agreement to justify not only a state order, but the principles of justice themselves.

people and firms subject to antitrust scrutiny have never been asked their opinion of the law and have not given their assent; yet the argument holds as a theoretical construct. Accepting the rules of the game is implicit in playing the game itself, or receiving the benefits it generates. Of course, this is true only where an option existed *not to accept* the game, or when exit is possible.[60]

On an individually realistic level, none of us truly has the option to exit the social order into which we were born. Even if exiting to another society were possible (one existed that was both different with respect to the relevant rules and was willing to accept us), the cost (both real and psychological) would be prohibitively high. One might generate a hypothetical thought experiment to compare the world we live in with an alternative one bereft of the rules of antitrust. If it could be shown that the alternative is clearly inferior, we might construe a hypothetical implicit agreement on behalf of monopolists to current antitrust doctrine, negating the argument that they are improperly treated. One prevalent framework for examining such scenarios is the Rawlsian 'original position', examined above, but here I focus on two alternative conceptions for deducing monopolists' agreement to antitrust rules: historical and game theoretic.

The historical argument goes as follows: since all current producers entered the market knowing that antitrust rules govern the legal and economic arena, they are enjoined from arguing against it. A caveat might be in order, as some existing firms (or economic institutions) preceded the antitrust laws. Such firms cannot be said to have agreed to game-rules that have so drastically been changed in mid-game. Quite the contrary, this type of argument could be used *against* antitrust, since consumers and other players in the pre-antitrust day entered the economic arena knowing that those of superior economic power use it freely, thus *their implied agreement* is to markets free of state intervention on their behalf. Not to belabour the point, differentiating between types of firms is definitely not helpful in justifying competition policy. Furthermore, not all game-rules are necessarily *just*. If antitrust is to rely on fairness arguments, we must come up with something better than saying 'we were here first'.

Antitrust as the safe-keeper of competition may promote the welfare of some, but it cannot be said that all participants in the market benefit from its existence. Here again the exit/voice paradigm is relevant: those who would prefer the market with no antitrust regulation have no viable exit option. Thus, they cannot be said to implicitly agree by mere fact that participation is the only option open to them.

[60] See AO Hirschman, *Exit, Voice, and Loyalty: Responses to Decline in Firms, Organizations, and States* (Cambridge, MA: Harvard University Press, 1970), arguing that as the opportunities for exit from a society increase, so does the loyalty owed to that society by individuals who declined to exercise their exit options and chose to participate in it. It is interesting to note that the 'retroactive change in the rules of the game' argument has been applied to the context of regulatory takings, positing that unilateral changes in regulation may be construed as governmental breach of contract. See JG Sidak and DF Spulber, *Deregulatory Takings and the Regulatory Contract* (Cambridge: Cambridge University Press, 1998) at 106.

The game-theoretic conception of implicit agreement relies on coordination costs, and society's members implicitly agreeing to governmental solutions to coordination problems. In situations where a prisoner's dilemma can be discerned, there is a strong argument in favour of external intervention to 'force' all parties to make the collectively superior choice. This coordination would lead not only to efficiency being achieved, but to the maximal satisfaction of the parties' individual interests.[61] But is the coordination argument appropriate for the antitrust context? For it to be so, such coordination must be of value both to producer and to consumer. Furthermore, for such an account to justify an implicit agreement theory it must be in principle applicable to *all* consumers and producers—otherwise it cannot be said that their consent is implied.[62]

What do monopolistic producers gain from the antitrust laws? Not much, actually. They are limited in business conduct, perpetually pressured by competition and must devote serious consideration to avoiding actions that, while pro-competitive, might raise the suspicion of antitrust enforcement agencies. On the other hand, every firm seriously contending to be a monopoly surely buys inputs from other firms. If asked whether it would prefer (forgive the anthropomorphizing) the chance of extolling monopoly profits with the risk of paying monopoly price, or antitrust laws precluding both—the choice is far from obvious. Surely, some would gladly assume the risks together with rewards, being in a position to enjoy the 'freedom to monopolize' much more than competition in their input markets would benefit them.

Another aspect of the gain to producers from antitrust laws is not in horizontal relationships, but rather in vertical input markets. The possibility of attaining monopoly profit drives many a firm to large expenditures in the hope of achieving such a position. This is exactly the basis for the 'rent-seeking rectangle' argument assessed above.[63] What drives firms to 'go for gold' are reasons of the prisoner's dilemma prototype. Multiple firms engage in a costly race for monopoly, which aggregately costs them more than they can hope to attain. Separately, though, it's a totally different ball game. To clarify, assume each firm invests X, assuming that with probability p, it will achieve monopoly profits M. If entry barriers, or strategic options exist so that monopoly may be maintained over time, $pM > X$ is

[61] See DG Baird, RH Gertner and RC Picker, *Game Theory and the Law* (Cambridge, MA: Harvard University Press, 1994) 31–35; RA Epstein, *Principles for a Free Society: Reconciling Individual Liberty with the Common Good* (Reading, MA: Perseus Books, 1998) 44–47; S Rose-Ackerman, 'Inalienability and the Theory of Property Rights' (1985) 85 *Columbia Law Review* 931, 957–59.

[62] Here we diverge from the standard game theoretical models used in efficiency analysis. There, the aggregately superior result is sufficient for justifying a solution. In the implicit agreement model, though, we attempt to prove that those *limited* would themselves opt for this solution in a perfect world. Only by securing their interest maximization, will *fairness* constraints be thus justified.

[63] See generally, Posner, *Antitrust Law* (n 1) 17–21, arguing that the classic study of monopoly's social cost [AC Harberger, 'Monopoly and Resource Allocation' (1954) 44 *American Economic Review* 77] is grossly understated; Epstein, 'Private Property and the Public Domain' (n 27) 52; But see M Glick, 'Is Monopoly Rent Seeking Compatible with Wealth Maximization?' (1994) *Brigham Young University Law Review* 499 arguing that rent seeking expenditures, while real, are not to be regarded as a social cost.

a very real possibility, holding that discounted monopoly profits are larger than investment in their attainment. Allowing for N firms, $NX > M$ is also possible (indeed, probable), holding that collective investment in the race-for-monopoly exceeds monopoly's gain. If both inequalities hold true, the race for monopoly is both individually rational, and aggregately inefficient.

Individually, a firm is interested in the first inequality alone, as aggregate effects are externalized. In order to successfully argue for implied agreement of *all* firms, $pM > X$ must be shown. But if that is true, will rent-seeking be attempted?

It might. The fault with the above analysis is its static setting. It assumes that the firms enjoy competitive returns, C, and merely decide if to invest in rent-seeking or refrain from it. A more realistic model would include two periods. In the first period, a firm chooses whether to act competitively, enjoying returns C, or to invest in rent-seeking and receive first period returns of $C - X$. In the second period, returns are determined by first period investments, so that those who did not invest in rent-seeking receive F, returns for fringe firms in a monopolized market, and first period investors in rent-seeking expect $pM + (1 - p)F$, the first term denoting monopoly profit (discounted by their chance of achieving it) and the second term denoting the alternative of receiving the fringe firm's profit.

If $F < pM + (1 - p)F - X < C$ holds true, first period investment in rent-seeking is individually rational for all firms, while a cooperative limitation on such rent-seeking would be to *all* firms' benefit. Competitive returns are higher than expected returns from rent-seeking (taking into account probability of success), and both in turn are higher than the fringe firm's expected profit. Thus firms *would* invest in an option they prefer ex ante to be unavailable to them—provided that it is not available to *all other firms* as well.

This is the classic prisoner's dilemma. In contrast to the standard rent-seeking rectangle argument reviewed above, here *even the successful monopolist* would have preferred precluding rent-seeking ex ante. It is only due to the fear of another firm attaining monopoly that the race starts in the first place. Thus, in cases such as these, coordination mechanisms unite the interests of *all players*, attaining aggregate efficiency to boot. Of course, this argument is neither universal (one can surely imagine cases where specific circumstances render the assumptions untrue), nor is it relevant to *consumer* protection. The implicit agreement that can be read from this account is between producers, so that when analyzing fairness considerations dealing with *competitors*, the argument may be used.

Of great significance is that this prisoner's dilemma analysis of producers proves quite detrimental to *consumers*' interests, since the horizontal coordination mechanism which firms would choose in lieu of the wasteful race for monopoly is not *competition*, but *collusion*.[64] Were the competitors to collude in order to

[64] Thus allowing not multiple investments in rent-seeking for one firm attaining monopoly profits, but investment in collusion (which may very well prove to be lower than unilateral rent seeking) by all firms, and sharing of monopoly profit. Furthermore, an industry-wide cartel, if successful, would be able to extract full monopoly profit (and divide it among participating firms), while one monopolist

share monopoly profits, the prisoner's dilemma would be solved and the *relevant* players would be better off. This, of course, is due to the current focus on those suffering from a coordination problem—as it is their implicit agreement the counter-argument sought to deduce. The argument for producers' implicit agreement to the *current doctrines* of antitrust (rather than for their right to collude) thus fails.

Of course, our mission here is not to justify collusion, and the result above is consistent only with producers' interests, not with those of consumers or other players yet to be examined. We can, though, add two more serious reasons against turning to the expenditures of rent-seeking for justification of antitrust law. First, the references brought as to monopolization costs which may be economized, are studies of the *current situation*, in which the antitrust laws already exist. There is nothing to suggest that these costs will be as high under a non-interventionist regime. On the contrary, it may very well be that allowing 'free' monopolization will economize on costs thereof, since activities that are currently under a veil of secrecy, would be conducted openly and perhaps more efficiently. Furthermore, costs associated with legal protection from antitrust enforcement are extremely substantial, and these could be saved completely (of course, some of those most interested in the issues this book addresses would then be out of a job).

The second reason for being suspicious of using rent-seeking as a justification for antitrust law is due to our analysis of 'public choice' in chapter two. When a firm, or group of interested parties, finds the legal regime non-optimal for their needs, they may choose to invest quite heavily in its repeal or adjustment. In the realm of antitrust, this may be in lobbying for an exemption, or for more stringent enforcement within a certain industry.[65] Such public choice activities are extremely costly (both in themselves and in their results) and are relevant only in a world where antitrust law is a realistic option. It would not be enough to repeal the antitrust laws in order to avoid this phenomenon, since as long as the *option* for them exists, there will be those willing to invest in lobbying for their enactment and others investing in preventing such a result.

in a market with fringe competition may be constrained. If we follow through with the argument that a prisoner's dilemma justifies intervention and state-mandated cooperation, a legally binding cartel is thus justified—cutting down on enforcement costs and maintaining stability of monopoly power.

[65] See the discussion in ch 2, section I.E.ii, as well as FS McChesney, 'Rent Extraction and Rent Creation in the Economic Theory of Regulation' (1987) 16 *Journal of Legal Studies* 101; R Sherman, *The Regulation of Monopoly* (Cambridge: Cambridge University Press, 1989) 59–62; JM Buchanan, RD Tollison and G Tullock, *Toward a Theory of the Rent-Seeking Society* (College Station, Texas: Texas A&M, 1980). For an exceptionally strong critique of this trend, see FL Smith, 'The Case for Reforming the Antitrust Regulations (if Repeal is not an Option)' (1999) 23 *Harvard Journal of Law & Public Policy* 23. Finally, it is interesting to note corporate funding of academic conferences with specific policy implications, eg, WE Kovacic, 'The Antitrust Paradox Revisited: Robert Bork and the Transformation of Modern Antitrust Policy' (1990) 36 *Wayne Law Review* 1413, 1433–35 and CE Mueller, 'The Anti-Antitrust Movement and the Case of Lester Thurow' (1981) 13 *Antitrust Law & Economics Review* 59.

vi. Antitrust as Securing Social Justice for Consumers

Some might argue that consumers ought to be protected from wealth transfers, not as a general protection of individual rights (property or contract), but due to a duty binding society to respect a minimal level of welfare that cannot be denied them. While up to now the focus was on *corrective justice*, arguing that monopolists are 'taking away' something belonging to the consumers, here we focus on *distributive justice*, dealing with deserved endowments and relative position in society. The same argument could obviously be made by other groups as well, thus I develop it here on behalf of consumers and apply it as relevant to other groups later on.

The argument for redistribution through antitrust relies on broad conceptions of social justice, with our current context serving merely as one specific implementation of this notion. The two questions this section focuses on are: can consumers point to a justification rooted in social justice to substantiate their argument against wealth transfers? And if they can, is antitrust an appropriate instrument to uphold their interests?

We turn first to a part of the Rawlsian argument previously left out. Based on the hypothetical veil of ignorance, Rawls concluded that society would choose to embrace principles improving the welfare of those worst off. Included among these selected principles would be some redistribution of assets (not our focus here) and some limitations on economically powerful actors so that weaker ones are not harmed. Competition policy, it could be argued, serves the specific capacity of this second type.

But what exactly are the consumers' interests requiring protection? Merely avoiding wealth transfers cannot be enough, since even without them many consumers will not be able to secure their needs in a competitive market. As seen above, competitive markets may price even basic goods above the ability of some consumers to pay, rendering antitrust under such circumstances unhelpful for them. Competition policy, however, is not alone in securing consumers' needs, but is accompanied by a variety of other legal norms redistributing wealth, ensuring that no individual would fall below a certain level of economic ability. Still, this claim for antitrust protection fails due to it being both too broad and too narrow.

The redistribution argument for antitrust is *overly broad* due to its lack of differentiation between different types of consumers and different types of goods. As seen above, varying elasticities of demand cause some consumers to suffer more than others when prices rise, or enjoy a higher surplus when prices fall. If intervention is aimed at protecting consumers, there is no justification for protecting the interests of some while ignoring others, or indeed, expending social resources (paid for by all) to increase the surplus enjoyed by those lucky enough to be inelastic purchasers of a monopolized good, such as those shopping for luxury cars in the example above. While social intervention is often focused on specific groups, applying it to help an extremely broad category of individuals due to a small part of them needing and deserving assistance is both wasteful and wrong; it is wasteful by investing social resources in circumstances where they are unneeded to attain the proscribed goal, and wrong, by essentially subsidizing consumption by well-off individuals (for example, purchasers of luxury cars) using resources garnered from those in an economically inferior position (taxpayers financing competition agencies).

Consumers whose demand is inelastic at a certain price possess a greater interest in seeing that price fall. The problem is that the consumers whose demand is inelastic (those benefiting the most from antitrust intervention) are not necessarily those worst off. It may be that others, economically weaker, have a more elastic demand due to their different preferences and willingness to substitute other products for the one in question. 'Beggars can't be choosers' it is said, and economically this translates into those worst off exhibiting a higher cross-elasticity of demand between products more affluent individuals would not consider substitutes.

Consider, for example, the market for premium brands of bread. Inelasticity of demand might be observed in well-to-do consumers, as they would rather pay a higher price than substitute with breads they perceive to be of lower quality. Consumers lower on the economic ability scale would easily convert to other products, substituting cheap bread for expensive, and baking their own or eating potatoes rather than paying exorbitant prices. Of course, this is not to say that the poor always exhibit more elastic demand, but rather that effects are ambiguous and shift across product categories. Indeed, empirical studies show that there is no reason to assume a correlation between elasticity of demand and economic affluence.[66] Antitrust, with its micro-market focus, protects the inelastic with respect to narrowly defined product categories rather than those with more limited resources—a result incongruent with the principle underlying the social justice argument.

Furthermore, if antitrust were aimed at protecting the financially weak, it could concentrate on products relevant to their needs rather than being applied in a context-neutral fashion. An antitrust regime treating the market for bread in the same manner as it treats the market for luxury cars, or the market for computer software, is not justified by a social justice conception of protecting the poor.

On the other hand, competition policy can be seen as having *too narrow* an implementation than social justice would call for. Intervention is aimed at

[66] See, eg, SJ Hoch, B-D Kim, AL Montgomery and PE Rossi, 'Determinants of Store-Level Price Elasticity' (1995) 32 *Journal of Marketing Research* 17, who found that increasing wealth (as measured by home equity) and education serves to reduce price-sensitivity, while increased family size and minority status (Black or Hispanic) increased price-sensitivity. Thus, protecting those with inelastic demand would act in favour of the privileged, contrary to common assumptions. Another interesting case is the demand for health services. See, eg, R Sauerborn, A Nougtara and E Latimer, 'The Elasticity of Demand for Health care in Burkina Faso: Differences across Age and Income Groups' (1994) 9 *Health Policy and Planning* 185 who found that elasticity was highest for those of the lowest income quartile.

attaining competitive markets, not at maintaining some predetermined price. If competition delivers pricing that places certain products deemed necessary to the group in question above their reach, it does not secure the results aimed for under this reasoning. Antitrust prohibits collusion regardless of its distributive effects, even in cases where social justice might be said to be promoted. For example, a horizontal cartel of supermarkets agreeing to set low prices for basic food products, and high prices for other products, would be prosecuted in the same way as any other horizontal cartel. Antitrust suits may not (overtly) refer to the position and opportunities that luck, merit, or society have bestowed upon either plaintiff or defendant if those are not *directly* a part of the antitrust offence. Thus, an extremely wealthy and advantaged individual has every right to sue a small and teetering family owned firm, if the latter has engaged in illegitimate conduct. The fact that the individual 'has enough money of his own' is of absolutely no interest to antitrust law.

Antitrust, thus, is both too broad to be justified by social justice and too narrow to achieve the goals such a concept demands; goals of redistribution would be much better attained by policies with discriminating abilities, such as subsidization, progressive taxation and regulation of basic products' prices.[67] These practices are not only beyond antitrust enforcement, but at times directly contrary to competition, the primary focus of antitrust. It seems that justifications for antitrust should be sought elsewhere.

a. Wealth Transfers as a Justification for Competition Policy: Summary

Competition policy is often described as protecting consumers from wealth transfers, implicitly assuming both consumers' property right to 'their share' of the surplus and state intervention as the appropriate enforcement mechanism. As shown above, these assumptions are difficult to justify. Notwithstanding the important roles competition serves as *social* policy (assessed in chapter two), the *individual rights* perspective underlying the wealth transfer argument has turned out to be less convincing than commonly assumed, especially given the broad definitions used for 'consumers' and the varying economic conditions governing their interactions (as to the types of goods covered and differing elasticities of demand).

All this is not to say that consumers have *no* right deserving protection, but that an assessment of their rights requires more examination and comparison with other relevant parties before a conclusion can be reached. The following sections turn to other victims of monopoly, whose protection was historically argued to justify antitrust intervention, though current emphasis on economic efficiency and consumers has relegated their claims to the sidelines of the debate. While important in their own right, the role of non-consumer victims of monopoly will

[67] See Posner, *Antitrust Law* (n 1). Another possibility is industry specific guidelines; see OE Williamson, 'Economies as an Antitrust Defense Revisited' (1977) 125 *University of Pennsylvania Law Review* 699, arguing for the possibility of distributional concerns, but suggesting that industry-specific qualifications are more appropriate at addressing them. See also Calvani (n 24) 9.

be attended to in a manner much more concise than that afforded consumers, both due to the latter's centrality in the literature and due to the current chapter's supporting role in the main argument to be developed later on. The criteria developed in the preceding discussion pertaining to consumers' rights within antitrust will also be employed in this context to deduce how other actors affected by antitrust are to be treated.

vii. Innovation and Product Variety as Consumer Rights

Innovation is usually seen as creating several positive results: new and better products, more variety, lower prices and accelerated economic growth. Pricing has been tackled above within the wealth transfer argument, thus even if innovation is an indirect route to similar results, this lends no *additional and independent* justification to that already assessed. The interest in 'new and better products' may be substantial, as they introduce not only the satisfaction of preferences, but the creation of new ones. Together with product variety, these interests focus on non-price issues, with consumer choice as the main beneficiary.[68] A common intuitive assumption is that the wider the variety of existing products and the more often new developments enter the market, the broader the scope of individual choice available to each consumer. As a society which regards individual choice as a primary good, product variety is valuable indeed. From the individual consumer's point of view, personal preferences and values can be better achieved when choosing the products best suited to her subjective individual demands from a wide selection.

On the other hand, as the previous chapter pointed out, innovation is not always aggregately efficient and often creates cross-subsidization, pitting some consumers against others. The aggregate concerns regarding excess innovation and its costs were outlined above, but the distributional issues and cross-subsidization argument bear fleshing out.

Innovation is expensive. It involves investing money today in order to come out with a better product tomorrow. In that sense, it raises the price of today's product, burdening current consumers with higher total costs that the firm needs to defray, with today's consumers being the main source of income for the firm. Future consumers (some of which are also current) may enjoy the fruits of such investment, but assuming that *all* consumers are always interested in research and development is an overly broad generalization. Obvious examples include one-shot consumers, or older consumers not anticipating enjoying the benefit for

[68] For emphasis on this interest, see Averitt and Lande (n 6). On the other hand, there are those who would argue that this is not necessarily a good thing. The market economy our society extols is seen by some to detract from the personal or contemplative domain, substituting mass-produced images which consumers are conned into accepting as their own. This poses a distinct and broad question as to individual autonomy and how it is best achieved. See, eg, MA Starr, 'Saving, Spending, and Self-Control: Cognition versus Consumer Culture' (2007) 39 *Review of Radical Political Economics* 214 and citations therein.

which they currently pay. Beyond these, we must keep in mind consumers who are satisfied with the way things are, and would rather have more of the same (potentially cheaper) than be assuaged with newly introduced products bearing their own switching costs and 'improvements' that are not always needed.[69]

Furthermore, increased product variety is not always a good thing. Expanding the choice-set is seen as intuitively good and most economists would see in it the potential for finding a better fit between idiosyncratic personal preferences and existing products. Yet increasing choice comes at a cost, both pecuniary and psychological. When we speak of product variety as inherently valuable, we often forget that carrying a large inventory of differentiated products is an expensive endeavour, which at least for some consumers would have been better forgone.[70] The psychological issue is addressed in the literature on cognitive load, where choice requires mental resources at a personal cost.[71] For some, benefits exceed costs; for others, the reverse is true. In some cases, increased choice causes cognitive overload which can be exploited by firms anticipating consumer responses, using excess variety to drive consumers towards more expensive products or less optimal purchasing patterns. Choice, then, does not always increase with variety and neither does consumers' utility.[72]

In some cases, specific market attributes raise questions as to innovation's role as an obvious public good. Consider, for example, the case of razors, with the commonly-known dynamic of firms selling cheap handles and expensive disposable cartridges.[73] As firms innovate in razor quality and type, consumers used to older razors and happy to continue using existing types find themselves in a quandary. Early adopters switch to 'new and improved' razors, leading to variety *at the store* shifting to include more of the newer versions (at higher prices) and less of the older ones. Similarly to what has become familiar in the software industry, those preferring to stick with 'old and proven' products often find them disappearing from the major outlets. Thus, even consumers preferring the older and cheaper models feel compelled to pay more for products they don't really want as much.

[69] Herbert Simon developed a framework assessing the benefits of such 'satisfying' rather than 'optimizing' forms of decision-making, calling for the development of economic models based on individuals who search for a good only until achieving a threshold level of utility, rather than maximizing returns. See HA Simon, *Models of Man: Social and Rational* (New York: Wiley, 1957). The current proliferation of behavioural models assuming bounded rationality owes much to the groundwork he laid, though goes much beyond it as well. For sources and discussion, see A Ayal, 'Harmful Freedom of Choice: Lessons from the Cellular Market' (2011) 74 *Law and Contemporary Problems* 91.

[70] See, eg, C Huffman and BE Kahn, 'Variety for Sale: Mass Customization or Mass Confusion?' (1998) 74 *Journal of Retailing* 491–513.

[71] Barry Schwartz expanded and popularized this issue in a series of studies. See generally, B Schwartz, *The Paradox of Choice: Why More is Less* (New York: Ecco, 2004).

[72] I have addressed this issue elsewhere, focusing on the market for cellular calling plans. There, cognitive overload was related to competition in the market and increased variety was shown to lead directly to sub-optimal choice, used by firms to mitigate competitive forces operating in the market. See Ayal (n 69).

[73] Though commonly-known and true are not always identical. See RC Picker, 'The Razors and Blades Myth(s)' (2011) 78 *University of Chicago Law Review* 225 showing that, counter to conventional wisdom, Gillette followed a different strategy during much of its rise to market prominence.

Aggregately, we might say consumers' benefit is apparent through their purchasing decisions, but some consumers are harmed so others' preferences might be satisfied—to say nothing of the role of firms in shifting those preferences and resulting buying behaviour towards more profitable opportunities for them.

The bottom line is that enhancing innovation and product variety may be aggregately good, but due to distributive concerns such a conclusion is far from obvious. We should bear in mind that the question is not whether innovation as such is good, but whether we require a state backed policy pushing it beyond what firms and consumers would achieve absent such intervention, which is another question entirely. Of course, consumers differ on many dimensions, and perfection in public policy is almost never attainable, but since our focus here is on *fairness* issues rather than total welfare, it bears keeping in mind the conflicting interests involved. Nonetheless, since our aim is in substantiating justifications for antitrust, we shall proceed based on the assumption that consumers as a group prefer more innovation and antitrust is a relevant mechanism for furthering this goal. How far this takes us down the path of a fairness-justified antitrust policy is yet to be seen.

Assuming that consumers do have an *interest* in promoting innovation and product variety through competition, do they have a protected *right* on which to base a claim for state intervention? The previous discussion outlining the basis for rights and their distinction from interests will serve us in this context as well.

Claiming a property right to the existence of ample choice among products is more difficult than the argument for consumer surplus. In the consumer surplus debate, we had in mind a direct and (at least hypothetically) measurable amount of money that consumers would have attained were competition present, one the monopolist had managed to transfer to himself. In the product variety context, the argument is not for the existence of products that consumers would necessarily *use*, but for those that would be there for them to *choose from*. Even if we were to frame the claim from the perspective of those who *would* use these products, the relevant group is much smaller than those suffering monetary loss from consumption of all monopolized products.[74]

A property right to variety entails a duty on someone to provide that variety, raising once again the 'forced labour' problem encountered above, and developed more fully in chapter six below.[75] There, the problem was circumvented by making the right to consumer surplus contingent on trade itself taking place,

[74] Eg, the consumer surplus argument can be made on behalf of all consumers of monopoly-priced products. Product variety arguments can be made on behalf of those consumers of monopolized markets, who, had there been alternative products, would have preferred those to the monopoly-provided one. The latter may be seen as a relatively small subset of the former, becoming even smaller if the issues of excessive choice outlined above are taken into consideration. Some argue that consumers' interest in choice is already incorporated in the general welfarist conception guiding economic analysis in antitrust, and positing choice as an independent goal would lower consumers' utility overall; see JD Wright and DH Ginsburg, 'The Goals of Antitrust: Welfare Trumps Choice' (2013) 81 *Fordham Law Review* 2405.

[75] See n 30 and accompanying text.

thus preventing a claim that monopolists are compelled to produce the good in question. Is a similar route available here? Variety, as distinct from consumer surplus, is beneficial even as a potential yet unrealized. The interest in variety stems not from a wish to experiment by buying a specimen of every single brand of product (although there might be those who do just that), but more often in having a large group of products from which to choose. The existence of such products, then, must necessarily be prior to trade itself and in any case, their number necessarily exceeds the number of those purchased. Indeed, the consumer interest in variety may be exercised by 'shopping around' with the individual subsequently concluding that no product is of sufficient interest to warrant a transaction (and some enjoying the process more than the result). A property right to variety thus necessitates someone offering these products, essentially externalizing onto the producer the consumer's 'right' to choose, embodying the forced labour problem. Furthermore, competition is not necessarily variety intensive, thus a direct right to variety might require far more than mere antitrust law and prevention of monopoly.[76]

There is another possibility. We may argue that while no right exists to *obtain* the maximal variety, a would-be monopolist should be prevented from 'getting in the way' of variety. While this result is more intuitive, it still does not answer the question of the *basis* of the right. 'Getting in the way' implies a process which precedes the monopolist's interference, and limiting such interference implies a right to this process. Once again we return to our basic question: where does the *right* consumers claim to a competitive process come from? Aside from the general interest that consumers have in increasing their satisfaction, are there aspects specific to product variety that might help in substantiating such a claim?

Perhaps so. Consider, for example, consumers whose religious or moral beliefs lead them to require products of a certain nature (kosher foods, non-CFC aerosols, or cosmetics not tested on animals come to mind). Consumers such as these might be slighted by a monopolistic firm which finds it unprofitable to manufacture the specific goods, resulting in the religious/moral minority group not being provided for. In such a case, product variety is more than a preference; it is justified by moral rights or religious freedom. On the other hand, cases of moral preference exhibit very inelastic demand (as consumers *need* the product rather than merely *want* it, raising willingness to pay). Thus, dominance in a market niche of this type would be extremely profitable, attractive to monopolists and prospective entrants regardless of legal duties.

Furthermore, if this need gives rise to an independent right justifying intervention, is antitrust law really relevant? Even if some cases exist where opening

[76] Competitive pressures may lead to cost-cutting and 'meeting the competition', generating uniformity in product offering, while monopoly power allows producers to price-discriminate, often by offering low price/quality products side-by-side with high price/quality combinations. Furthermore, if consumers value variety, and if niche markets exist, monopolists (as well as fringe firms) may profitably service these markets regardless of competition.

up a monopolized market to competition may satisfy such needs, it is far from clear that such cases are prevalent. Cases such as these merely steer us once again towards differentiating between types of goods and consumer elasticities, calling for specific regulation rather than general antitrust law.

What then remains? Consumers' interests in antitrust protection are not in dispute; their *right* to such protection, though, is more dubious. If antitrust is to be defended on fairness grounds, we may have to turn to other affected parties for justification.

II. ANTITRUST AS A TOOL FOR PROTECTING COMPETITORS

> Trusts have made products cheaper, have reduced prices; but if the price of oil, for instance, were reduced to one cent a barrel, it would not right the wrong done to people of this country by the *trusts* which have destroyed legitimate competition and driven honest men from legitimate business enterprise.
> (Representative William Mason, arguing for enactment of the Sherman Act, 1890)[77]

One of the more controversial themes to rise in antitrust debate is the need for and justification of protecting competitors. Even within the broader definition of 'monopoly' used here, referring to all practices strengthening or maintaining market power, there is no doubt that in most cases one firm acquiring monopolistic status entails another being pushed aside. The question, therefore, is whether competing firms *as such* are entitled to protection (rather than being allowed to compete merely for instrumental reasons, for the benefit of consumers).[78]

While the slogan of 'protecting competition and not competitors' is well known,[79] efficiency considerations may demand protection of competitors to maintain the competitive process and its advantages. Of course, under this approach competitors are merely a useful means to another end.[80] Here we deal

[77] Congressional Record, 51st Congress, 1st session, House (20 June 1890) 4100.

[78] Interestingly, in some cases it is antitrust law itself that harms competitors. Monopoly with a competitive (or oligopolistic) fringe entails the existence of other firms competing with the monopoly for the same consumers. Firms within the competitive fringe enjoy a unique status of attaining close to monopoly profit without holding monopoly power themselves. The phenomenon is known as a 'price umbrella' and is relevant whether the dominant player is a monopolist or cartel (in the latter case, non-members enjoy the cartel's existence). When the monopolist raises price, small players undercut slightly or match prices, sharing monopoly profit—until antitrust enforcement steps in. In such cases, 'protecting competitors' might necessitate *encouragement* of monopoly rather than fighting it. Of course, this is not the sort of 'protection' most commentators have in mind when claiming it as a justification for antitrust law.

[79] See *Brown Shoe Co Inc v United States*, 370 US 294 (1962). But see H Hovenkamp, 'Antitrust's Protected Classes' (1989) 88 *Michigan Law Review* 1, arguing that competitors *as such* are entitled to antitrust protection as well.

[80] See, eg, JW Burns, 'The New Role of Coercion in Antitrust' (1991) 60 *Fordham Law Review* 379, reviewing the doctrine of 'trader freedom' in antitrust litigation. While the doctrine's application is almost a thing of the past, Burns argues that even within an efficiency perspective it should not be dismissed.

with the question whether antitrust law should attach importance to competitors' *as such* and not the instrumental role they may play in the attainment in other goals.

From a fairness perspective, competitors may be bearers of rights deserving a place in the analysis, but the question at hand is whether these rights automatically include the right to a competitive market in which they may participate. The competitive market is not the creation of any single participant; it exists solely as a series of interactions among various actors, so that each may attempt to participate within—profiting or not according to circumstances, foresight, merit and chance. A player's profit in itself is not protected as a vested right, as losing money or even going bankrupt are viewed as potential and legitimate consequences of competition. But is the competitor's 'right to compete' protected against would-be monopolists driving him out? It seems the answer depends on the means employed to achieve this result.

A competitor driven to bankruptcy (or merely leaving the market) due to market price falling below his cost of production is considered merely an inefficient victim of the free market. While some social justice conceptions call for a communitarian support system, few automatically assume that the burden must fall on those competitors who managed to cut costs or reorganize according to shifting market conditions. It is not, then, the players remaining in the market who are responsible for those leaving it.[81]

Does the fact that monopolization was the cause of a competitor's commercial demise change this assessment? In some cases it does. While the free market system guarantees no one success or profit, it does create a system of game-rules that players can rely upon. Any individual wishing to compete is (supposedly) subject to the same rules, allowing all players access to markets, both as sellers and as buyers. This ideal picture complements our view of modern democracy, where all people are subject to the same laws, and free expression is allowed in the competition for political influence. The 'marketplace of ideas' allows one and all to present their views in public, and argue for their implementation. Just as democracy assures no one that their ideas will be *accepted* by others, competition assures no one success. The right to be protected, then, is not competitors' right to a specific result, but a right to *the process.*

The process, rather than its consequences, should be the focus of our analysis. The right to free trade has long been considered an extension of the right to property and autonomy. The state refrains from unnecessary interference in commercial relations, and it stand to reason that the same freedom of trade should be protected from private parties hindering it.

[81] But see JA Schumpeter, *Capitalism, Socialism and Democracy*, 2nd edn (New York: Harper & Bros, 1947) ch 8. There, Schumpeter deals with monopolistic practices in a different way, as one possibility for slowing down the destructive 'race of capitalism'. This competitive race results in firms going bankrupt in their eagerness to cut costs and maintain profit, bringing down with them their workers, dependent communities, and the like.

Competitors arguing for a 'right to compete' must justify not only their right of participation, but their right to *government intervention* aimed at maintaining the market competitive. What is the property that competitors point to warrant such protection? Their products (or capital, plant, etc), are undisputedly theirs, but this is irrelevant for competition policy. If it is the producer surplus that competitive markets promise them (mirroring the previous claim by consumers), the problem is compounded, since now they must argue not only for limitation of monopolists, but also for similar implementation as to consumers (otherwise no producer surplus will be created).

Competitors may claim an interest in competitive markets based on their right to freely dispose of their property, a right that would be devoid of content if no market existed in which they could sell. But accepting such an argument would expand disposition of property to placing duties upon others, so that the property owners can attain their desired benefits. We must therefore ask: what constitutes the substantive difference between a competitor blocked from enjoying profits by a more efficient (or simply luckier) competitor, and the same result caused by a more powerful monopolist? In both cases, identical profit is lost, no forceful of fraudulent interference existed and the unlucky competitor's hopes are frustrated.

There is one distinguishing factor which may operate in competitors' favour. While they have no justifiable claim to protection from an external process, they may have a right to protection from specific injuries aimed at them. For example, imagine a case where a monopolist aims to maintain his market power by offering to buy out a potential competitor. Under standard contractual analysis, this represents an agreement between two consenting parties, and therefore should not be interfered with (assuming away, for a moment, the existence of antitrust). If the monopolist uses his market power to *force* the competitor to sell (or threatens to do so, explicitly or implicitly), such a contract would be void as the competitor was compelled, and no free will was exercised.[82] It is through this doctrine that we may target predation as well. If a monopolist harms a competitor in order to cause the latter to sell his business, leave the market, or refrain from entering it, the monopolist's action should be analyzed under the harm principle.[83] Under this principle, the competitor has a right to protection of his property, not because he *owned* the niche in the market which he occupied, but because force was used to 'push him out' of a market belonging to no one. Since the market belongs to no one, space within it may operate on a principle similar to Locke's 'first possession' rationale.[84]

When this principle is applied to property, first possession grants ownership when the new owner does something to improve a property (for example,

[82] Economic duress being an example of performance-excusing compulsion assessed above. See Farnsworth (n 53) 264–66.
[83] See Epstein, 'Private Property and the Public Domain' (n 27) 71–76.
[84] Ibid, 25–31; John Locke, *Second Treatise of Government* (1689) 40.

cultivating previously barren land) and enough property remains for others as well. Under this view, the market is not property, both in the sense that it does not exist physically and in the sense that its existence is not protected over time. The existence of a market depends on the free will of buyers and sellers within it, and each of these parties is free to alter it, shifting preferences for consumption or supply. Thus, no party can claim ownership of the market, but all may gain from its existence. Any player is thus free to alter his contribution to the market, and if others are affected, they may claim no property right to their previous market share.[85]

Like consumers, competitors enjoy the benefits of market participation as well as the difficulty in arguing that they *deserve* a certain portion of the surplus created by trade. While modern competition doctrine centres on consumers and regards competitors as instrumental, means rather than ends, viewing the market as a process in which all have an interest restores some of the esteem in which competitors' rights were once held. Applying the Rawlsian criterion developed above, if we are to imagine a discussion behind a veil of ignorance, the question is whether the polity would agree that market participation is important—beyond the result of competitively priced products to be consumed. Trade induces creativity in attempts to offer marketable products, creating both profit opportunities and circumstances allowing for the expression of ingenuity and foresight. Furthermore, trade within markets goes beyond materialistic interests in achieving products or profit, encompassing much of modern living and labour-related self-expression and identity. It is hard to believe that monetary compensation and consumption would alone dominate discussions in Rawls' hypothetical. These issues will be attended to in chapter five below, where the Rawlsian thought experiment will be applied to all parties affected by competition policy as well as the type of society we seek. Competitors, viewed instrumentally within the consumer welfare framework, may very well deserve independent standing in such a setting.

III. WORKERS, LOCAL COMMUNITIES AND SMALL BUSINESSES: THE LOST CLASSES OF ANTITRUST

While those being introduced to competition law in today's intellectual climate might never realize it, in the early days of antitrust multiple constituents were named as beneficiaries. Workers in plants closed down due to price cutting by large, out-of-state conglomerates, communities devastated by local unemployment and small businesses losing out to huge chain stores, were all thought to

[85] For criticism of Locke's lack of definitive answers to cases of dynamic changes, see J Gray, 'Liberalism and the Choice of Liberties' in J Gray (ed), *Liberalisms: Essays in Political Philosophy* (London: Routledge, 1989) 148–49. Notice that the author refers to changes similar to the market changes described here, and finds no substantial answer to the problem of clashing interests. In the same way, my present analysis points out that no one person may claim a property right to a future market-produced result.

benefit from an interventionist regime aimed at protecting them.[86] Following much 'mom-and-pop store' rhetoric, large businesses were perceived as driving out local competition by exploiting superior economic power, a result antitrust law was supposed to prevent.

Over time, it became clear that competition law was not only ineffective at solving these problems, it may actually exacerbate them. Antitrust's focus on efficiency led businesses enjoying economies of scale and scope to be viewed as beneficial to the economy at large, and to consumers specifically. Gone are the days of mergers being blocked merely due to their increasing business size, and smaller firms losing their businesses. While the 'efficiency defence' is still consumer-centric (allowing efficiencies only insofar as these are passed on to consumers), arguments focusing on the role and importance of local businesses or independent entrepreneurs would not be entertained in today's antitrust climate.[87]

Furthermore, even firms' size and power were thought to be a social concern; antitrust is far from the appropriate solution. Not every antitrust offence affects local communities, just as not every multiregional (or multinational) firm commits antitrust offences or enjoys a monopolistic position. Much was said above, and shall not be repeated, regarding the problematic nature of opposing specific objectionable results with the broad tool of antitrust law. As reluctant as we would be to target a mosquito with a cannon, so we are with combating the specific nature of local community life with the broad stroke of forbidding monopolization or regulating mergers. If the concern of local communities is closed-down plants or employment within impersonal outside firms, it is not antitrust in general or monopolistic firms in particular that should be turned to. It will not help local communities if the acquisition of their businesses is carried out by a competitive out-of-state firm, rather than a monopolistic one.[88]

Furthermore, since the focus of antitrust law is on the monopolization of distinct markets, many local firms and townships would be precluded from creating entry barriers so that their local market remains local. Instead, such segregated local markets, insulated from outside competition, are themselves often the object of antitrust enforcement.[89] Realistically, the firms posing greater competition to

[86] See, eg, R Hofstadter, 'What Happened to the Antitrust Movement?' in *The Paranoid Style in American Politics and Other Essays* (New York: Vintage Books, 1965); Lande (n 3); SF Ross, *Principles of Antitrust Law* (n 16); RJ Peritz, 'A Counter-History of Antitrust Law' (1990) *Duke Law Journal* 263; RJ Peritz, *Competition Policy in America: History, Rhetoric, Law*, rev edn (New York: Oxford University Press, 1996).

[87] See OE Williamson, *The Economic Institutions of Capitalism* (New York: Free Press, 1985), as well as his discussion of the Proctor and Gamble merger case in *Antitrust Economics* (ch 2, n 78).

[88] This assumes that 'bigness' as such is not an antitrust concern; rather its focus is on market power. This issue was questioned in ch 2, section II.A, and shall be returned to below, in chs 5 and 7 setting out the balancing test for antitrust.

[89] It is an interesting fact that protection of small, locally owned, businesses is many times attempted by townships. These, for example, place obstacles in the path of large mega-stores (not necessarily monopolists!) wishing to open a branch within city limits. Ironically, it is these larger firms that turn to antitrust for protection of their right to compete with the small businesses. Of course, the

(and thus in more danger from) monopolists, are not small businesses, but firms which would be 'second best'. Such firms are usually the large, established and efficient ones, very far from the intuitive 'mom-and-pop stores' considered here. The mental picture conjured by small businesses as victims of large predatory monopolies, is likely rooted more in public perception than fact. In any case, small businesses' interests are often best be served by *allowing* monopoly to flourish, since a protective 'umbrella' of monopolistic pricing would allow the small (and usually less efficient) businesses to price at or higher than their own costs of production.[90]

As to workers and local communities, these operate on both sides of the debate. Workers of monopolistic firms enjoy their firm's market power, and monopolists, too, have plants and stores located in local communities that enjoy (part of) the spoils of commerce. Insofar as these groups would be considered relevant to competition policy (currently they are not), arguments on their behalf could be made both for stringent enforcement and for lax standards, depending on context and application. In sum, relying on these constituencies to provide a normative justification of antitrust law is a mistake, as their position is indeterminate and they require a legal doctrine more tailored to their specific needs. For them, competition is not necessarily what the doctor ordered…

public choice perspective is relevant here as well, as local merchants may turn to local authorities for protection from competition. See TW Ross, 'Store Wars: The Chain Tax Movement' (1986) 29 *Journal of Law and Economics* 125. See also SF Ross, *Principles of Antitrust Law* (n 16) 516–20, focusing on local authorities' antitrust offences, where explicit protectionism carries legal liability that overcomes 'state action' immunity.

[90] See n 79 for a similar argument relevant to competitors in general, large or small.

4

Monopolists' Rights

Who are the monopolists, and why do we love to hate them? Of course, many would balk at the emotional assertion, and explain at length that monopoly is not necessarily bad, monopolists not evil and hatred is far from the determinant of appropriate competition policy. Yet I contend that two main approaches are prevalent as to competition policy and appropriate antitrust rules: First, that of the pro-consumer and anti-monopolist persuasion which views monopolists as exploitative producers who should be limited by law. Second, that of modern antitrust aficionados who focus on economic efficiency and view monopoly as inherently wasteful, and monopolists as greedy rent-seekers who should be limited by law. The first focuses on fairness issues and implicitly assume that consumers deserve the wealth created by competition (even when they did nothing to contribute to it). The second focuses on efficiency and reaches a similar result, albeit for society's gain rather than that of the consumer. Both view monopolists as having no relevant rights or claims when assessing appropriate antitrust rules, at most being able to claim an instrumental role as fostering economic growth during their race for monopoly or 'creative destruction'.

All of the above might make sense if we were discussing only large exploitative firms engaged in pushing around poor unorganized consumers. This is far from the case in modern a-contextual antitrust. Those versed in modern efficiency analysis might contend that I exaggerate the moral content of antitrust, that these laws deal with economics and efficient social rules rather than sentiment. But these ignore the elephant in the room: that antitrust is often associated with criminality, and that its enforcement enjoys a huge consensus as to its appropriateness and moral value. Those violating it are not seen merely as harming economic efficiency, but violating moral principles and stealing something that does not belong to them. The term 'wealth transfer', so basic to antitrust analysis, assumes that this wealth *belongs* to consumers and is extracted by monopolists (in the broad sense of the term). This claim is so obvious and widely accepted that state intervention returning such 'property' to its rightful owners seems justified with almost no compunction. Monopoly *is* viewed as inherently unfair, if not outright evil. The source of this view, as detailed in chapter one, is the historical use of the term and the laws regulating it: royal grants of monopoly and powerful robber barons misusing power bestowed on them by political elites, always at the expense of 'the little guy' who could never sufficiently protect himself.

This chapter aims at highlighting the opposite: those instances where antitrust is used not to protect the weak from the strong, but posits the strong state with its legal monopoly on the use of force against the weaker monopolists. Obviously, the most well known cases of antitrust intervention are reminiscent of the paradigmatic powerful monopolist. One needs only think of Standard Oil, AT&T, IBM, Microsoft and the like to understand the need for a powerful state enforcing the rules of competition when faced with large firms whose economic power overshadows that of the state. Yet these are extreme cases, a small minority of antitrust. The current framework prevalent in competition regimes worldwide applies rules based on the 'powerful monopolist paradigm' to *all* markets, no matter how large or small, and no matter how important to consumers or other social interests. This is what I refer to as '*a-contextual antitrust*', tackled below. The economic paradigm dominating competition policy worldwide is that all markets can be identically assessed using similar microeconomic models, leading small manufacturers to be subject to the same rules as huge conglomerate firms. The result is that context matters very little in modern antitrust jurisprudence. In order to promote the idea that context *should* matter, and set up the need for a case-specific balancing test (to be developed in the following chapters), I shall first focus on non-paradigmatic monopolists and the case they might make.

We begin with the story of one individual, call him Tom, who starts a business in order to realize personal and financial goals, such as the manufacture of iron girders with various construction uses. Over the years, Tom expands production to meet the growing needs in his area, raising funds both internally and via financial markets. Obviously, as the company grows, more and more markets must be sought to make use of expanded production and make up for seasonal slumps in local markets. Tom is successful, partly through luck, but mostly because of foresight in planning and careful risk-taking. As more funds become available, he invests wisely and runs a profitable business for himself and his investors. The industries relying on his products (by now including steel and other alloys) thrive, and their mutual dependence allows all to flourish. When the local construction company (his main customer) goes under, Tom buys it—saving both the industry and his supply of orders. When out-of-state companies seek business cooperation, he expands by shipping his products and slowly increasing dominance in neighbouring regions. By this point Tom controls 70 per cent of total steel and iron production in the relevant geographic market, and his prices, though often undercut, are the law of the land. His size and capabilities allow him to promise supply even in times of input slumps, and he manages to weather every storm cast his way.

At what time did Tom transform from a successful and daring entrepreneur into a money-guzzling monopolist? He didn't. Although no business can be run and maintained without externalities harmful to others in some way, no maliciousness should be assumed because of size alone. Tom, and his shareholders (creditors and workers), deserve success and progress no less than any other. If the state is to intervene and limit his business practices (by, for instance, offering rebates for repeat business and bundling steel with transport), or limit his growth (by acquisition of other companies), strong reasons are needed to justify that decision. Even if consumers, or society at large, would benefit from limitations imposed on Tom's business, his claims deserve standing and his interests are not to be ignored. In short, Tom would argue that his property rights entail the right to profit, and the state should not limit his contractual abilities without balancing the harm caused by him to others, with the harm caused to him by state intervention. Tom would argue for a balancing test, claiming that limiting his business endeavours is akin to a governmental taking requiring compensation and clear justification.

Now, a nice story must be transformed into a solid argument.

I. WHY THE *VERIZON* CASE IS UNHELPFUL: BASELINES IN ANTITRUST

Some might argue that my characterization of common disdain for monopolists is unfair, citing *Verizon v Trinko* as a prominent case where the US Supreme Court pronounced monopoly profit to be not only lawful, but actually beneficial:

> The mere possession of monopoly power, and the concomitant charging of monopoly prices, is not only not unlawful; it is an important element of the free-market system. The opportunity to charge monopoly prices—at least for a short period—is what attracts 'business acumen' in the first place; it induces risk taking that produces innovation and economic growth. To safeguard the incentive to innovate, the possession of monopoly power will not be found unlawful unless it is accompanied by an element of anticompetitive conduct.[1]

Careful reading of the text, though, drives home the point made above, namely that monopoly profit is not protected due to the monopolists' *right* to enjoy the fruits of their labours, but due to *society's* interest in achieving innovation and economic growth. Monopolists are thus allowed to profit in order that society gains, and not for their own sake. This is in accord with the efficiency justification for antitrust, assessed in chapter two above, and limited in this respect as well. While consumers are commonly assumed to *deserve* the fruits of their labours, *as well as the fruits of societal economic growth*, monopolists are viewed as merely instrumental: means to an end rather than ends in themselves. Monopolists—and producers more generally—are protected only insofar as they show that their actions create no competitive harm, or that a sufficiently high pass-through rate exists, so that consumers benefit from their actions. In this respect, efficiency analysis is actually fairer than standard fairness analysis, as the former affords monopolists 'a place at the table' within the social maximization imperative, while

[1] *Verizon Communications Inc v Law Offices of Curtis V Trinko LLP*, 3540 US 398, 407 (2004).

the latter considers consumers alone (with occasional references to competitors and other groups assessed in the previous chapter).

The *rights* of monopolists, as opposed to the benefit derived from their existence, are almost never discussed. Were competition policy truly interested in monopolists' rights, limitation of their business conduct would be limited to cases where this is demonstrably necessary to avert greater evils. When government determines that it is necessary to make public use of private property, such takings are accompanied by compensation and by serious deliberation regarding the necessity of such intervention.[2] Thus, determining that competition is necessary for societal growth, and that monopoly inhibits this worthy goal, is insufficient to justify competition policy as currently practiced. The fact that no one seriously considers compensation to monopolists shows that on no level is monopoly profit considered their property. Not only is their interest in such profit insufficient to thwart intervention, but the monopoly profit motive is considered problematic in itself, if not downright evil. The question posed below is who these monopolists are and what justifies treating them differently from others whose property is protected by the state. Tom, our entrepreneur above, is thus raising the issue of his own rights, the manner in which he might be considered deserving of the profit created by him, beyond his contribution to society.

One might ask why contemporary antitrust scholarship has so little to say on the subject of monopolists' rights. One possible answer referred to above is the path by which antitrust developed, dealing with royal grants and powerful conglomerates. Another might relate to the prominence of economic analysis within competition scholarship. Economic analysis is oblivious to rights and intuitive differences between large and small firms or producers and consumers. Discussion of fairness within antitrust was thus focused on those cases where economic efficiency was insufficient to justify intervention. Fairness was usually referred to only by those seeking to induce intervention on behalf of consumers where economists were ambivalent as to social benefit.

As is well known throughout the antitrust community, the Chicago School proponents of limiting traditional antitrust intervention carried much weight both within the court system and within public discourse. As with most social movements a pendulum effect can be discerned whereby a wind of change sweeping through the discipline is met by a 'boomerang effect', initiated by those whose position (intellectual or otherwise) is threatened. First, 'left-side' arguments were made that economic analysis of antitrust loses sight of the human issues affected, sacrificing fairness in the name of efficiency.[3] Then, those versed in economics

[2] Indeed, the argument calling for compensation has been applied to situations where the governmental taking is indirect, such as when a regulated firm is subjected to rate-decreases, new limitations are imposed, or increased competitive pressure is created by governmental regulation set to induce entry and limit the incumbent's competitive response. See JG Sidak and DF Spulber, *Deregulatory Takings and the Regulatory Contract* (Cambridge: Cambridge University Press, 1998).

[3] The term stems from Hughes; EJ Hughes, 'The Left Side of Antitrust: What Fairness means and Why it Matters' (1994) 77 *Marquette Law Review* 265. See generally, ch 3, nn 2–3 and accompanying text.

and able to use more complex models to show that equating efficiency with non-intervention is overly simplistic, generated 'Post-Chicago' scholarship. And then, arguments between 'schools' were assimilated into more general knowledge that none can afford to ignore, so that antitrust scholarship as a whole became more inclusive and less prone to ideologically induced automatic responses. When all modes of analysis are sufficiently grounded so that none can be ignored, the different perspectives are taken into account regardless of who conducts the analysis, and the schools of thought mesh into a less decisive, but more mature, debate.[4]

Or so one would hope.

It is illuminating to note the arguments made on behalf of monopolists' rights in early Sherman Act litigation. Early American antitrust jurisprudence dealt with constitutional claims of property rights made on behalf of those convicted of antitrust offences. The claim then raised was relatively straightforward: that the Sherman Act (as well as state antitrust laws) limited their use of property, effectively an unconstitutional taking. Admittedly, there were judges who found the Sherman Act undesirable, and opted for its repeal. Justice Holmes, for example, is famous for his statement that the Sherman Act is 'nothing more than a noxious humbug'.[5] Still, support for the unconstitutionality contention was limited. Holmes, for example, is famous for his dissent in the *Northern Securities* case which extended the Sherman Act's reach to encompass mergers, though there he focused on common and statutory law rather than on constitutional interpretation.[6] While the Act proscribes contracts 'restraining trade', it says nothing directly about competition. Thus, Holmes construed the Act as focusing on freedom of

[4] An example of such inclusiveness, going beyond 'for' or 'against' arguments, can be found in R Pitofsky (ed), *How the Chicago School Overshot the Mark: The Effect of Conservative Economic Analysis on US Antitrust* (Oxford: Oxford University Press, 2008). There, a commendable effort can be discerned to include economists and lawyers, practitioners and scholars, those averse to the ideology inherent in 'Chicago' discourse and those wary of 'fighting fire with fire'—an attempt to both answer Chicago and make use of its revelations. Daniel Crane reviews the contributions, setting a broader historical background against which to assess the school's rise to prominence and the different claims made on both sides; see DA Crane, 'Chicago, Post-Chicago, and Neo-Chicago' (2009) 76 *University of Chicago Law Review* 1911. It is especially interesting to compare this current historical assessment with the work of Eleanor Fox, a prominent scholar on the 'Beware Chicago' side. See, eg, EM Fox and LA Sullivan, 'Antitrust—Retrospective and Prospective: Where are we Coming From? Where are we Going?' (1987) 62 *New York University Law Review* 936. For a different perspective, see JD Wright, explaining the Roberts Court acceptance and implementation of 'Chicago-style' antitrust in 'The Roberts Court and the Chicago School of Antitrust: The 2006 Term and Beyond' (2007) 3 *Competition Policy International* 24; as well as commenting on Pitofsky's book, in 'Overshot the Mark? A Simple Explanation of the Chicago School's Influence on Antitrust' (2009) 5 *Competition Policy International* 179, where he rejects the claim that 'post-Chicago' alternatives offer a better theory (or a coherent one, for that matter) that should guide antitrust doctrine.

[5] See *Letter from Oliver Wendell Holmes, Jr to Lewis Einstein* (28 October 1912) reprinted in RA Posner (ed), *The Essential Holmes* (Chicago: University of Chicago Press, 1992) 141. See also AS Neely, 'A Humbug Based on Economic Ignorance and Ignorance—Antitrust in the Eyes of Justice Holmes' (1993) *Utah Law Review* 1.

[6] *Northern Securities Co v United States*, 193 US 197 (1904). See also G Bittlingmayer, 'Did Antitrust Policy Cause the Great Merger Wave?' (1985) 28 *Journal of Law and Economics* 77, ch 2, n 40 and accompanying text.

trade *of the parties to the trade*, rather than any benefit that society as a third party to the contract might receive. This was in line with Holmes' jurisprudence in general, favouring the consistency of common law interpretation and the gradual evolution of society's standards over statutory provisions owing more to populist trends than coherent policy.[7] Thus, interfering with the right to trade and the right to property was construed as well within the power of Congress, but it was 'trader freedom', rather than competition or societal concerns, that was to benefit from such intervention. While early American antitrust jurisprudence focuses on such 'industrial freedom',[8] making that argument today would seem very much out of place.[9] What one must remember, though, is that at the time American jurisprudence was struggling with precisely such contentions, mirrored in the literal reading of the Act and its per se implementation. The issue of infringement upon the right to property found zealous adherents in Lochner era courts, but suffered from the overreaching interpretations prevalent at the time. It seems that those arguing for monopolists' property rights were perceived as anti-antitrust altogether, thus lost legitimacy and effect as consensus materialized regarding the need for state-sanctioned competition policy.

Rudolph Peritz characterized this as the ultimate clash between the turn-of-the-century property rhetoric favoured by the court, and the focus on competition that developed later on.[10] It is due to the strict interpretation advanced by those who strove for a decisive victory of one over the other, that antitrust doctrine leaned on 'the winner' of these formulations—the defence of competition. Once competition gained prominence in judicial and scholarly writing, arguments for protection of monopolists were understandably less compelling, especially within the American constitutional framework where the limitations on protecting private property and freedom of contract might lead to calls for outright annulment of the antitrust laws.[11]

[7] See SW Waller, 'The Antitrust Philosophy of Justice Holmes' (1994) 18 *Southern Illinois Law Journal* 283.

[8] See RJ Peritz, *Competition Policy in America: History, Rhetoric, Law*, rev edn (New York: Oxford University Press, 1996) 15, characterizing John Sherman as focusing on this concern, rather than the cheap products consumers might enjoy as a side benefit of his proposed Bill.

[9] See JW Burns, 'The New Role of Coercion in Antitrust' (1991) 60 *Fordham Law Review* 379, describing the previously central role of 'trader freedom' in antitrust jurisprudence, and its subsequent rejection. On the other hand, see AJ Meese, 'Economic Theory, Trader Freedom, and Consumer Welfare: State Oil Co v Khan and the Continuing Incoherence of Antitrust Doctrine' (1999) 84 *Cornell Law Review* 763, arguing that the rejection of trader freedom as an independent goal of antitrust is unwarranted, though realizing that contemporary judicial opinion is not expected to change: 'Although it appears that the Court will have to determine explicitly whether trader freedom merits normative significance under the antitrust laws, history suggests that it will not do so any time soon', ibid, 786.

[10] RJ Peritz, 'The "Rule of Reason" in Antitrust Law: Property Logic in Restraint of Competition' (1989) 40 *Hastings Law Journal* 285; 'A Counter-History of Antitrust Law' (1990) *Duke Law Journal* 263.

[11] As some did. See G Hull (ed), *The Abolition of Antitrust* (New Brunswick, NJ: Transaction Publishers, 2005); Dominick Armentano is a prominent contributor to this line of thought, see D Armentano, 'Time To Repeal Antitrust Regulation?' (1990) 35 *Antitrust Bulletin*, as well as *Antitrust: The Case for Repeal*, 2nd edn (Auburn, AL: Ludwig von Mises Institute, 1999). More recently,

Here, we need not go so far. The purpose of this chapter is not to claim that monopolists' rights justify allowing any and all monopolistic practices to go unhindered, but that fear of such an extreme result should not inhibit us from examining the whole picture. What is sought is a complete analysis of the justifications of antitrust, requiring assessment of the interests and rights of *all those involved*, perpetrators and victims alike, as well as the interests of society at large. Conceptions that demand ignoring one party to the dispute in order to protect the other seem foreign to philosophical debate in general and modern jurisprudence in particular. I shall therefore carry on with the analysis of affected interests and rights of monopolists, all in order to adequately include them and their counterparts within a general balancing test later on.[12]

II. WHO ARE THE MONOPOLISTS?

As stated at the outset, I use the term 'monopolists' in the very broadest sense to include all those whose conduct might be limited by antitrust law. This includes those with market power who are forbidden from bundling their products, those vying for market power limited in the business strategies they might employ and those battling with economic downturn or increased competition who are trying to save their (monopolistic) business. It also includes businesses hoping to merge in order to cut costs or increase market penetration, as well as competitors wishing to cooperate in order to combat increasing labour costs or prevent a downwards spiral in service quality (for example, due to consumers' focus on price). Markets large and small are affected, for luxury items as well as basic goods, new and innovative ideas along with staple items and those slowly becoming extinct. While public enforcement may target the larger and problematic cases, private litigation applies to all. Since competitors as well as consumers may bring suit, the

Richard McKenzie argued against antitrust intervention due to its chilling effect on innovation. See RB McKenzie, 'In Defense of Monopoly' (Winter 2009–10) 32 *Regulation* 16, as well as RB McKenzie and DR Lee, *In Defense of Monopoly: How Market Power Fosters Creative Production* (Ann Arbor, MI: University of Michigan Press, 2008). Austrian economics is a bedrock for those arguing along these lines; see, eg, W Block, 'Total Repeal of Antitrust Legislation: A Critique of Bork, Brozen, and Posner' (1994) 8 *Review of Austrian Economics* 35 and citations therein.

[12] By juxtaposing the rights of monopolists with those of their victims, I consciously call for a move away from what has been described by Daniel Crane as a move towards technocracy in antitrust. This tendency focuses on professional implementation of what are (mistakenly, in my view) objective standards, and relies explicitly on a lack of necessary balancing between the interests of affected parties. See DA Crane, 'Technocracy and Antitrust' (2008) 86 *Texas Law Review* 1159. For a discussion of the interplay between economic and non-economic influences, and how economic expertise is relevant in the interpretation of supposedly non-economic issues as well, see JE Lopatka and WH Page, 'Economic Authority and the Limits of Expertise in Antitrust Cases' (2005) 90 *Cornell Law Review* 617, as well as H First and SW Waller, 'Antitrust's Democracy Deficit' (2013) 81 *Fordham Law Review* 2543, 2546, who argue that this move towards technocracy 'puts too much control in the hands of technical experts, moving antitrust enforcement too far away from its democratic roots'.

rules of competition govern even when specific circumstances make their application to the case at hand doubtful from a public interest perspective.[13] When speaking of monopolists, we implicitly include people like Tom, our entrepreneur from the example above, as well as the paradigmatic Standard Oil and firms of its kind, though normative discussion implicitly centres on the latter, to the detriment of the former.

Each of the monopolists included in our broad definition may bring a similar claim: that the business they operate is their own, that the profits accrued are theirs and that they should be free to sell their wares as they please. Their claims would be based on two prongs, long accepted as basic rights in our society yet denied to monopolists: the right to property and freedom of contract. Both are severely constrained by the rules of antitrust, in many cases perhaps rightly so. It is exactly the justification of these limitations that we explore here, with the main question being whether current antitrust rules are correct in denying standing to monopolists' rights. The claim raised is not that monopolists should be free to exploit at their discretion and force consumers into unwanted deals, but that *in some cases* the right claimed by the monopolist is important enough to constrain the way in which the general antitrust rule applies. The claim is simply that monopolists' rights are relevant, should be part of the debate and that a balancing test comparing both sides should be applied in a contextual manner.

In order to clarify and focus the issue, I remove from consideration basic goods and cases where no real choice remains if the monopolist is unconstrained. While paradigmatic of antitrust and the source of public sentiment, these are the extreme (and rare) cases and should not taint discussion of the rest. In the following sections I outline two basic rights monopolists might argue for: the right to property, and freedom of contract. The point is not to delineate them completely, but explain through them the need for a balancing test that would take them into account on a basis similar to that afforded consumers in current competition policy. The balancing itself, and the types of contextual analysis employed therein, will be the subject of the next chapter.

III. MONOPOLY PROFIT AS A PROPERTY RIGHT, OR COMPETITION AS CREATING PROPERTY?

Arguing for monopoly profit and conduct as justified by conceptions of property and freedom of contract is counterintuitive and perhaps even heretical, yet this is precisely my aim here. The right to property is usually accepted as including the

[13] As discussed in ch 3, private enforcement in the presence of per se rules leads to a powerful limitation on practices deemed anticompetitive, even when the specific circumstances of the case make such a characterization dubious at best. Given the strong public sentiment regarding competition as good, and antitrust offenders as bad, the effects of an antirust suit are magnified and many a business fears litigation even where eventual dismissal of the claim might be expected.

power of disposition, the owner's choice as to how to use his property. It follows that a simple yet powerful statement can be made: just as any owner of property may choose whether to utilize it in production or let it lie unattended, so the monopolist may choose not to maximize production at his whim. The harm done to society by reduced output due to monopoly pricing, as well as the harm to consumers from resulting price-hikes, are then justifiably within the domain of the owner's discretion.

Since the reduction of output (and thus efficiency) is the most often cited social harm from monopoly, it is worth dwelling on its implications. Essentially, antitrust (at least with its current focus on efficiency) is aimed mostly at preventing the output reduction and price increase associated with monopoly. Granted, in the US (as opposed to the EU) monopoly pricing is not considered an offence *in itself*, but even there competition policy is in place to prevent similar results. Essentially, merger control is used to prevent market power, commonly and openly citing monopoly pricing as the evil forestalled by public enforcement. Monopoly pricing is seen as a problem to be managed and prevented, not a right to be respected. European competition law goes further than its American counterpart, condemning monopoly over-charges as 'abuse of dominant position'.[14] In both, the state constrains monopoly power by forcing current and potential holders of monopoly power to employ their resources only in directions that would benefit society, akin to public management of personal property.

Any conception according to which the state limits the use of private property in order to increase social wealth (or protect consumers) must compensate the original owners, or at least spell out the limitations according to which the system operates. The fact that competition law is enforced without such consideration makes it clear that the governing legal paradigm *does not* consider monopoly as a legitimate source of profit. The implicit assumption governing competition law is thus that competition is not only a framework in which private property is employed for personal gain, but the *source* of property itself, or at least the external constraint operating upon it. In other words, *competition is taken to be a precondition for the existence of property.*

Within the property law scholarship, Hanoch Dagan has argued along similar lines, although without specific application to antitrust.[15] According to his conception, property is meaningless as a basic construct, and should be viewed as an amalgam consisting of interests protected by the state. Private property is then a

[14] For comparisons among the two along these lines, see EM Fox, 'Monopolization and Dominance in the United States and the European Community: Efficiency Opportunity and Fairness' (1986) 61 *Notre Dame Law Review* 981; EM Fox, 'Monopolization, Abuse of Dominance, and the Indeterminacy of Economics: The US/EU Divide' (2006) *Utah Law Review* 725.

[15] H Dagan, *Property: Values and Institutions* (Oxford: Oxford University Press 2011); 'The Craft of Property' (2003) 91 *California Law Review* 1517. See also GS Alexander, *Commodity and Propriety: Competing Visions of Property in American Legal Thought: 1776-1970* (Chicago, IL: University of Chicago Press, 1997) for a presentation of traditional conceptions of property as pointing to a similar result.

result of the underlying interests deserving protection, and where these do not apply, it is not a *limitation* of property but the lack of such a right altogether. This would help explain current competition policy. If the right to property is in itself justified by the importance of creating competition, monopolists are not harmed nor their property taken, but merely limited to the natural contours of their right. In other words, their property is a social construct rather than a natural right, and the social construct includes within it an implicit 'do not monopolize' caveat. One might take this another step towards the implicit agreement argument outlined above, and hold monopolists as agreeing that their property is limited in this way. One might alternatively sidestep the issue of agreement altogether and hold property in itself to justify only certain types of claims by owners, with freedom to monopolize distinctly excluded.

While appealing theoretically, it is important to delineate the underlying assumptions of such an argument. First, it assumes that property is bestowed by society, thus may be granted or limited at society's whim. Protection of property is then no longer an independent right, but one which must be earned by following certain minimal guidelines. Property cedes its status as individual right, becoming instead a state-created normative order serving collective concerns. Second, it assumes that one of the mandated guidelines is utilizing the capability of full production, or at least refraining from strategic under-production aimed at extracting monopoly profit (or refraining from actions leading to a position where this could be carried out—acquisition of monopoly).

While the second assumption follows an intuitive conception of refraining from harm to others, this assumes those 'others' have a right deserving of protection. Such rights were assessed in the previous chapter, and will be brought to bear on the monopolists through the balancing test in the next chapter. The first assumption, though, is much more difficult to swallow. True, there are conceptions of property (and even of natural endowments) that negate any individual ownership per se. These conceptions usually deem such endowments as granted to the individual through chance, thus society is justified in 'taking them back', or at least taxing them, so that others would benefit.[16]

Some property scholars argue that property should not be thought of as 'belonging' to its owner, but a concept delineating rights *and obligations*, a concept through which society defines relations (commercial and otherwise) between its

[16] David Gauthier, for example, argued that morality should be founded on a hypothetical agreement similar to the one proposed by Rawls (and examined in the previous chapter). See D Gauthier, *Morals by Agreement* (Oxford: Clarendon Press, 1986). Gauthier's experiment, though, did not assume a 'veil of ignorance', but allowed each individual to assess their own true state of affairs. While endowments remained intrinsic to the individual ('belonging' to them), the rents they allowed him to extract were not. Thus, taxing natural capabilities would be justified to the extent that the individual's motivations were not altered. For a critique of this conception based on the reduction of 'ownership', see E Mack, 'Gauthier on Rights and Economic Rent' in EF Paul, FD Miller and J Paul (eds), *Economic Rights* (Cambridge: Cambridge University Press, 1992). See also the 'forced labour' argument by Nozick and Richard Arneson's response in ch 3, n 29. Ch 6 returns to this issue from a different perspective.

members.[17] Under this conception, ownership of property does not necessarily imply its free disposition, but inherently entails limitations for the benefit of society, due to considerations which may be aggregate or distributional in nature.[18]

Such a conception deviates quite extremely from the common ground assumed by most antitrust scholars (not to mention legislators). If we were to go this far, we would end up arguing not only for a different conception of antitrust, but for a society much different from the one we currently live in. Even if we accept a richer conception of property which stems from multiple criteria with differing levels of protection and rights of disposition, the balancing argued for here is even more necessary. What are we left with? Property rights of monopolists to the assets currently in their possession are clear. If we are to force a monopolist to change a decision as to utilization of that property, we need to point to harm caused to another, or a positive right some other person has which should limit the monopolist's discretion. In other words, there is balancing to be done, and it will be—in the next chapter.

IV. FREEDOM OF CONTRACT

Again, we need not repeat discussion of this concept's basic attributes as set out in the previous chapter. Two subsets of claims can be made based on the right to freedom of contract: the freedom *to* contract, and the freedom *from* contract. The first refers to a person's discretion as to disposition of his property, including what price to demand for relinquishing that hold. The second refers to the basic decision whether to enter into contract or refrain from trade altogether. Current antitrust doctrine infringes upon both.

If the owner of property may decide at what terms to sell that property, it follows that a monopolist may decide to sell his merchandise at any price he chooses. A businessman's interest in maximizing profit leads to seizing any opportunity to sell at a price exceeding costs of production. For a monopolist to seek monopoly profit, is in itself (in the US at least) no antitrust offence. Long-term planning to achieve this result, though, is commonly considered 'monopolization' or 'abuse of dominant position'—barred by competition policy across the world. If a firm chooses to sell below cost due to long-term goals (removing competition), it will be charged with predation. If two firms seek mutual benefit through merger, they must attain governmental approval. When several manufacturers of similar products get together to work out a mutually benefiting contract as to future business practices, such contracts are not only unenforceable, but often subject to criminal

[17] See J Singer, 'Property and Social Relations: From Title to Entitlement' in C Geisler and G Daneker (eds), *Property and Values: Alternatives to Public and Private Ownership* (Washington DC: Island Press, 2000) 3–19.

[18] See J Singer, 'No Right to Exclude: Public Accommodations and Private Property' (1995) 90 *Northwestern Law Review* 1283.

charges. This is true even when cooperation is necessary to combat devolving industry standards, difficulties in enforcing intellectual property rights, or ruinous competition that pushes price to cost—but at the expense of quality.[19]

Innovative business practices, when practised by those holding market power, may also be constrained by competition law due to their effect on others. In some situations, technological innovation may be curtailed as well, due to monopolists fearing state intervention in what could be perceived as raising their rivals' costs, engaging in predatory innovation, or excessively raising switching costs or entry barriers. In previous chapters, innovation played a key role in *justifying the use* of antitrust law, protecting innovators from monopolistic constraints and society from the reduced incentives to innovate that monopolists might have. Here, I go further. Surely, an unhindered monopolist may choose to chase his innovative competitors out of the market, but it is also possible that a firm holding a dominant market position, limited by antitrust law, will refrain from innovations enlarging its market share due to its fear of legal repercussions.[20] While most support the view that innovation has positive externalities and therefore should be encouraged, monopolists may find themselves in a double bind: legal norms aimed at protecting others from the monopolist's superior economic power sometimes inhibit the same monopolist from socially beneficial innovation.[21]

A monopolist taking care not to commit antitrust offences may pre-emptively limit itself even when an enforcement agency would have considered the action harmless, resulting both in societal loss and in individual harm. This is due to the general and ambiguous nature of most of the antitrust laws, the downside of broad definitions that facilitate context-specific enforcement.[22] The gist of the matter is that monopolists aiming at developing their business through devising new methods of contracting with consumers or collaborators should be wary of antitrust intervention and are thus limited in disposition of their property through contractual means. The freedom to contract is thus seriously undermined.

The freedom *from* contract suffers similar infringement. A monopolist wishing to avoid dealing with his competitors, might be subject to an 'essential facilities'

[19] See, eg, CS Hemphill and J Suk, 'The Fashion Originators' Guild of America: Self-Help at the Edge of IP and Antitrust' (22 March 2013): ssrn.com/abstract=2237799.

[20] This is true when enforcement agencies see market share as a criterion for their intervention, or when they are perceived as such, regardless of the perception's accuracy. Similarly, a firm under antitrust scrutiny will fear that successful product or marketing innovation will be labelled 'monopolization'—with all accompanying legal repercussions. Of course, there are also the direct claims of 'predatory innovation', see ch 2, n 15 and accompanying text.

[21] See WJ Baer and DA Balto, 'The Politics of Federal Antitrust Enforcement' (1999) 23 *Harvard Journal of Law & Public Policy* 111, fn 45.

[22] Already in 1936 the US Supreme Court expressed this view: 'we have said that the Sherman Anti-Trust Act, as a charter of freedom, has a generality and adaptability comparable to that found to be desirable in constitutional provisions. It does not go into detailed definitions'; *Sugar Institute v US*, 297 US 553 (1936). See also, MB Garland, 'Antitrust and State Action: Economic Efficiency and the Political Process' (1987) 96 *Yale Law Journal* 486, fn 157; NO Fitts, 'Note: A Critique of Noncommercial Justifications for Sherman Act Violations' (1999) 99 *Columbia Law Review* 478, fn 118.

ruling or one of exclusionary conduct, while a group of traders seeking to enjoin another from participating in their events, might face a 'group boycott' suit. Monopolists have no general right to refuse contractual relations they don't want, just as they are subject to a host of limitations on their business conduct once their market power is recognized. With monopoly status come obligations and limitations due to potential effects on competitors and consumers. The monopolist may thus be forced into commercial relations because this benefits the other party or society at large.

The result is clear and unambiguous: antitrust intervention limits monopolists' freedom of contract. While such infringement may well be subsequently justified in order to protect others, harm to contractual freedom is clear. In order to justify such intervention, the state should compare costs and benefits, as well as the distribution thereof between those paying the costs and those enjoying the benefits. This is precisely where the proposed balancing test comes in.

V. THE ROLE OF FIRMS

The paradigmatic view of weak consumers versus strong monopolists conjures a mental picture of individuals (consumers) versus powerful firms. While most private antitrust litigation is brought on behalf of plaintiff firms as well, the issue of whether firms enjoy similar rights to individuals needs to be addressed. Three strategies are available: the first compares pro-consumer arguments with those made here on behalf of monopolists. Since antitrust protects consumers broadly, including firms as buyers and especially given the current bar on indirect purchaser suits, symmetric arguments can be posed on behalf of monopolistic firms. The first strategy thus forgoes debate regarding firms' rights, relying instead on symmetry: 'if consuming firms have standing in the rights debate, so should producing firms'. The second approach views firms on both sides as the 'long arm' of classes of individuals with interests in the firms' success, thus viewing the firms not as bearers of rights on their own but instrumental in the protection of individuals. The third argues directly for corporations as bearers of rights, to be granted equal (or at least equivalent) protection to that afforded the affected individuals in our debate. The first and the third approaches both argue for rights being afforded to firms. The difference being that the first is an equivalence claim ('if consuming firms have rights, so do producing firms'), while the third is a substantive claim ('firms do deserve rights'). Thus accepting either the first or the third claims leads to antitrust being required to respect firms' rights (including monopolistic ones), while accepting the second claim avoids the corporate rights debate and deals directly with affected individuals on either side. If even one of the claims has merit, the rights outlined in this chapter deserve a place alongside consumers' rights, and a balancing test should be applied prior to approval of antitrust intervention.

A. The Parallel Definition of Consumers and Producers

In our discussion of consumers' rights above, we saw that the consumers of one product were often the producers of another. Antitrust protection is not limited to end users of a product, both for practical reasons (it may be very difficult sometimes to assess the influence on end users, as well as distinguish between them and producers buying the same product as an input) and as a general principle—that monopoly power should not be used to extort supra-competitive profits from any buyer whatsoever.[23] Also, competition law does not discriminate between consumers who are firms, and those who are individuals. The guiding premise is that all consumers of a product are to be afforded equal protection, with no weight given to their status or individual circumstances. If this is the case with consumers, identical consideration should be afforded producers, or in this case, monopolists.

Of course, a diametrically opposed argument could be made. If protection of rights is deserved by individuals only, and not firms, the same should apply to consumers as well. In such a case, we would need to find a format of antitrust law that could differentiate between different cases, both as to consumers and as to monopolists. In such a case, much of the current antitrust doctrine would need to be modified, as every claim of protection would demand proof of individuals affected by it. Such a framework might be extremely difficult to implement, though this is no reason to shy away from the effort, at least as a theoretical endeavour. I prefer to proceed along a different line, exploring the justifications for affording firms rights-based protection, and applying these across the board—to consumers and producers alike. The main point here is one of symmetry—that treating firms and individuals differently cannot in itself justify antitrust intervention or be used against it, as both sides to the debate are similarly affected.

B. Monopolistic Firms as Proxies for Individuals' Rights

Firms do not exist in and of themselves; they are created by individuals seeking to advance their own personal goals, and are allowed by a legal framework defining these goals as worthy. Corporations are not merely an efficient means of attaining material benefits for different classes of individuals, but are majors players in a variety of non-economic debates as well. The previous chapter highlighted the various categories of victims monopoly might have. This section assesses the converse, the different classes of individuals that have a material interest in the monopolistic firm's *success* and the effect antitrust intervention might have on them.

[23] This was discussed in the context of the indirect-purchaser rule. See ch 3, nn 4–15 and accompanying text.

i. Shareholders' Interests

The group whose financial welfare is perhaps most closely related to that of the firm is the collection of its shareholders. Being residual claimants to corporate assets, they have a material interest in the firm's success and stand to lose the most from its failure.[24] Monopolistic firms' shareholders are occasionally referred to in the antitrust debate, justifying an argument that wealth transfers are not 'all bad', since the producer surplus is distributed in profits to shareholders.[25] The fact that it is individuals (rather than firms) who benefit, makes it perhaps easier for some to regard wealth transfers as less problematic, an issue between different classes of individuals rather than one in which the state must intervene.

It is not enough, though, to compare individuals to individuals or firms to firms. If consumers are to be preferred (or shareholders for that matter), it should be based on a substantiated argument explicating their rights. A right to property, including disposition and profit, may be defended directly or through the use of an intermediary such as a corporation. If shareholders have a right to invest their resources in a business enterprise, it stands to reason that the same right to the profits they would enjoy should be afforded to them when they assemble and appoint managers to conduct their business for them.

If firms are seen as proxies for enhancing shareholder wealth, it is necessary to provide serious arguments for limiting the firms' conduct. Such arguments as were attempted in the previous chapter may be compared and balanced with the property rights shareholders enjoy in their (monopolistic) stock, and indirectly, in the firm's ability to freely manufacture and trade according to its own interests.

Of course, shareholders' property right is in the share itself, and not in the corporation's assets or commercial opportunities. Normal property rights entail a veto power over sale and use of the property. Affording such power to shareholders would debilitate the firm and contradict their stated (or implied) wish of collective management through agents. It is precisely the personal veto power that shareholders forgo through contractual agreement implied both in the corporation's bylaws and in the maxims of corporate law under which they interact.[26] Thus, a second-order property right may be discerned. Under this right, a shareholder forgoes her claims to direct control over the firm's assets, as a procedural

[24] See AR Pinto and DM Branson, *Understanding Corporate Law* (New York: Matthew Bender, 1999) 93. For focus on the harm caused to monopolistic firms' shareholders (along with their workers) by 'trust-busting', see D Dewey, 'Romance and Realism in Antitrust Policy' (1955) 63 *Journal of Political Economy* 93.

[25] See, eg, T Calvani, 'What is the Objective of Antitrust?' in T Calvani and J Siegfried (eds), *Economic Analysis and Antitrust Law*, 2nd edn (Boston: Little, Brown & Co, 1988) 8, fn 7; EO Correia, 'Antitrust and Liberalism' (1995) 40 *Antitrust Bulletin* 99, 136–37.

[26] This question rises often with regard to shareholders 'rights' to dividend allocation. There also, individuals might claim a right to profits made through the corporation, though such claims could pose a 'prisoner's dilemma' whereby all prefer to forgo such a claim, contingent on others doing the same. The common solution is to stress the contractual nature of corporate bylaws defining shareholders' rights to assets only pursuant to the corporation's internal decision to dissipate these through dividends.

safeguard against collective action problems. Forgoing the veto power, though, does not entail forgoing the right to enjoy maximal profit maximization. The property rights that shareholders may claim include any and all circumstances affecting the share's value, while the discretion as to the *method* of value maximization, is granted to corporate management.

Shareholders are materially affected by loss of potential corporate profits, and thus may claim individual harm justifying their protection. Any rule detrimental to corporate profit maximization, may not be instated without attention being given to the rights of those affected.

A counterclaim may be raised that shareholders are players in a game with predetermined rules, one of which is antitrust law. Their decision to invest in stock implies agreement to the game-rules of corporate conduct, including the game-rules of antitrust. Such a claim, however, is similar to the claim that producers as such have implied their agreement to the game-rules of competition. This claim was assessed at length and rejected above, and there is no need to repeat the analysis here.[27]

ii. Workers' Interests

Monopolistic firms employ workers as well. These workers have an immediate and substantial interest in the financial well-being of their employer, since they are invested heavily in its success. Workers invest their human capital and are usually less able to diversify their investment than those who invest monetarily.[28] This lack of diversification places workers at greater risk in the case of firm-specific business failures.[29] Antitrust enforcement is undoubtedly firm-specific,[30] and thus should worry workers to a great degree.[31]

[27] See ch 3, section I.B.iv.

[28] The term 'human capital' refers to the investment of their time, expertise, loss of alternative sources of income and specialization in the firm's business. Usually, the longer an employee remains with one firm, the more specialized he becomes in that firm's operations, and the less able he is to relocate to other firms in case of employment termination. This is one of the justifications for employee representation on the board of directors. Often workers have capital invested as well. When a firm offers workers benefits including stock or options in the firm, they come to have a direct financial investment that may be adversely affected by antitrust regulation of the firm.

[29] See, MA O'Connor, 'The Human Capital Era: Reconceptualizing Corporate Law to Facilitate Labor-Management Cooperation' (1993) 78 *Cornell Law Review* 899, 903. Diversification as a means of risk reduction is much easier to attain in an investment portfolio. The workers are most often employed by one firm only, and any harm coming to them through that firm cannot be mitigated through a benefit accruing from other employment. It is unnecessary here to distinguish between the different types of employees, such as between managers and other employees, since the present argument unifies them all, albeit to a different extent as to diversification and future employment prospects.

[30] Admittedly, enforcement sometimes targets several firms at the same time (eg, refusing to approve a merger, or breaking up a cartel), but specificity could then be argued as to those firms, as distinct from others. Beyond direct enforcement, there is the chilling effect on potentially regulated firms who limit their conduct (and profits) preventatively. Still, workers within such firms are singled out relative to workers in general, and have little opportunity for diversification.

[31] See Dewey (n 24). Of course, this is relevant to workers within the monopolistic firm alone. If antitrust enforcement is aggregately efficient, it will usually cause production to rise necessitating more working hands than were previously employed, thus beneficial for workers generally. In this

What harm may come to the workers of a monopolistic firm? At worst, antitrust enforcement will cause massive termination of jobs, either due to forgone profit which leads to 'downsizing', or due directly to a state-ordered divestiture. In less extreme cases, loss of profit for the firm will mean fewer benefits for the employees, either immediately or in the future (for example, less frequent, or smaller, rises in salary). While not every case of antitrust enforcement will lead to workers being harmed, their interests should clearly be examined as one of the relevant parameters in antitrust debate.[32] I mention harm caused to workers by antitrust rather than possible benefits, not as a result of prejudice, but of focus. Justifying antitrust by referring to its benefits was the focus of the previous chapter, while this one aims at the other side of the debate. Conclusions naturally will be justified only later on, after analysis of both sides and balancing have taken place.

Do workers have a *right* to be protected from antitrust intervention? Their interests may be clear, but any contractual rights they have place claims on their employer alone. These contractual rights protect many of their interests, but do not justify claims made on outside parties. It is likewise unclear what property justification they may raise that will produce an obligation on the state or any other party to refrain from actions harmful to the firm in which they are employed.

One claim that workers may raise, is that of worker protection as an independent value. According to this argument, a worker as such is entitled to state protection, as employment is a right in and of itself. Worker protection is well established as a principle of law, and antitrust may have to take it into account as well. Yet even if we were to accept the argument of protecting society's economically threatened classes, and were we to include worker protection as so justified, it seems antitrust law (or its abolishment) would hardly be the appropriate candidate for affording such protection. As seen in the previous chapter, distributive arguments demand more differentiation between affected groups, and precision of corrective measures, than antitrust law offers.[33]

It follows that while workers of monopolistic firms might be adversely affected by antitrust enforcement, their protection is merited by specific circumstances

section, however, we deal with the side of the monopolist alone, while workers 'from the other side' are dealt with as victims of monopoly, justifying intervention. For empirical support of the contention that antitrust enforcement entails a cost borne by workers, see WF Shughart and RD Tollison, 'The Employment Consequences of the Sherman and Clayton Acts' (1991) 147 *Journal of Institutional and Theoretical Economics* 38. It must be noted, though, that their study did not differentiate between workers of monopolistic firms and those employed by their victims.

[32] In fact, in some cases workers will *benefit* from state intervention. If, for example, the monopolistic firm operated inefficiently due to lack of competitive pressure, the effect of antitrust enforcement may lead to the firm increasing its efficiency and perhaps increasing worker compensation as an incentive. On the other hand, increasing efficiency on part of the firm is often *at the expense* of individual employees (being fired or pressured to produce more). The contention that monopolistic firms are less productively efficient came under attack, which was referred to above in the discussion of X-inefficiency.

[33] Similarly, distributive claims for protection of consumers, workers and small businesses are better addressed by other fields of law more able to focus on deserving cases, such as taxation, regulation and subsidization; see ch 3.

and appropriate of specific measures. Such workers' claims against antitrust cannot guide us in the general debate.

iii. Creditors' Interests

Creditors of the firm (whether directly as lenders of capital, or suppliers granting credit, etc) are investors of capital, similar to shareholders, only with different contractual agreements and statutory protection. The similarity is that if a firm faces antitrust enforcement, these investors may suffer through the firm's inability to repay its debts in full (and on time). In case of the monopolistic firm's suppliers, any enforcement limiting expansion by the monopolist may lead to reduced buying power and loss of business for the relevant suppliers. Of course, not all antitrust enforcement will lead to such difficulties that harm a firm's creditors and suppliers, but these *are* specific groups facing *potential* harm, and their interests merit consideration.

Do creditors have a right to back up their claim of interest? It seems not. Any rights they have gained impose obligations on the firm itself, through contractual agreement. The fact that outside powers influence the firm's ability to meet its obligations is true, but expanding protection to encompass all such instances is extreme to say the least. Competitive pressures may also bring firms to bankruptcy and injure creditors (and probably more often than antitrust measures will). Are we then to consider a successful competitor liable for another firm's demise? It is clear that there is no end to the argument that 'someone affected my debtor's liquidity'. If one were to take this argument as justifying antitrust, it could be used to justify regulation of all markets, forced employment and state-backed commercial insurance as well.

The fact of the matter is that creditors' rights are contractual in nature. The only relevant exception allowing bringing suit against a third party for contractual failure is that of tortuous interference.[34] As that requires a showing of intent to cause the breach of contract, it is hardly relevant here.

It may be said that creditors' rights have been the subject of favourable review in corporate law. Creditors are no longer considered 'outsiders' to the corporation, but one of the communities materially affected, and deserving of more than contractual rights alone. This holds as to claims creditors bring *against the corporation* and not to claims against third parties. Generally speaking, it is the corporation itself that must maximize wealth, debatably taking into consideration all communities (or 'stakeholders') affected by it.[35] While conceivably creditors may gain an even stronger foothold in corporate debate, so that infringements on the firm's

[34] See EA Farnsworth, *Contracts*, 3rd edn (New York: Aspen Law and Business, 1999) 763; RA Epstein, *Torts* (New York: Aspen Law & Business, 1999) 578–79.

[35] Generally taken to include shareholders, creditors, workers and arguably the general public or the community in which the firm operates. The division of benefits among these groups, and preference issues are far beyond the scope of our discussion here.

interests may grant them standing as well, I find it unnecessary to explore this issue further here. For every creditor of a monopolistic firm, we may find a creditor of a competing firm harmed by the former's actions. Introducing an argument that everyone indirectly harmed by an action may claim an infringement of rights is akin to allowing every member of society a say in almost every dispute. For rights to maintain their meaning, some line must be drawn separating relevant parties directly affected from those indirectly affected and excluded from the debate. Creditors by definition invested in a manner protected by contract at arm's length, thus separating their interests from those of the firm (as opposed to the shareholders). We shall respect the same separation in this discussion as well.

iv. Local Communities

The final group to be discussed in this context is that of the community in which the monopolist operates. Local communities are usually considered on the 'other side' of the equation, whose livelihood and character are injured by a monopoly taking over the market and foreclosing local production.[36] Here we take a different view, that of the local community in which the monopolist's production is based. What should be remembered is that monopolists are not necessarily huge impersonal corporations, but sometimes a local producer who has 'cornered' a local market. Even the huge corporation has plants producing its products, and these plants are located within communities depending on them for their livelihood. The 'community effect' is strengthened in cases where the firm is not only one workplace among many, but the central one in the area. In such cases the community as a whole may be harmed by antitrust enforcement.[37] Assuming an injury to local communities, do their interests in non-intervention rely on a right to be protected?

The discussion here mirrors that of the local communities who would benefit from antitrust intervention. Without expounding again the same arguments, our conclusion there was that the material interest did not rely on basic rights, and that even if such rights were justified, antitrust law would be the incorrect mechanism to address them. The same applies here, and thus local communities are excluded hereafter from our discussion.

C. Firms as Independent Bearers of Rights

Attaching rights to non-living legal entities is troublesome. On the one hand, rights are assumed to be a human attribute (or at least an attribute of living

[36] See ch 3, section III.

[37] Of course, the opposite is possible as well. It may be that the downfall of the monopolist will create an opportunity for local entrepreneurs to succeed, and for the community to escape an all too powerful hold that the monopolist had on local development. This is not the stage to juxtapose these considerations, but merely to raise the need to examine each side carefully.

creatures). On the other hand, modern society has delegated to corporations of every sort many of the duties and privileges formerly associated with individuals. When people turn to associations and corporations for their political expression, leisure activities and perhaps most obviously—making their livelihood, a simplistic distinction between humans and non-humans is not enough.

The theory of the corporate personality has long dealt with the diverse powers a corporation enjoys. That corporations may own property and enter into contractual obligations is uniformly accepted. But is corporate ownership akin to personal ownership? In other words, in a conflict of rights between a person and a corporation, are the two on equal standing?

Modern property law and corporate law answer these questions with an unequivocal 'yes'.[38] There is no serious suggestion of arguments to the contrary, that a corporation's claim should a priori make way for that of an individual, despite a recently emerging view that allowing corporations free reign has gone too far, and is detrimental to society.[39] Yet in every field of commercial law, we find corporations owning assets, entering into contracts, suing others and being sued themselves.

Some go as far as arguing for corporations as ultimately political organizations, more akin to states than to individual businesses.[40] Others have debated long and hard over attaching rights of the most personal nature—such as freedom of speech—to corporations.[41] While it is possible (and interesting) to argue this

[38] The US Supreme Court made this abundantly clear in *Citizen United v Federal Election Commission*, US 130 S Ct 876 (2010), see discussion in n 41. The issue itself, though, has developed over time and seen much controversy; see Note, 'Constitutional Rights of the Corporate Person' (1982) 91 *Yale Law Journal* 1641, 1641–51 and citations therein. While this view was not always the case, the late nineteenth century saw the US Supreme Court accept corporate constitutional protection of property and liberty (to conduct business) against unreasonable laws, on equal standing with natural persons. See ibid, fn 35.

[39] See, eg, J Bakan, *The Corporation: The Pathological Pursuit of Profit and Power* (US: Free Press, 2004) and K Greenfield, *The Failure of Corporate Law* (Chicago: University of Chicago Press, 2006). Even there the argument is not that corporations' rights as such are always inferior to those claimed by any individual, but that due to their distinct mechanisms of governance they should be regulated differently and held accountable more than they are today.

[40] See J Hill, 'Changes in the Role of the Shareholder' in R Grantham and C Rickett (eds), *Corporate Personality in the 20th Century* (Oxford: Hart Publishing, 1998) 185–89; E Latham, 'The Body Politic of the Corporation' in ES Mason (ed), *The Corporation in Modern Society* (Cambridge, MA: Harvard University Press, 1960).

[41] The issue is far from universally accepted. See DJH Greenwood, 'Essential Speech: Why Corporate Speech is not Free' (1998) 83 *Iowa Law Review* 995, arguing corporations are not independent actors, thus their speech is compelled and not subject first amendment protection; AJ Meese, 'Limitations on Corporate Speech: Protection for Shareholders or Abridgment of Expression?' (1993) 2 *William & Mary Bill of Rights Journal* 305, arguing for limitation of corporate speech in order to *protect* shareholders; D Shelledy, 'Autonomy, Debate, and Corporate Speech' (1991) 18 *Hastings Constitutional Law Quarterly* 541, showing corporate speech to be a public interest, though analyzed not as corporate autonomy, but reflecting interests of shareholders and the general public; SL Ross, 'Note: Corporate Speech on Political Issues: The First Amendment in Conflict with Democratic Ideals?' (1985) *University of Illinois Law Review* 445, explaining the difference between commercial and political speech and arguing for a compromise entailing limited political speech. See also M Dan-Cohen, 'Freedoms of Collective Speech: A Theory of Protected Communications by Organizations, Communities, and the State' (1991) 79

issue, we need not delve into it for the purposes of our current debate; our focus is on justifying antitrust law. The relevant arguments are related to economic rights, namely the right to property and freedom of contract. Rights of a more personal nature may give rise to different issues, but that is an issue for corporate law and discrete fields of social policy where specific applications merit more debate. Here, in order to justify antitrust law, we must address only firms' capability of arguing for the rights of property and contract, specifically the right to run a business unimpeded.

Within the framework relevant here, corporations act within their core rights. In civil cases, firms are legal persons capable of suing and being sued. In administrative law, firms argue for compensation when their property is seized, as well as for respect of their rights and constraining such takings within the same parameters with which individuals are protected. Firms may even be considered criminally liable in various cases and some argue about firms' morality, the question of their 'having a heart'.[42] For our purposes here, we need not look that far. With hearts or without, corporations undoubtedly have rights, and can justifiably complain if these are ignored.

D. Conclusion: Monopolistic Firms' Rights

As far as claiming rights to be considered in an equivalent manner to those of consumers, competitors and the like, monopolistic firms stand on steady ground. This result may be based on the prior acceptance of firms as consumers and competitors, thus justifying parallel treatment of monopolistic firms. It may be based on the firm as a procedurally convenient proxy for stating the claims and rights of

California Law Review 1229, arguing that institutional characteristics affecting corporations should be taken into account, with most mirroring similar traits of political organizations and states. In 2010, the Supreme Court decided *Citizens United v Federal Election Commission*, US 130 S Ct 876 (2010), ruling that corporations as such have a constitutional right to freedom of expression, allowing Congress some forms of regulating it, but not banning it altogether, or enacting policies with that effect. The decision whirred up a storm of responses, critiques and analyses too broad to assess here. See generally, F Abrams, 'Citizens United and its Critics' (2010) 120 *Yale Law Journal Online* 77; for an application of the ruling to other constitutional rights of corporations, see DAH Miller, 'Guns, Inc: Citizens United, McDonald, and the Future of Corporate Constitutional Rights' (2011) 86 *New York University Law Review* 887. David Yosifun goes further and argues that *Citizens United* implicitly revokes the shareholder primacy assumption common in corporate law; see 'The Public Choice Problem in Corporate Law: Corporate Social Responsibility after Citizens United' (2011) 89 *North Carolina Law Review* 1197. Susanna Kim Ripkin reviews the more extreme contentions arising from this case, including cries for revoking corporate personhood altogether, see 'Corporate First Amendment Rights after Citizens United: An Analysis of the Popular Movement to End the Constitutional Personhood of Corporations' (2011) 14 *University of Pennsylvania Journal of Business Law* 209.

[42] See LE Mitchell and TA Gabaldon, 'If I only had a Heart: Or, How can we Identify Corporate Morality?' (2001–02) 76 *Tulane Law Review* 1645; LE Mitchell, 'Cooperation and Constraint in the Modern Corporation: An Inquiry into the Causes of Corporate Immorality' (1994–95) 73 *Texas Law Review* 477.

shareholders affected by the firm's performance. It may be based on the argument that a firm *as such* may argue for an independent right to property.

Whichever path we follow, we reach the same conclusion. If the property rights and contractual freedom of monopolistic firms (and of course individuals) are to be infringed upon, this may not be due to ignoring their claims but superseding them with others. Antitrust thus must supply satisfying arguments for the infringement of rights it demands. Since rights are relevant on both sides of the debate, we must move on to a framework allowing for balancing the claims raised and the effects of state-mandated intervention.

After examining the different rights and claims on behalf of monopoly's victims, we assessed parallel rights and claims that monopolists themselves might raise. The high regard our society has for the right to property and freedom of contract should cause concern over the lack of similar attention by contemporary antitrust debate to the rights of those subject to legal restraint. This lack of attention can perhaps be explained by the sociology of antitrust scholarship, but such explanation does nothing to *justify* it. If antitrust is to be implemented not only as 'good for society' in its efficiency promotion, but as justified on fairness grounds, we must analyze both the rights of those clamouring for state protection and of those claiming a right to free trade, including the right to monopolize.

The wealth transfer argument—perhaps the most pervasive non-efficiency justification for antitrust—focused on harm to consumers. If our debate is to be complete, though, producers' rights must be equally assessed. Following the famous Coasian argument, the transfer of wealth may harm consumers, but legal restraint on monopoly harms (some) producers.[43] The term 'wealth transfer' itself assumes a prior ownership of the surplus by consumers and thus their preference. The consumers' right to such surplus was critically assessed in the previous chapter, while producers' claims were partially substantiated by this one. Any further use of this issue in antitrust debate, then, must be substantiated by a test balancing the clashing claims of both sides. The next chapter addresses this issue.

[43] R Coase, 'The Problem of Social Cost' (1960) 3 *Journal of Law and Economics* 1 highlighted the bilateral effect of externalizations. As *A* affects *B*, so does *B* asking for state protection affect *A*. One cannot automatically be assumed to be the 'active' or 'harmful' party without a prior substantive decision as to whose interest should be preferred. The normative conclusion thus requires substantiation as to whose interests to prefer rather than technical argumentation as to transfer or infringement.

Part III

The Balancing Act of Antitrust

5

Towards a Constitutional Balance in Antitrust

I. THE NEED FOR A BALANCING TEST

The preceding chapters presented legitimate and persuasive arguments that might be made on behalf of monopolists as well as on behalf of their potential victims. This chapter will thus examine the possibilities for a balancing test taking into account all relevant interests and prescribing the appropriate action according to the different circumstances.

The need to balance between clashing interests and claims that individuals make is nothing new. Almost every treatise concerning constitutional law deals with this necessity as one of the basic demands made on modern society and state by the rise of liberal ideologies, which include divergent points of view and protected rights. Indeed, the very recognition of different persons as holding equal standing before the law, or equal claims to moral rights, makes such clashes inevitable. One question that must be addressed is whether the claims raised by the different players who were recognized as relevant, stand on a common ground and thus demand equal respect—or perhaps these claims are of a totally different nature, and thus a lexical ordering is possible.[1]

A. The Case for Balancing

The argument supporting a balancing test rests on the premise that the issue at hand involves different legal persons, each bearing rights and with interests to be protected. These rights, while deemed as deserving protection by the state, conflict

[1] A lexical ordering is one in which issues are considered sequentially, the first being infinitely more important than the second—thus the second consulted only if the first does not lead to a clear solution. The clearest example is the ordering of words within a dictionary, where words beginning with 'B' will appear only after all words beginning with 'A' have been exhausted. Thus, the first letter 'trumps' the second and 'Az' will appear before 'Ba'. One such lexical ordering might be the distinction between 'rights' and 'interests', discussed in ch 3. If one side has a protected right, and the other merely an interest in protection, the right shall 'trump' the interest, and no balancing test will be necessary. Other theoretical possibilities exist as well, such as always preferring one type of right over another, or always preferring collective interests over personal ones (or vice versa).

with each other—so that they cannot be simultaneously protected in full. In order for the existing rights to be respected and protected optimally, their underlying sources of value must be compared, and context-specific decisions must be made in each case.

Despite this obvious argument, monopolists' rights are not often considered in and of their own. Two basic contentions substantiate the need for a balancing test: that monopolists as such are bearers of rights, and that these are not forfeited with the advent of market power.

i. Monopolists as Bearers of Rights

As the previous chapter showed, 'monopolists' include various groups and individuals, each with a claim to state protection from interference in their rights.[2] This does not automatically mean that *the nature and content* of these rights are of equal standing to those of the victims, but that a balancing test must be devised and carried out in order to distinguish between the different cases. Allowing one side (the victims) to present right-based arguments, without allowing the other side (monopolists) to do the same would amount to improper and unjustifiable favouritism. This is reprehensible in political dispute, and unforgivable in philosophical debate. If fairness is to have any standing whatsoever in the antitrust debate, any conclusions must be based on assessing all relevant parties' arguments.

ii. Assessing the Rights and not the Person

Even if the person claiming state protection (or the right to state non-intervention) is one who deserves moral admonishment, this does not void her claims. Even in the extreme case of a criminal, we acknowledge her right to be treated according to an acceptable code, both with regard to method of punishment and with regard to other moral claims she might make. Thus, while specific characteristics of the person making moral claims may influence the way these claims are treated, such influence must be separately assessed rather than automatically negating the claim.

This is almost undisputed when such claims are unrelated to the crime (or moral wrong) attributed to the person, and most would agree that even when a person commits a moral or legal wrong, we are not exempt from respecting other claims that person may raise in *the same* context. Consider, for example, the case of a small political party whose members believe in the superiority of a fascist regime over the existing democratic state. These fascists attempt to convince

[2] Again, I use the term 'monopolists' broadly, to encompass all those limited by antitrust law whether it be due to existing or potential monopoly, agreements that might cement collective market power, or merging parties constrained due to public policy of preventing monopoly rather than merely constraining it.

others of their views, both in order to convert 'new believers' and in order to gain the political clout necessary to bring about the change desired by them.

We assume that the democracy in which they live has rules respecting the right to free speech and that the anti-democratic group wishes to rely on these rules in order to gain access to the public 'marketplace of ideas'. If the aims of this group contradict the democratic structure, may we automatically assume that it has forfeited its right to participate in democratic debate? This question has been debated heatedly by many, most famously during the *Skokie* case in the US.[3] There, a group of Neo-Nazis applied for a permit to march on the anniversary of Adolph Hitler, their ideological leader's birthday. Without delving too deeply into the specifics of the case, legal debate focused on their right to free speech—including the right to march in public wearing Nazi uniforms and insignia—as guaranteed by state laws and the federal constitution. Some argued that a democratic society must respect even those views found most abhorrent, at least as far as allowing freedom of speech to their proponents; others argued that a group such as this should not be allowed to march through a community of holocaust survivors—a measure aimed not at political speech, but rather at antagonizing those most vulnerable to emotional distress. The march was finally allowed by the Court, with the argument for free speech triumphing over all other considerations. The sole reason that would justify limiting free speech was held to be a 'clear and present danger' posed to others around them.

Of course, one may disagree with the Court's decision in that case, or the final balancing of rights that justified it. What is important, is accepting the *possibility* of such groups to argue for their right to speech, or any other right for that matter. I submit merely that such a claim must be thoroughly analyzed before a decision is made, and offhand dismissal is not an option—regardless of the group's moral and legal position.

The question at this point is not whether a monopolist should categorically be allowed to act unhindered (indeed we shall see cases where severe limitations are necessary); the question is merely whether monopolists *as such* may claim rights to be considered along with their victims'. In this context, there is no reason to ignore possible moral claims that monopolists might raise. Therefore, such claims must be compared with contradicting claims made by other parties (the various victims) through some method of balancing the clashing rights.

B. The Case against Balancing

Some might argue that fairness considerations do not necessitate considering the monopolists' side, but only that of their victims. Moral claims by the perpetrator

[3] *Village of Skokie v National Socialist Party of America* [1978] 69 Ill 2d 605, 373 NE 2nd 21; *Collin v Smith* [1978] 578 F 2d 1197, cert denied.

of the harm being considered should, according to this view, be dismissed a priori and any view to the contrary would again place those deserving protection at the mercy of those wielding superior power. These views may be founded on the following arguments.

i. Monopolists can Protect Themselves

By definition, monopolists are more economically powerful than their victims, thus it is unnecessary to protect them in the first place. Beyond that, the 'evils' against which the monopolists cry for protection, are those that they can avoid in the first place. Monopolists are not sought out as pariahs to be punished, but only reprimanded in cases where their actions are improper and should not have been committed in the first place. A monopolist clamouring for protection can protect himself by avoiding anticompetitive actions.

ii. Monopolists Misuse their Rights

The existence and use of market power is an excessive misuse of the basic right to trade. True, the right to trade (predicated on property and contract as considered above) protects monopolists as well as any other owner of property, but this is not what they argue for here. Here, the claim being made by monopolists is for the right to extort, to demand exorbitant prices and limit competitors attempting their own trade. In short, monopolization is not a form of trade, just as running someone over with your car is not an expression of your freedom of movement.

Market power, thus, serves as a turning point. A seller without it may fully enjoy the right to trade, since market forces ensure that his demands create no compulsion for buyers. Freedom of trade, then, allows for personal idiosyncrasies whose price is borne by the person himself. If one prefers not to trade with certain partners, this is allowed due to other alternatives being open for those excluded. The same is not true of the possessor of market power. Once this threshold has been passed, it is no longer freedom of trade which is exercised, but a freedom to exclude or compel, neither of which justifies state protection and both of which may be limited.

iii. The Rights are Incomparable

The rights juxtaposed here are incomparable. One cannot compare the right of a monopolist to 'trade freely' and profit extensively, to the right of his competitor to stay in business. One cannot put on equal standing the right of the victim to be protected from harm, and the right of his oppressor to cause it. Even if we accept that both sides are bearers of rights, it is the *nature* of these rights that demands separate analysis; to do otherwise would be to reduce the concept of balancing rights to a farce, allowing bullies to go unscathed due to their claim of 'expressing their strength'.

C. Answers to the Case against Balancing

i. Monopolists can Protect Themselves

This claim relies on two focal points. The first is the strength of monopolists in relation to that of their victims, and the second is the monopolists' ability to avoid antitrust prosecution in the first place. Let us address each separately.

Monopolists are 'strong enough': as shown in chapter one, not all monopolists have great economic power. A monopolist is such only in relation to the market in which he operates. That market may be a very small geographic market, a limited product market, etc. The party bringing suit may be a small consumer requiring protection by the state, but it may also be a strong competitor wishing to utilize a legal opportunity.[4] In some cases, the plaintiff possesses even more economic power than the defendant does—although of course this does nothing to show whether the complaint itself is justified or not.[5]

Even if we assumed that monopolists possess economic power, we must remember that in the realm of antitrust law, the victims require protection from the monopolist, but the entity from which the *monopolist* needs to be protected is *the state*. It is the state that would limit his actions, require him to deal with people and organizations contrary to his wishes, or order his firm to divest itself of certain departments or business endeavours. In this context, then, the monopolist may be as weak as any other subject of statutory regulation. In a nutshell, once state enforcement is at issue, the 'self protection' argument fails. State intervention brings with it the full force of the law, legal agencies and the firepower behind them (both literal and figurative). Of course, there are cases where the defendant in an antitrust case is a huge, economically powerful firm, rivalling the state in influence and power. These cases are not the focal point of normative analysis, as one would be loath to reach general conclusions based on extreme specific cases. Furthermore, when such extreme circumstances do exist, justifying antitrust is far from sufficient—as its implementation may be constrained by *real politic*, the sense that even independent state action is limited when accosting superior economic power. In any case, antitrust has far too broad a reach to be justified on the basis of singularly extreme cases, however colourful and intuitive they may be. This tendency is precisely the one outlined in chapter one above, where historical (and irrelevant) precedent still guides current intuitive judgments.

While the argument relies on monopolists' relative strength as an issue to be addressed, this premise can be questioned as well. Why should power matter

[4] See, in this context, WJ Baumol and JA Ordover, 'The Use of Antitrust to Subvert Competition' (1985) 28 *Journal of Law and Economics* 247. See also the discussion of public choice in ch 2, section I E ii.

[5] Eg, a large buyer exploiting monopsony power would still be entitled to argue against the merger of two of its suppliers, or sue them for collusion (relying on per se rules!) if they seek cooperative solutions to their common misfortune.

in questions of rights? What makes 'strong' monopolists less deserving of legal protection than 'weak' ones? The fact that a monopoly possesses great economic power does not absolve the state or the legal philosopher from the duty to respect its right-based arguments. If the monopoly is deserving of protection due to its right to property, contract, or any other claim, that claim should be assessed independently of the monopoly's relative strength. Just as the rich are entitled to protection of life and property no less than the poor, so the fact that one possesses market power with regard to a specific good does not dissolve its property rights. Consider a case where a thief breaks into a store and the (monopolistic) proprietor calls the police. Is it at all possible that the police officer taking the call will answer along the lines of 'sorry, but no protection for those possessing market power'?

Of course, the relative strength of a monopolist may be relevant when devising the balancing test, applying it, or deciding upon remedies. Where it is not relevant is in the question *whether to balance the clashing rights*. Where two sides have rights, both are to be assessed: it really is as simple as that.

What we do have to take into account is that in cases where the monopolist is significantly more powerful than its victims, the latter may need more protection, and the former might justifiably be limited more severely. This, however, will be *the result* of applying a balancing test that deems relevant all parties' rights and specific circumstances. Thus, the 'strong enough' argument fails as a preliminary objection.

Monopolists can avoid antitrust enforcement: while some monopolistic practices are undeniably voluntary and undertaken after intensive deliberation, this is not always so. It is possible for a monopoly to be 'thrust upon' a business through sheer luck (for example, public taste changes so that its brand or product suddenly becomes so fashionable that previous competitors are not considered viable alternatives); mismanagement by their competitors (for example, bankruptcy or even inefficiency bringing about high costs and pricing); or superior business acumen.[6] Since there are many methods of creating a monopoly, we cannot judge all monopolists equally. So, while predatory pricing or refusals to deal may be avoidable on the monopolist's part, not every monopolistic practice is of the same nature and the issue of 'false positives' creating a chilling effect on business behaviour by would-be monopolists looms large.[7]

[6] The language of course draws from *US v Grinnell Corp*, 384 US 563, 571 (1966). There, such monopoly was explicitly referred to in order to explain that monopoly is not forbidden. The fact is, though, that while formally no illegal monopolization occurred, those now possessing of market power will find themselves subject to enforcement agencies' scrutiny, and might constrict their own business practices either due to the legal obligations monopoly entails (eg, the US doctrine of per se illegality of tying when in possession of market power or the EU doctrine of legal duties applying to holders of dominant market positions).

[7] The fear of 'chilling effects' has been much discussed and was a focal point in the US Supreme Court's discussion in *Verizon Communications Inc v Law Offices of Curtis V Trinko LLP*, 3540 US 398, 407 (2004). See the discussion in ch 3, n 34 and ch 4, n 1.

ii. Monopolists Misuse their Rights

Let us begin with the extreme: 'monopolization is not a form of trade, just as running someone over with your car is not an expression of your freedom of movement'. This example was used rhetorically as an obvious case where none would argue to the contrary. But I will. Running someone over with a car is an example of using the basic freedom of movement in a manner incompatible with its justification. A driver arguing for freedom to run over others will be restricted not because he lacks the freedom to drive as he pleases, but because this freedom is balanced with other people's rights to freedom of their own movement, protection from bodily harm, etc. What this example proves is that freedom of movement is not absolute, but requires a balancing test with conflicting rights so that where clashes arise they will be resolved through optimal fulfilment of the different parties' interests.

Similarly, in the case of monopolists' freedom of trade, I do not argue for an absolute right to supersede all conflicting claims, rendering helpless the victims of monopoly. My sole contention at this point is the necessity of a formal balancing test, as no conclusion can be reached without addressing *all* relevant claims, and any decision to allow one group to harm another must be justified in context.

The mere existence of market power does not obliterate pre-existing freedom of trade. Not all manifestations of monopolistic phenomena are evil attempts at stifling others. Consider, for example, a local jeweller operating one out of three shops in a secluded region. Over the years, he has refused to deal with his next door neighbour, due to a personal dispute between them. The neighbour himself gladly took his business elsewhere, as he too preferred not to deal with the jeweller. Next, assume the other two jewellery shops suffered misfortune and closed, due to a combination of personal and market conditions. Now our jeweller enjoys a monopoly position in the region. Are all manifestations of his freedom of trade, including barring his neighbour from the shop, automatically nullified? When pushing his neighbour into his competitors' arms, his refusal to deal was one of the personal idiosyncrasies allowed by his legal freedom in trade. This personal aspect has not changed with the introduction of market power, and the same reasons for allowing it to begin with are relevant now as well. What has changed, though, is the effect on the neighbour. It may be that in order to protect the neighbour from these new circumstances, we shall be forced to compel the jeweller to accept his neighbour's business despite the personal discomfort he will suffer. We may not. The decision, in any case, will be made according to a balance reached between each party's interests, as protected by legal rights.

The point made, is that market power neither nullifies all the monopolists' interests, nor does it automatically restrict freedom of trade. What it does do is give weight to the counter-arguments presented by those on the other side, whose options may be severely limited due to the monopolist's stronghold. This may necessitate careful consideration of the victims of monopoly when devising the balancing test and implementing its results, but not rule out balancing altogether.

iii. The Rights are Incomparable

To this I answer twofold: first, even if the rights claimed are of a different nature, this is true for most cases of clashes of rights discussed in constitutional contexts.[8] The fact that the rights are different is not an impediment to the need for a balancing test—but rather the main justification thereof. It is because the rights are not of an identical origin and nature that an *external* balance needs to be struck: one taking into account each right's place in the political and social order. Precisely because different types of rights are claimed, it is necessary to define exactly their nature and extent, so that they may be assessed within our context of choice. The question then will be: what actions may (and indeed must) the state undertake, so that the democratic principles our society wishes to live by will be best achieved?

The second response to this argument is that in fact many of the rights claimed *are* similar in nature, though not identical in implementation. The monopolist's right to property, justifying her claim to non-intervention, is not totally dissimilar from her victim's right to property, on which he bases his plea *for* state intervention on his behalf. The argument for recognition of a right to free trade may equally be used by the monopolist against a court order compelling her to deal with her competitors, and by her victims—against the limitations placed upon them by her excessive market power. The most striking similarity was found in the previous chapter, when we examined the specific individuals and groups that make up the 'monopolist'. There we saw that sometimes the community in which a monopolistic firm manufactures has a strong interest in its success, and antitrust action may cause severe harm to members of that community as well as to workers, stockholders, etc. The same types of communities stand on the other side of the equation, as potentially harmed by monopoly—only their recognition on the victims' side has become more commonplace.

There is a need, then, for balancing of both kinds: between rights of a different nature that each side claims and between similar rights claimed by the different sides. The 'incomparable rights' argument fails.

II. STRIKING A BALANCE

The basic premise for our discussion is that where (non-lexical) rights clash, we shall never reach a permanent, all-encompassing, solution fitting for all contexts. Since the rights examined are personal and the circumstances change case-by-case, we must seek a process that will allow for taking into account the relevant differences. For the question at hand, the main purpose of the proposed test is to

[8] Eg, the right of individuals to be protected from criminal harm versus the right of criminals to receive a fair trial, or the right to freedom of expression clashing with the right to protection from malicious emotional distress in the *Skokie* example above.

balance among competing claims, each justifiable on its own, but unattainable simultaneously. The balancing itself will, of course, rely on the system of values and priorities relevant to the legal and cultural framework within which the claims arise. Our balancing test, therefore, must allow for 'fine-tuning' according to the shifting tides of political morality, while maintaining the basic themes constant. Without holding some basic premises constant, there is no sense in devising a test—as public sentiment and political opportunism will triumph anyway. Without allowing for 'fine-tuning', a model based on today's consensus will be inappropriate and inapplicable tomorrow. The 'golden path' between these is not easily defined, but then again, no one promised us an easy task …

A. The Setting: Constitutional Law

In the modern democratic state, questions of conflicting rights and the state's proper role of intervention are commonly analyzed within constitutional boundaries. Here too, constitutional law must provide the setting for the formulation of an appropriate standard. There are several reasons why the constitutional setting is appropriate for antitrust-related balancing between rights.

B. Laying Down the Ground Rules

The basis for any constitution is setting the ground rules for subsequent legislation and litigation, so that society has a basis for its future development of legal norms. Similarly, the dispute analyzed here is not a particular one. The argument pertains to the very basis that will guide antitrust law from the ground up, affecting an extremely broad range of firms and individuals. Exactly as we expect basic rules of property to be subject to constitutional review, here too the ground rules are set according to society's conception of what property is, where its boundaries lie and how to understand competing claims—not to a particular asset, but to the basic standards of state protection. The same is true for our analysis of contractual freedom and social goals, as set out in the previous chapters.

Put simply, if antitrust law is to be understood coherently as a facet of general commercial law, it must be examined according to the basic norm substantiating such law in the first place. Of course, this is not the first time antitrust law was questioned in light of constitutional standards. The early days of the Sherman Act saw various attacks on its constitutionality by those who would have it repealed altogether.[9]

[9] See ch 4, nn 6–12 and accompanying text.

The claims made there, though, were of the *illegitimacy* of Congress interfering with economic rights altogether. When viewed through the lens of present-day knowledge of economic and legal history, these arguments seem destined for failure, but it serves well to point out their underlying legal rationale, and their inherent difference from our discussion here. The unconstitutionality of the Sherman Act, if so found, would reside in its interference in the contractual freedom of the parties to trade or the uncompensated taking of private property belonging to those limited by the Act. These claims seem relevant, as a basic tenet of antitrust law is that monopolists' freedom of disposition as to their property results in harm to various parties denoted above as monopoly's victims. The early (and some recent) claims of unconstitutionality were doomed to failure, not because of a mistake in assessing the infringed rights of monopolists, but due to their ignoring the parallel rights of monopoly's victims. Were the claim of unconstitutionality accepted, regulation of monopoly would be abolished altogether, leaving both the victims and society at large unprotected. Judges forced to decide between a total commitment to monopolists' rights and the protection of their victims, understandably chose the latter.

My claim is more humble, and I believe more realistic: allowing monopoly to flourish without legal intervention is wrong and foolhardy, yet regulation of monopoly need not ignore monopolists altogether. The stated purpose of this book is to argue for *balancing* among the competing rights, affording respect to both sides of the conflict. Thus, our focus (after identifying the competing rights in the previous chapters) should be on devising a workable standard that would take into account *all* relevant constitutional rights, and balance among them in a manner coherent with standards from other realms of legal thought. It is with this in mind that we proceed.

C. Limitation on State Intervention

The state's role in society is obviously a concern of constitutional law. Similarly, the limits imposed upon the state's ability to interfere in private relations are a matter for constitutional debate. Some societies may prefer a more active role, others a more passive one. The differences may be across countries, as in comparing the US and the European Union (or countries therein), or they may be across time, comparing local antitrust rules in one era to another. In any case, it is within the basic framework of legal institutions that these decisions are made, and the most fundamental legal norm—the constitution—should address these issues. Even within a country (and across time), constitutional discourse is dynamic, shifting with political tides and social consensus. This is true in countries with and without a written constitution, as in both cases constitutional discourse evolves through implementation, with courts considering modern cases through the lens of political theory and modern needs.

Many times the written constitution (if such exists) fails to directly address the pertinent issues, either due to lack of foresight on the part of its framers, or the contrary: foresight as to the possibility of shifting social consensus. In the latter cases, framers of written constitutions may wish to leave the definition vague in order to allow future generations to implement their own conclusions. Implementation over time is then conducted according to constitutional standards developed by the courts.

Countries without a written constitution operate according to similar principles. While only some of the 'constitutional' questions are formally addressed in legal documents, courts routinely must answer questions as to the proper role of state intervention and the balance of rights made necessary by conflicting claims. Regardless of the statutory framework, it is clear that questions regarding the proper level of state intervention in protected basic rights must follow guidelines set out by constitutional discourse. We should remember that any standard developed here is not intended as an interpretation of an *existing* rule within antitrust law, but as a guideline to be followed by the field as a whole. Theory regarding optimal competition policy thus combines with considerations stemming from moral and political discourse regarding basic rights and the individual's right to protection from, and by, the state.

D. Policy versus Principle: Can Societal Goals Supersede Fairness?

The preceding analysis regarding antitrust goals and their justifications included two themes: fairness considerations and societal goals. The fairness considerations refer to the rights-based arguments raised by all groups involved in the debate, and were analyzed in-depth in chapters three and four. The societal perspective includes aggregate efficiency considerations, and various conceptions of a 'good' society that antitrust law may help protect, analyzed in chapter two above. The standard to be developed here needs to address not only the clash of different parties' claims to fairness protection, but also society's collective interests in shaping commercial relations.

In short, the fairness claims are questions of principle: what is 'right' and who shall triumph. The societal goals raised are questions of policy: what is aggregately superior and how reality may be shaped to allow it.[10] The question whether policy issues can supersede principle is a basic debate, fundamental to the type of legal

[10] Of course, many see fairness as an interest of society as a whole, not just those affected, eg, for us to live in a just society is no less important (at the very least) than the total amount of goods that society can bestow upon its members. Living in a just society, though, can be valued only *after* determination of what 'just' means. Since our discussion of fairness claims of the different groups aims precisely at this result, we focus on societal goals that may contradict fairness. Once the fair result has been determined, we shall remain with the question if other non-fairness goals may supersede the former. For discussion of the policy versus principle issue in a general, non-antitrust, context, see, eg, RM Dworkin, *A Matter of Principle* (Cambridge, MA: Harvard University Press, 1985) 72–103.

regime we wish to live in. The answer is not specific to the realm of antitrust, but part of a coherent and comprehensive view of law, and its place in society.

I cannot hope to provide a full answer to this fundamental query, since that would demand philosophical investigation far beyond the scope sketched out here. What we can and must do, however, is make sure that the balancing test proposed coincides with current learning of this issue. It is in constitutional law that this question is addressed, as part of the basic framework in which legal institutions operate. Our antitrust debate, thus, must follow constitutional guidelines.

III. BOUNDARIES TO BE RESPECTED

Before we delve into the standard setting itself, some ground rules should be set. There are certain preconceptions that will guide the proposed standard, some implicit in the previous discussion and some that require clarification in order to deal with initial objections that might be raised.

A. No One Side may be Preferred A Priori

Following the analysis so far, a balancing test must take into account all relevant parties and assess their claims in an objective manner. The test may not at any point assume that there is a 'bad guy' to be sanctioned versus a 'good guy' deserving protection. Monopolists should receive the same initial treatment as their victims, notwithstanding the fact that in many cases the final result of the analysis might be to limit the implementation of those rights.

B. Protection of Monopolists while not Abandoning their Victims

Initial non-preference of one side sounds nice, but does it not merely camouflage non-intervention that benefits monopolists? In other words, do victims stand a chance without strong state support?

Optimal regulation of antitrust must consider fairness arguments of all sides, as well as other relevant social goals. By definition, a formulation that would benefit only one side of the equation would fail to achieve such optimality. Can we hold the stick at both ends? Perhaps. A balancing test is devised exactly for this purpose, to find a golden path between two incompatible claims, so that the total harm done is minimal and implementation can be case-specific, aiming at optimal balancing according to realistic circumstances. Our test, therefore, must find a way to protect the monopolist from unwarranted intervention, while simultaneously allowing swift and firm state action when necessary to protect others from that same monopolist.

IV. DEVELOPING THE STANDARD

What type of standard is justified for this sort of dilemma? In formulating the standard we will need to take into account fairness claims of the different groups affected, societal goals deemed appropriate, our setting within constitutional debate and ramifications of state intervention versus non-interference. While my aim at this point is to provide a general framework and not specific answers to concrete questions of law, one cannot ignore practical implementation of the proposed standard later on. The general themes guiding discussion should thus allow for formulation of concrete rules and overarching standards, with modern competition policy providing context even for the initial considerations of theory. We thus begin by spelling out the broad contours of an acceptable standard, moving later on to implementation and examination of such a standard's practical results. This allows for a re-examination of implicit assumptions we may hold, together with a reality check of where theoretical considerations may lead us in practice.

A. State versus Private Interests

Setting antitrust law within a constitutional context may be misleading as to the forces to be dealt with. Many constitutional issues deal with the state's proper role in restraining personal liberties. A common example is the justification of restraining the right to freedom of speech in the interest of maintaining national security, and limitations on such restrictions due to the right's importance. This type of question juxtaposes the common interest, as represented by the state, with individual interests. Consequently, 'liberalist' conceptions tend to limit state intervention, focusing on protecting individuals from the relative near omnipotence of the state.[11]

Our context is different. Juxtaposition of state versus individual interests is but one aspect to be dealt with, and not necessarily the central one. The discussion of antitrust above showed that most cases deal with specific monopolists versus specific victims of monopolization; thus the fairness considerations are argued by two distinct groups of private individuals rather than one individual versus the state as a whole. State intervention here is an answer to the calls of one category of affected individuals, at the direct expense of another. On the other hand, there are interests broad enough to be categorized as common interests represented by the state.

Since two types of instances occur, our discussion of justifications for intervention (and limitations thereof) should follow the same structure, assessing each case separately: that of the state intervening to protect the rights of those who otherwise will be overwhelmed by the monopolists' superior economic power,

[11] See, eg, J Tomasi, *Free Market Fairness* (Princeton, NJ: Princeton University Press, 2012) chs 1–2.

and that of the state protecting common interests that cannot be ascribed to a specific category of individuals. The first case is related to the discussion of fairness above, where monopoly's victims' desire protection, while the second relates to policy considerations assessed in the discussion of societal goals. Of course, following our inclusive method of analysis, monopolists' rights will be balanced with the interests in their limitation, but the balancing test itself might differ between the two contexts.

B. State versus Private Action

Having described the interests at stake, we turn now to the actions argued for. There is a great difference between an individual arguing for his right to act in a certain manner (unlimited by the state), and the same individual arguing for his right to the *result* of such action, necessitating at times that the state act for him.[12] For example, freedom of speech might on its own justify allowing a person to express his views, but a claim for *effective speech* might entail a subsidized means of promulgation (so that his views have more realistic chances of affecting others). Similarly, when the victims of monopoly argue for their right to trade, or the benefit thereof, it does not automatically follow that state intervention in order to protect them from private parties (the monopolist) is also justified. In order to implement such a freedom in our context, a positive right to state action must be substantiated, including the limitation to be placed on the monopolist's freedom as well. While we saw in chapter three that many of the intuitively appealing claims on behalf of monopoly's victims ultimately failed to justify intervention, here I give them the benefit of the doubt, assuming protection is initially justified. This allows for assessment of the limits imposed on governmental intervention due to balancing the competing claims, even if the arguments against victim rights are subsequently rejected.

i. The Market Correction Hypothesis

A common argument against intervention in economic matters is that the market tends to correct itself over time. At its extreme, this would justify laissez faire capitalism, with no need of antitrust whatsoever.[13] Assessed more carefully, a

[12] If the argument is for freedom of action, what the individual craves is a 'freedom' in the Hohfieldian sense. Thus, a lack of duty on his part to refrain from the action will suffice. If, on the other hand, the argument is for the *result* of such action, this constitutes a Hohfieldian 'right', necessitating an outside party to bear a duty to act on the individual's behalf if he cannot create the sought result on his own. See WN Hohfeld, *Fundamental Legal Conceptions* (Westport, CT: Greenwood Press, 1978). For modern applications, see L Fiorito and M Vatiero, 'Beyond Legal Relations: Wesley Newcomb Hohfeld's Influence on American Institutionalism' (2011) 45 *Journal of Economic Issues* 199.

[13] This being a basic and well-known argument, there is no need of reiteration here. See generally, R Bork, *The Antitrust Paradox: A Policy at War with Itself* (New York: Basic Books, 1978); FH Easterbrook,

preference for non-intervention is usually justified only when the relevant market failures are such that they tend to self-correct, and taking into account the duration of interim efficiency loss. Our rights-based analysis may lead to different conclusions: if a victim of monopoly suffers now, it is of little value to him that the market promises future correction. A *right* to protection places demands upon the relevant authority to act immediately or as soon as possible and not wait for 'natural occurrences' to make the problem disappear. This is so due to the right-bearer seeking redress for a wrong, and expecting to reap the resulting benefits himself, rather than have the market correct over time and have the benefits accrue to some lucky individual later on.

Despite the above, since antitrust intervention is subject to costs and delay, ignoring the market alternative is not an option. Where market forces exist, that will eliminate monopolistic practices, *society as a whole* might be better off if antitrust recedes in favour of market correction, obviating the need both for direct costs and for the indirect expenses associated with antitrust.[14] The *individual rights* claim, on the other hand, remains intact, since the good of society does not necessarily triumph over individual rights.

Consider a monopolist arguing that governmental intervention infringes upon his rights: following our symmetry of analysis, it seems there is a correlation between the harm monopolists may cause their victims and the harm the state may cause monopolists. Some argue that this symmetry is unfounded, since it is the monopolists who cause the harm. This, though, relies on a conception challenged here from the start. The analysis in previous chapters showed that both monopolists and their victims have justifiable claims, and only after balancing between them, will we arrive at an answer as to who is to be afforded protection in specific circumstances.

There is, however, a second challenge to the symmetry proposed, this time from the monopolist's point of view. The harm caused by the monopolist to others cannot be compared to the harm he suffers from state intervention due to the basic distinction between private and state action. Two arguments can be made that state actions should be more severely constrained than private actions: one instrumental and one of moral standing.

ii. The Instrumental Argument: State Action Causes more Harm than Private Action

Briefly stated, the argument goes as follows: state action is more harmful due to the superior power of the state over other players in the market. If the state issues an injunction on a certain type of commercial behaviour, normal market forces

'Does Antitrust Have a Comparative Advantage?' (1999) 23 *Harvard Journal of Law & Public Policy* 3; FL Smith, 'The Case for Reforming the Antitrust Regulations (if Repeal is not an Option)' (1999) 23 *Harvard Journal of Law & Public Policy* 23.

[14] See ch 2, section E.

will not overturn it—thus any harmful effects will be sustained for a long time. A monopolist constraining commercial behaviour, on the other hand, is constantly subject to market forces that in most cases will find a way to circumvent the constraint.[15]

An example should help to clarify this argument. Assume a monopolist sets supra-normal prices in order to maximize profit. Market forces would normally attract new entrants, thus substantial entry barriers are necessary in order to sustain monopoly. Unless barriers are impregnable, the market will not sustain monopoly indefinitely. Thus, any harm caused by monopolists will eventually be remedied by the market. Furthermore, the same dynamic may constrain monopolistic behaviour ex ante.[16] Of course, only proponents of the strong version of the efficient markets hypothesis will carry this argument to its extreme, ie, that monopoly pricing is perfectly constrained a priori, and thus may be safely ignored. Still, even if we reject the more optimistic views of market efficiency, it is difficult to argue that monopoly can be sustained indefinitely without state protection. Indeed, it may be argued that it is precisely the state protected monopolies that pose the most danger; thus patents, regulated industries and licensing requirements should be carefully scrutinized.[17] Regarding 'standard' monopolies, then, our focus should be on the interim period in which monopoly is sustained—how long is this period, and how much harm is caused therein.

Assume now a state decree constraining the freedom of monopolists. Our inclusive analysis dictates that harm to monopolists be assessed similarly to the harm to their victims, subject to the conditions set out in chapters three and four. What will overturn the state's decision? Either internal revision—which means that decision-makers within state authorities reach a conclusion that the decree was unjustified—or market forces of such a nature that even the state, with all its might, cannot constrain for long. The first option is relevant in cases of a mistake being made (and admitted) and the second deals with either the collapse of the rule of law, or a certain area thereof—hopefully not a very frequent occasion.

It thus follows that when assessing the relevant harms imposed by state versus private actions, the different time frame of their relevance as well as the possibility of change due to adjustment to market dynamics, should be considered, with state action deserving stricter scrutiny.

[15] Here we refer to the famous 'false positives' versus 'false negatives' distinction, see ch. 2 n 37 and accompanying text. The former denote mistakes by courts proscribing harmless practices as monopolistic, and the latter denote mistakes allowing truly monopolistic practices to go unhindered. On the other hand, see H Hovenkamp, 'Antitrust's Protected Classes' (1989) 88 *Michigan Law Review* 1, fns 118–21, for a contradictory view.

[16] Since eventual entry becomes more likely the stronger the incentive for potential entrants is, monopolists may rationally decide to constrain pricing even in the initial stage, so that its duration is lengthened, see ch 2, n 24.

[17] See RB McKenzie and DR Lee, *In Defense of Monopoly: How Market Power Fosters Creative Production* (Ann Arbor, MI: University of Michigan Press, 2008) using this argument to criticize both antitrust and state intervention in the economy more generally.

iii. *The Moral Argument: The State is Bound by Higher Standards*

When the state interferes with an individual's rights, it stands on different ground from when private actors do the same. While an individual is assumed to act on her own behalf, the state enjoys the presumption of representing the common interest. Even the public choice literature examining the private interests guiding legislators and policy makers does so as an acknowledgement of an imperfect reality to be dealt with accordingly. Consequently, state action against an individual usually carries with it social stigma above and beyond the legal sanctions imposed.

State action imposing sanctions on monopolists must thus pass more stringent tests then when one private party causes another a similar harm in a non-legal context. Antitrust law imposes both criminal and civil liability on monopolists in most jurisdictions. When examining its justification and limitations, we must take into account this fact: that the state is creating a context where harm might come to monopolists in order to protect their victims or societal goals. This does not mean that society must refrain from legal sanctions, only that these must conform to the more stringent criteria relevant for state intervention. Furthermore, we must take into account the state's unique status as creator of law and special power regarding the creation of social norms. Laws have an expressive effect, following but also creating widespread consensus regarding value judgements.[18] When monopolists are limited by law—indeed as soon as they are named—social stigma can often be an immediate by-product. Firms prosecuted by antitrust agencies, or even defendants in private antitrust suits, may find themselves designated 'public enemies' by consumer groups, economic reporters and others. Insofar as this causes them economic harm (and one could argue for a reputational effect for employees and managers as well), state action requires special care.

In the context of balancing, when assessing the harm caused by monopolists on one hand, and the harm caused by state interference on the other, it is not enough to conclude that monopolists are more harmful. State intervention must do much better in the balance when we know that some harm invariably follows (as do some mistakes), taking into account the unequal position the two sides occupy, and the higher expectations from the state.

Before moving on to the formulation of the standard itself, let us add an alternative (potentially complementary) view of fairness analysis, one less often seen in legal writings: formalization of fairness. While terminology and modelling differ from our discussion so far, it is my hope that, viewing things from a different perspective, enriches and clarifies concepts upon which we rely.

[18] See, eg, E Posner, *Law and Social Norms* (Cambridge, MA: Harvard University Press, 2002); CR Sunstein, 'On the Expressive Function of Law' (1996) 144 *University of Pennsylvania Law Review* 2021; R Cooter, 'Expressive Law and Economics' (1988) 27 *Journal of Legal Studies* 585. But see MD Adler, 'Expressive Theories of Law: A Skeptical Overview' (2000) 148 *University of Pennsylvania Law Review* 1363 for a contrary view.

6

Formalization of Fairness: Keeping Everyone Envy-Free

Fairness has traditionally been discussed within the realm of moral philosophers and theologians. Interest in the issue by economists, though, has introduced an alternative method of analysis, adding mathematical formalization of the sort less common among philosophers. Real life complexity precludes exact implementation of quantitative models, yet this type of analysis may offer important insights regarding the balancing of claims by monopolists and their victims.

Fairness theory in economics generally focuses on the allocation of goods among members of society, while attempting to avoid the problems of interpersonal comparisons of utility. The basic question posed is, how should the available resources be distributed, achieving (hopefully) both efficiency and fairness? People have subjective and heterogeneous preferences, not merely about goods, but about social values as well. Thus, the goal is to describe 'fair' allocations, without ascribing to a particular moral viewpoint regarding 'who deserves what' or which values are more important than others.

In order to do so, we focus on process rather than substance, while treating all preferences as equally legitimate. Similar to the way Rawls focused on the procedure for attaining agreement on principles of justice behind a veil of ignorance, here we focus on a hypothetical procedure for inducing an allocation that would be considered fair by all participants. From a moral standpoint, such a procedure strives for neutrality among world views, insofar as this is possible.[1] It is presented not as *the* correct view, but as an interesting one which will add to our perspective on the broader issues in antitrust.[2]

[1] The search for a neutral theory of justice reaches far and wide, yet the term itself is contentious. For a discussion of the term and its inherent connection to liberalism, see CE Larmore, *Patterns of Moral Complexity* (Cambridge: Cambridge University Press, 1987). For a critique of this notion and specifically of the Rawlsian formulation, see MJ Sandel, *Liberalism and the Limits of Justice*, 2nd edn (Cambridge: Cambridge University Press, 1998).

[2] Even within antitrust, using 'objective' and 'value free' criteria may be itself construed as an ideological choice. See, eg, F Rowe, 'The Decline of Antitrust and the Delusion of Models: The Faustian Pact of Law and Economics' (1984) 72 *Georgetown Law Journal* 1511; H Hovenkamp, 'Fact, Value and Theory in Antitrust Adjucation' (1987) *Duke Law Journal* 897; EM Fox, 'The Politics of Law and Economics in Judicial Decision Making: Antitrust as a Window' (1986) 61 *New York University Law Review* 554.

I. THE FRAMEWORK OF ENVY-FREENESS

We begin by considering a society of heterogeneous people with exogenously given preferences. Our goal is the satisfaction of these preferences to the greatest degree, while maintaining an allocation which all can consider fair. Preferences are assumed to be subjective, and information regarding individuals' preferences to be private. Thus, each member of society knows what they prefer, and thus the value ascribed to each potential bundle of goods, but they need not share private information. While the construct is obviously hypothetical, we seek real insights implementable in the real world of antitrust, affecting the way each side's claims are treated.

The basic question such discussions often start with is, 'do we deserve what we have?', or the justification of the initial endowment with which we enter this world. More directly, within our context, we focus on the common conception of monopoly as infringing upon fairness, and ask what about it is biased by our history and antecedent 'common sense', and what survives radical re-examination in light of objectively assessed parameters. In other words, we delve into the theory of allocative fairness in order to subject classic antitrust justifications to a test. Hopefully, theoretical ideal will grant us a novel view on practical reality.

Ronald Dworkin made this hypothetical move famous within the debate regarding equality of resources.[3] Suppose, he said, a group of shipwrecked survivors reach an uninhabited island. The island has numerous resources, to which none of the immigrants bears a claim larger or smaller than that of his peers. How would they divide up the loot, in a way that respected each equally? Equal division seems intuitively appropriate, but assume the goods are not divisible, thus splitting them is not an option, nor are they equally valuable. Theoretically, we could divvy up the goods in bundles of comparable worth, but then we encounter the problem of heterogeneous preferences, ie, 'worth' is itself subjective. We could thus divide the goods into bundles, and allow survivors to self-select by choosing the bundle dearest to them. If each selected a unique bundle, with none wishing to trade places, all could be said to be satisfied and the allocation deemed 'fair'. Alternatively, we could seek a market mechanism which approximates this result (Dworkin focused on a semi-Walrasian auctioneer). Economists before Dworkin had been working on similar issues and have continued to offer refinements since, and I present some of these here.[4]

[3] See R Dworkin, 'What is Equality? Part 2: Equality of Resources' (1981) 10 *Philosophy and Public Affairs* 283.

[4] Hal Varian, one of the pioneers of this strand of literature, delved into the philosophical debate as well, while commenting on Dworkin's formulation. See HR Varian, 'Dworkin on Equality of Resources' (1985) 1 *Economics and Philosophy* 110. See also C Arnsperger, 'Reformulating Equality of Resources' (1997) 13 *Economics and Philosophy* 61, criticizing Dworkin's confusion of initial bundles serving as resources with final allocation of goods. This issue, which indirectly raises issues of production, will be assessed below. See generally, C Arnsperger, 'Envy-Freeness and Distributive Justice' (1994) 8 *Journal of Economic Surveys* 155.

Economic models require precise definitions, and dealing with fairness is no exception. In order to avoid interpersonal comparisons of utility, only the individuals involved assess their endowments, and as no commonly agreed metric exists, the question posed is whether they would like to trade places (bundles) with any other individual. An allocation is said to be fair if none envies the bundle another has, ie, envy-freeness implies fairness.[5] Obviously, identical bundles of goods generate no envy (as there is no better bundle to covet). Equality, though, can be extremely inefficient. This is true due to equality's disincentive effects (why invest effort if all are rewarded equally?) but in a more basic sense, due to heterogeneity of preferences. Since different people place different values on identical goods, it makes sense to allocate them in a way which maximizes utility rather then merely minimizing envy. For example, consider two players who have one orange. Player 1 wants the peel in order to make jam while player 2 wants the pulp in order to make juice. In this classic negotiation scenario, envy can be avoided by splitting the entitlement, the orange in this case, in half. Both, though, receive less than what they want, and inefficiency plagues the allocation. Allowing for unequal bundles can maximize utility without sacrificing fairness: allow player 1 to receive the entirety of the peel and player 2 to receive all pulp. Both will prefer this new allocation to the previous one—while neither envies the other's bundle. We shall therefore focus not merely on fairness in allocations, but ask that efficiency be attained as well.

Obviously, envy-freeness is not the ultimate, or only, criterion for fairness. It is due to limitations of the analytic tool that substance is constrained: in order for economic modelling to shed light on what is inherently fuzzy and debatable (what fairness really means), we limit ourselves here to one formulation, one clear-cut definition which allows for modelling and development. When using a microscope, one is required first to cut off a sliver of material and place it on a glass plate so that its details might be brought into focus. Similarly here, only with the help of a narrow definition susceptible to measurement (at least hypothetically), will we be able to garner the analytical prowess of precise models. After conducting the thought experiment and assessing in detail its results, I shall return to practical implementation, taking into account both the inherent limits of economic models and the limits of the definitions used therein.

The most basic beginning point for 'envy-free' allocation models is equal allocations, where envy is impossible by construct. As mentioned above, goods may be bulky and resist divisibility, a problem causing Dworkin to posit clamshells as pecuniary stand-ins and Varian to suggest constructing negotiable shares representing joint ownership of entitlements. The Dworkinian construct requires that the auctioneer should allocate and reallocate the goods until an envy-free division is achieved, while Varian makes use of free trade. If each participant is granted an equal share in each good, players can trade shares, exchanging goods they value

[5] Developed in DK Foley, 'Resource Allocation and the Public Sector' (1967) 7 *Yale Economic Essays* 45, this standard served as a basis for several subsequent developments, to be reviewed below.

less for those they value more. Goods would thus 'gravitate' towards those valuing them most highly—precisely the 'most efficient user' efficiency with which free trade is associated.[6]

This hypothetical process was dubbed 'people's capitalism', denoting the duality of initial equality reminiscent of communist ideology, intertwined with the uninhibited free trade of capitalist methodology. Following a 'people's capitalism' process facilitates both Pareto efficiency and fairness. The process is Pareto efficient since all those involved start out equal, and the only changes they undergo are by choice. Thus, any consensual exchange leads by definition to a Pareto superior result, and trade will continue until Pareto optimality is achieved. Fairness is maintained, since initial division was equal (ie, envy is impossible), and any player could have traded for the exact same bundle as another did. It is easy then to conclude that none envies another's bundle, even after trade, as each could have attained the same for himself.

William Baumol added the use of an Edgeworth box in order to assess possible divisions among two players with different preferences, showing a distinction between 'fair' divisions, where lack of envy is the criterion, and 'superfair' ones, where each player strongly prefers his own bundle to the other's.[7] Superfairness is possible where both players' preferences and the goods to be allocated are heterogeneous, generating unequal value.

The common example for superfairness, and its limitations, is the division of a cake. Everyone knows that 'one cuts, the other chooses' is a successful procedure to ensure fairness of division (those who grew up with a sibling, or raise children, are even more aware of this ...). The problem arises where the cake itself has part raisins and part chocolate chips. If one of the players prefers raisins, and the other cuts, the division may be unequal. The chooser will by definition receive the part that he prefers over the other (at least a weak preference), but the division will strategically take into account the chooser's preferences (insofar as the divider is aware of them). Thus, the divider might cut the cake so that one part includes mainly raisins but is smaller, and the other includes mainly chocolate chips and is larger. The chooser's preferences deem the smaller slice more valuable than the larger, due to its content, thus he will choose it. While fairness as lack of envy is

[6] H Varian, 'Equity, Envy, and Efficiency' (1974) 9 *Journal of Economic Theory* 63. While initial equal division is by definition fair, a question arises as to alternative fair allocations with subsequent trade. Feldman and Kirman analyze this question, to conclude that equal division maintains stability in subsequent trade, thus resulting in a fair allocation, while unequal (yet fair) allocations satisfy initial demands, but are unstable over subsequent trade, thus will eventually result in an unfair (ie, envy inducing) allocation. See A Feldman and A Kirman, 'Fairness and Envy' (1974) 64 *American Economic Review* 995. An alternative model was developed by Schmeidler and Vind, focusing on surplus gained from trade rather than the allocation itself. If fairness is defined as lack of envy as to the *surplus* gained, initial allocation need not be equal (relaxing the model), but a market with prices and uninhibited trade would suffice. See D Schmeidler and K Vind, 'Fair Net Trades' (1972) 40 *Econometrica* 637.

[7] WJ Baumol, 'Applied Fairness Theory and Rationing Policy' (1982) 72 *American Economic Review* 639. Extension of the model and its application was thereafter included in WJ Baumol, *Superfairness: Applications and Theory* (Cambridge, MA: MIT Press, 1986).

maintained, the allocation of tasks between the parties (divider/chooser) affects the final result, with strategic use of information possible.[8] One might then argue about the fairness of allocating tasks, as being chosen to divide grants the first player an advantage whenever he is aware of the other's preferences.

Superfairness theory allows for repeated analysis of the allocation of goods, so that after initial fairness is assured (each weakly preferring his own slice to the other party's), the excess is again allocated according to the same criterion. Thus, in our cake example, the divider and chooser both get a slice they weakly prefer to the other's—with a possibility that part of the cake remains undivided. Thereafter, a second division takes place, again according to a weak preference standard, continuing the process until the entire cake is spoken for. What this repeated division ensures is that at each stage the parties are assured of a fair result, with no strategic use of information or possibility for one to take advantage of the other's preferences. Superfairness thus attains true equality as well—a division of goods not only precluding envy, but assuring that subjective valuation, or actual enjoyment, is equal for all participants.

The paradigmatic benefit this type of fairness analysis offers is the ability to avoid interpersonal comparisons of utility (as each party here chooses according to their own preferences without divulging them to the other or measuring one's utility against the other), while at the same time ensuring subjectively envy-free allocations. In a way, this achieves a proxy for equality of welfare while respecting the view that welfare as such is incommensurable. Here, we need not compare one's utility to another, only allow them to exercise choice with respect to bundles. The only comparison conducted, originates within each individual and focuses on the different bundles observed. Comparisons are thus *within* and according to subjective valuations, and not *across* individuals.[9]

As fairness goes, this shows great promise (provided a suitable means of implementation to our context will be found): such a model deals with enlarging the 'pie' and worrying about its division in separate steps. The possibility for using efficiency analysis to maximize aggregate welfare, without sacrificing fairness in its division, lends itself to a multitude of implementations, antitrust included. Prior to delving into practical applications to our context, a number of theoretical pitfalls are first examined.

[8] Ayres and Talley observe that such procedures are inherently better when each side remains partially ignorant of the ultimate role they will play. Thus, when it is possible to conduct a type of double auction where each submits a price without knowing if this will turn out to be their buying or their selling price, countervailing forces operate to generate a 'fair' offer. They suggest splitting entitlements between potential users in order to facilitate such trade between them. See I Ayres and E Talley, 'Solomonic Bargaining: Dividing a Legal Entitlement to Facilitate Coasean Trade' (1995) 104 *Yale Law Journal* 1027.

[9] But see JE Roemer, 'Equality of resources implies equality of welfare' (1986) 101 *Quarterly Journal of Economics* 751, arguing that the two are mathematically indistinguishable. For a more general treatment, see JE Roemer, *Equality of Opportunity* (Cambridge, MA: Harvard University Press, 1998).

II. COMPLICATIONS AND EXTENSIONS

A. Dynamics of Time: Production of Goods and People

The basic framework considers the allocation of a fixed set of goods among a given number of people. In order to successfully implement the model to a realistic context, both assumptions must be relaxed, taking production of new goods as well as future generations into account.

Production introduces a problem. Following the initial equal division, players will begin using their assets, presumably in different ways. When assets are invested in production, new resources are created, benefiting some members of society more than others. This need not interfere with fairness as presumably investment options were known at the time of allocation (or at least probabilities for occurrence of such options), and preferences for investment over consumption were taken into consideration within the framework of subjective valuation employed. Those who chose consumption (or leisure) followed their own valuations, and cannot rationally be said to envy others who profited utilizing options available to all on equal terms.

All this is true where the initial allocation is indeed both fair and complete, encompassing all relevant goods. What we did not yet directly consider, though, is the question of natural endowments, including innate talents and handicaps. If these are not dealt with, dynamics over time will shift distribution of goods towards the more fortunate and able (for example, the more successful at whatever sort of production deemed worth paying for by other members of society). Some would argue that unequal endowments, in and of themselves, deem society unfair, even when society is unable to influence initial allocation.[10] Even if this extreme form of the argument is rejected, the fact that the value of goods allocated *depends on* these unequal endowments, should be taken into account. Granting differently situated people the same treatment does not absolve one of discriminatory effect, as is made clear in case law and public discussion regarding disparate impact.

If we attempt to incorporate inequality of natural endowments into the model, though, a forced labour result will occur.[11] Since we are not able to truly reallocate natural endowments, those born with superior talents would need to be taxed in

[10] This issue is reminiscent of the socialist/capitalist divide, but more recently central to the discussion of 'moral luck' in philosophy. See generally, D Statman (ed), *Moral Luck* (Albany, NY: State University of New York Press, 1993).

[11] Varian puts it more gently: 'Should we view labor time on an *individual* basis and give each agent the same amount of his individual leisure, or should we view labor time on a *social* basis and give each agent the same amount of "labor power"?' (emphasis in original); Varian, 'Equity, Envy, and Efficiency' (n 6) 75. If labour is viewed on a social basis, society has a property right in individuals' labour time, resulting in forced labour from the perspective of individuals. Compare with the discussion of forced labour in ch 3, n 29.

some way to compensate for their superiority, otherwise even equal allocation of goods would result in unequal welfare, and hence unavoidable envy. Since leisure itself may be considered part of the bundle of goods to be enjoyed, taxation cannot begin after production, but must be part of the initial bundle.[12] The result would thus be a formulation of bundles including natural endowments together with a tax on their enjoyment, so that those born without them need not envy those born lucky. The result is that positions are 'equalized', but some are taxed before they produce, thus must produce in order to pay their initial (inherited) debt. A different way of putting it would be to say that the most able are born into 'social slavery' that they must work their way out of—not a very endearing proposition.[13]

In short, a compromise must be reached. Either we agree to a forced labour result due to equalization of total utility (including endowments), or we settle for 'wealth-fairness' that equalizes asset utility while maintaining imperfections due to natural endowments.[14]

Regarding future generations, the problem is that of gifts or inheritance. Gifts are given at the owner's discretion, thus pose no problem upstream, but discriminate among the downstream beneficiaries in a way that jeopardizes both Pareto efficiency (there is no assurance of the good reaching its most efficient user) and fairness (non-recipients will envy recipients). Inheritance, again, manifests the wishes of the deceased, but jeopardizes society's interest in fairness and efficiency. Inheritance poses an especially important problem, as accumulation of wealth over time will tend to concentrate in specific families, generating growing inequalities and birthrights incompatible with fairness.[15] Envy-freeness demands that at any given time the subjective valuation of bundles is such that each weakly

[12] See HR Varian, 'Distributive Justice, Welfare Economics, and the Theory of Fairness' (1975) 4 *Philosophy and Public Affairs* 223, developing the argument only to finally prefer exclusion of endowments from the analysis rather than accept forced labour.

[13] This is reminiscent of Kurt Vonnegut's *Harrison Bergeron*, a story of a world where in the name of equality those born strong wore weights, and those born beautiful wore masks, or rubber noses. There, equality came at the expense of efficiency, as those high up were dragged down. Here, efficiency need not be sacrificed, as it is not holding the able down that the model proposes, but using their abilities. The problem, though, is that it is *society* deeming the ability worthwhile (insofar as it is worth paying for, thus the endowment generates income potential). The individual, then, is made to work off his 'unearned advantage'—even if he would have preferred not to consummate it in full.

[14] Varian prefers the latter, claiming that 'it can be shown that in general a fair allocation will *not* exist in this case' [of inequality in endowments], see Varian, 'Distributive Justice' (n 12) 243. See also EA Pazner and D Schmeidler, 'A Difficulty in the Concept of Fairness' (1974) 41 *Review of Economic Studies* 441. Dworkin considers a similar 'slavery of the talented' and attempts to solve it through an insurance mechanism. His suggestion is useful when considering the initial allocation, but fails to encompass production and dynamic effects, thus cannot help us here. See Arnsperger, 'Envy-Freeness and Distributive Justice' (n 4).

[15] Even more so if we consider the fact that inherited goods will allow recipients to enjoy economies of scale and scope, so that their initial endowment is made more valuable by combining it with inherited wealth. In such cases, benefits are supra-additive, causing the concentration of wealth issue to arise even more quickly.

prefers his own bundle to all others. If accumulation of wealth is allowed through gifts or inheritance, this ideal is compromised.

Of course, it may be argued that respecting the wishes of owners of property to grant others title (even posthumously) is just as (or more) important than maintaining an envy-free society. That is precisely Nozick's argument, which deems an allocation just if it originated in a just allocation and every shift in resources was conducted according to a just procedure.[16] The argument here is whether inheritance is a just procedure—being the exercise of the owner's discretion, or not—since it compromises the envy-free principle for future generations.

In general, the dynamics of time imply that either Pareto efficiency or envy-freeness can be preserved when production and future generations are taken into account, but not both simultaneously. The underlying problem is that individual preferences may differ from social gain, thus those best suited for one task may prefer another. If occupational choice is a basic right, the positive externalities one could create for society may be ignored and individual satisfaction maximized instead.[17] One could potentially perform life-saving surgery, yet choose to avoid medical studies and high-stress environments in favour of time spent with family or contemplative solitude. Essentially, efficiency and fairness collide, not merely in interpersonal comparisons and envy-freeness, but also regarding the question of who decides how social goods are utilized. This issue resonates with the takings analogy of antitrust considered in the previous chapter, and will be further explored in the next one.

B. Is Pareto Efficiency to be Desired?

One of the basic premises upon which very few dwell is the inherent value of a Pareto efficient allocation. Initially, who could argue with the claim that when it is possible to improve the position of at least one party, without harming any other, society should do so? Robert Sugden rose to the challenge in direct response to Varian's fairness theory.[18] Briefly stated, Sugden's critique goes as such: while it is clear that any Pareto inefficient solution could always be improved upon by a

[16] See R Nozick, 'Distributive Justice' (1973) 3 *Philosophy and Public Affairs* 45.

[17] Cappelen and Tungodden wrote a series of articles explicating this issue, focusing on tax-related methods of equalizing unequal endowments while rewarding effort and respecting occupational choice. They focus on interdependencies of individual choices, and show that allowing one to keep the marginal utility produced from investment of effort will always violate the liberal egalitarian framework. Interestingly, they assume that effort should always be rewarded, regardless of incentive effects. This result, while intuitive, is not obvious, as when individual choose to exert effort for its own sake, enjoying the process rather than the result, society might deem the utility gained reward enough. See A Cappelen and B Tungodden: 'Reward and Responsibility: How should we be Affected when others Change their Effort?' (2003) 2 *Politics, Philosophy and Economics* 191; 'Rewarding Effort' (2009) 39 *Economic Theory* 425; 'Distributive Interdependencies in Liberal Egalitarianism' (2011) 36 *Social Choice and Welfare* 35.

[18] R Sugden, 'Is Fairness Good? A Critique of Varian's Theory of Fairness' (1984) 18 *NOUS* 505.

move to a Pareto superior one, this does not imply the broader contention that any Pareto efficient allocation should always be chosen over any Pareto inefficient one. Furthermore, as Paretian theory does not allow comparisons of efficient allocations (since no efficient allocation is superior to another), choice *between them* is arbitrary, and cannot be justified on fairness grounds.

To clarify, consider an example: assume a market of two players, with one type of good, *G*, and 100 units to be divided between the players. Preferences are taken as increasing monotonously, so that where *X* and *Y* are amounts of *G*, whenever $X > Y$ all players prefer receiving *X* to receiving *Y*. Given 100 units, Allocation (45:45) is obviously a Pareto inefficient allocation, since 10 units remain undivided and Pareto superior allocations exist. Allocation (99:1) is obviously Pareto efficient, yet it is clearly not always superior to the first allocation, and some would argue that the equitable (yet inefficient) result is preferable, and a society of envy-free individuals is better to live in than one where some enjoy endowments dwarfing those of others.

Of course, for every Pareto inefficient allocation *there exists* a Pareto superior one that is preferable (such as 50:50 in our example), but since practical constraints may impede its realization, inefficient allocations are sometimes preferred and Pareto efficiency as such is not to be taken as a virtue. One may take the argument even further: if equality is an independent value, allocation (45:45) may be deemed preferable even to a Pareto superior allocation such as (55:45). This contradicts Paretian theory, as its stated assumption is that 'no one is left worse off'. The crux of Sugden's critique (though he doesn't take it this far) is that inequitable allocations are inherently unjust, thus improving only one player's bundle implicitly degrades the other's, or society at large is detrimentally affected.[19] His basic argument is thus not with the development of the envy-free criterion, but with its underlying premise that satisfaction of wants is *all* that matters (with envy being an embodiment of wants, one wanting the bundle that another has more than he wants his own).

While this critique may have merit if fairness is to be based *solely* on the envy-free principle, the economic theory of fairness here is but one of several claims to fairness criteria considered previously. Thus, we may focus the discussion at this point on envy-freeness and enjoy what benefit this theory has to add to our broader inquiry.[20]

[19] Another way of stating the same is through the language of social preferences in behavioural economics—that A's preferences include B's share as well as A's own. See generally, S DellaVigna, 'Psychology and Economics: Evidence from the Field' (2009) 47 *Journal of Economic Literature* 315. For a review of applications within game theory and an emphasis on reciprocity between individuals, see J Sobel, 'Interdependent Preferences and Reciprocity' (2005) 43 *Journal of Economic Literature* 392.

[20] Sugden's critique may be considered excessive (indeed, unfair), due to Varian's explicit admission that he has no intention of a complete ordering of alternatives, thus no comparison of fair allocations was intended. On the other hand, Varian implies that fair allocations are 'better' than unfair ones, a focal point of Sugden's critique.

C. Are Fair Allocations Fair?

An important critique of the branch of distributive justice that both Varian's and Baumol's theses rely on, is that they make improperly narrow assumptions, thus ruling out any imperfections in their analysis. Fairness, it is argued, is much more than lack of envy. Holcombe has argued that envy-freeness, while relevant for assessing some allocations, is an inappropriate criterion for assessing cases where differences in effort and investment lead to different results.[21] In short, granting equal weight to each party's envy of the other's bundle may unfairly discriminate in favour of those who did little to contribute to the creation of the goods divided.

The problem with this critique is twofold: first, it assumes a priori that a party who contributed more to the creation of a good deserves more of that good; second, it focuses on the static division problem while ignoring the dynamic aspect of 'people's capitalism' as well as the 'historical' aspect of economic fairness analysis. The first assumption is very reasonable, indeed almost obvious. Yet it is a moral statement that requires substantiation. Why is it that contributors should be rewarded more? On what presumptions does this contention lie? Previously we saw that the problem of natural endowments may bias any such analysis, so we must either accept 'natural' inequalities as fair, or equalize them ex post, thus relaxing the 'effort brings reward' principle. In essence, this principle should be the end result of a fairness criterion, rather than assuming that which is to be proven. In short, 'effort brings reward' is biased in favour of those born with more ability to exert effort, especially if it is not effort in itself that is rewarded, but some specific skill set upon which effort is exercised.[22] Which skill set is valued depends on the society into which one is born, returning us to the issues of moral luck considered above.

The second problem, of focusing on the initial static division rather than on dynamic aspects, may be ascribed to Holcombe's focus on Baumol's paper. Baumol refers to division of a set amount of goods, with the emphasis on going beyond freedom from envy, to the analysis of superfairness, ie, the surplus over an envy-free allocation. By nature of its focus, this analysis is static, ignoring the process by which such goods came into being. Other writers reviewed above, though, have offered their analysis of dynamic considerations, with explicit reference to allocation of goods produced with unequal contribution. Furthermore, the distributive justice conception within which fairness theory was developed has a historical context. Similar to Rawls' 'original position' and Nozick's 'initial just division', analysis begins at a hypothetical beginning (where equal division

[21] This argument is made by RG Holcombe in two papers: 'Applied Fairness Theory: Comment' (1983) 73 *American Economic Review* 1153 and 'Absence of Envy does not Imply Fairness' (1997) 63 *Southern Economic Journal* 797.

[22] See also R Piron, 'Fair Outcome/Fair Process' (1985) 75 *American Economic Review* 878, arguing that 'Holcombe has steered economists (inadvertently?) into a methodological morass they have tried hard and long to avoid for half a century'. Piron's difficulty is with Holcombe's shift from a predictive-positive emphasis still possible under Baumol's construct, to an imprecise ethical-normative one.

is fair), assessing the process that would maintain fairness and comparing the hypothetical results with current ones. Holcombe's critique assumes division is *after* production and investment decisions, while all writers reviewed have focused on division *before* production. It seems then, that what remains of this critique is a reminder to be careful applying fairness theory, so that initial allocation is not confused with subsequent trade and profit.

III. IMPLEMENTATION TO ANTITRUST

Can formal fairness analysis be incorporated into antitrust? Perhaps, as many of the justifications for antitrust centred on fairness claims made by the different parties to the debate, each essentially arguing for her 'fair share' of the surplus from trade, similarly to the formalized variant considered here. On the other hand, antitrust is more than achieving a fair division of cakes.

There are two reasons to apply fairness formalization analysis to our antitrust concerns. The first is striving for completeness of discussion. Just as we examined different moral and political philosophies in order to offer a 'round' assessment of the fairness claims in the antitrust literature, so is this unique strand examined in order to achieve implementation. Formalization of fairness offers a distinct outlook applicable to a wide variety of subjects, and while antitrust has never yet been so assessed, this may be the perfect opportunity. Second, and even more important, the focus of most of the fairness analyses in antitrust is on wealth transfers. As explained above, the wealth transfer argument arises when the surplus created by trade is divided by the relative bargaining power of the trading parties. Monopoly power distorts the division expected in competitive markets, so that monopolists are able to divert most of the surplus to themselves, 'cheating' the consumers out of their fair share. This is exactly the type of problem upon which proponents of formalization of fairness built their analysis. There, we considered a good to be divided between two or more parties in a manner barring envy, and here we consider the division of a good (the surplus) between the parties to trade, and speak of one party 'grabbing' more than his fair share. Previously, we saw this surplus as the crux of the wealth transfer argument, and asked whether consumers could claim a property right to a certain part thereof in order to substantiate their claim to fairness-based protection. Perhaps our failure there may be corrected here.

Consider the following argument: the surplus created by trade is similar to the allocation problem dealt with above. If we apply the envy-freeness principle, total welfare should be divided between producer and consumer in a manner which satisfies the preferences of both sides, so that neither would exchange her surplus for the other's. There are two basic reasons for the applicability of this principle:

1. The surplus is by definition created by both sides to the trade, as none would be created unilaterally. Thus it is similar to the initial allocation problem considered above where no side holds an a priori advantage.

2. In this manner we substantiate the common intuition of each side having a right to a part of the surplus, with the added benefit of a preliminary distribution between them (to be developed below).

How can the theoretical principle developed above to be applied to real life antitrust? Since it is impossible to assess the subjective preferences of each party to each trade, it is clear that we cannot assure individual envy-freeness on the part of all involved. What we can do, though, is assess the traits common to individuals on each side, and use them as an imprecise guideline, though obviously better than none at all. The relevant traits will not be preferences of the subjective type, impossible to generalize, but the relative contributions to production and preferences revealed through trade itself.

There remains a question regarding using the distribution expected from unfettered competition as a baseline. If this is the ideal against which we compare, any shift in distribution would give cause to the offended party to claim protection, as he has been treated unfairly. This, though, would be to assume that which is to be proven. Why should competitive distribution be considered fair? Why should anyone be entitled to claim it as a given right? In chapter three we assessed this claim independently and dismissed it, thus now it shall either be independently justified, as a *result* of the process rather than assumption.

The question of allocation of total welfare between the parties to trade may be assessed through revealed preferences. Obviously, both sides prefer trade to retaining their income, otherwise no trade would occur. Thus, allowing free trade is in any case a move towards a Pareto superior position, regardless of previous conditions. Pareto efficiency can be said to exist in any case where trade is allowed but no longer carried out, since each product has reached its most efficient user. Of course, several Pareto efficient equilibria exist, depending on initial allocations and even within each one. Any market failure can be analyzed in two manners: either as an inhibition on Pareto efficiency (preventing superior moves), or as a given factor of reality, existing constraints on the model. The second interpretation allows for realizing (a diluted form of) Pareto efficiency even in face of market failure, as we see no superior moves *granted existing conditions*. The difference between them is perhaps semantic, or one of definition—similar to the difference between stressing theoretical ideals or practical possibilities. Deciding which factors should be taken as given and which should be seen as obstacles to be overcome is the connection between model and reality, and the task of both theorist and practitioner.

Can we argue for correction of market failures in the name of Pareto efficiency? Not necessarily. Market failure may inhibit aggregate efficiency, but still grant one party an advantage, absent in perfect competition, that will be claimed as 'his' and worthy of protection. For example, informational asymmetries may preclude some efficient transactions, but one party may exploit them to raise her profit from existing transactions while claiming that they deserve the profit no less than the other party deserves the information they now lack. Similarly, a monopolist would hardly support correcting market failures that result in the loss of her monopoly. Furthermore, in the presence of multiple market failures, correction of some but not all imperfections will lead to second-best problems, so that even aggregate efficiency is not necessarily maximized by imperfect intervention.[23]

Returning to envy-freeness analysis, can we argue for a general consumer/producer division that would preclude envy? Here we need to distinguish between analysis of specific trades and analysis of the market as a whole. When each specific trade is considered in itself, the focus is on the surplus created alone, but when we broaden our analysis to the market as a whole, additional matters are considered. It is quite obvious that envy-freeness cannot be deduced for specific trades. Even if we get beyond the different subjective preferences present, why should is one side assumed to prefer his own surplus to the other's? Since surplus is assumed to be monetary (or at least money equivalent, as a basic premise allowing numerical analysis), the only envy-free distribution would be an equal one. It is easily shown that equal distribution of welfare is not the standard (or even common) even under perfect competition. Indeed, it would be impossible when taking into account the multiple buyers and sellers of each product. Competition distributes welfare according to subjective and individual factors, such as preferences (for example, consumer surplus), cost structures (for example, marginal cost for individual producers) and the like.[24]

The result is that just about any trade analyzed will show that different consumers come out with different results, even if they all bought the same product and paid the same price! Obviously, the same is true of the different producers as well.[25] Furthermore, even if we move to aggregate analysis of consumers as a group versus producers as a group, total welfare is divided according to case-specific supply and demand schedules, meaning that each group's relative part fluctuates with market characteristics. It seems that envy-freeness, especially when monetarily leading to equality, is not at all a natural phenomenon.

When we look at the broader market, though, other factors aside from price versus cost/enjoyment are relevant. The choices made prior to production and trade are relevant as well. A product's existence is not self-evident, but the result

[23] See ch 2, n 28 and accompanying text. I took on this issue in more detail in A Ayal, 'Musings on the Importance of Economic and Legal Analysis' in D Hakker and N Ziv (eds), *Law, Society, and Culture: Does Law Matter?* (Tel Aviv: Tel Aviv University Press, 2010).

[24] It serves well to remember here, that even the standard textbook model of perfect competition grants each consumer and each producer a different surplus, depending on each side's elasticities. Equality of total consumer surplus with total producer surplus is a very rare, knife-edge, result. It will occur when consumers are all identical, producers are all identical and consumers' preferences generate demand schedules that are the exact mirror-image of producers' costs—not a likely occurrence.

[25] This is easily shown graphically, relying on Figure 1 in ch 2. When consumers value the good differently, but it is sold at an identical unit price, each consumer comes out with a different surplus from the same trade. This is shown in Figure 1 by the vertical distance between the demand schedule and price, a distance that shrinks as we move to the right, from consumers very lucky to have found such a low price to those just marginally preferring purchase to non-purchase. Similarly for producers, with respect to their cost of production which determines the supply schedule.

of a producer making a conscious choice to invest the necessary funds, effort and innovative creativity, so that a product is realized from potential to reality. Incorporating these choices is possible through bundling of investment and consumption choices, together with labour/leisure decisions. Thus, any production is the result of multiple choices bundled together, that consumers comparing their lot to that of the relevant producer must consider in their entirety. Put simply, determining a consumer's envy would be based not on his willingness to exchange *surplus* with the producer, but exchange *places* with him—including time/effort/money expenditures.

In order to proceed with application of the envy-freeness criterion to antitrust, where consumers as well as producers are both numerous and heterogeneous, we need to differentiate between cases where markets are perfectly competitive (a theoretical benchmark rather than anticipated reality), and those where market failures exist.

A. Perfectly Competitive Markets

In a perfectly competitive market, opportunities are assumed to be available to all on equal terms. Ideally, this precludes envy, since similarly to the above formulation of the standard any individual could have chosen to produce rather than consume (or balance both), essentially switching places with the producer in question. Since labour specialization is aggregately efficient (allowing for economies of scale, learning-by-doing and the like), and no barriers or constraints on choice are assumed to exist, specialization is also Pareto efficient. Envy will thus occur only where initial allocation is unequal, granting an advantage to some at choosing their place in society, and possibly causing others envy.[26]

Inequality of initial allocation can be due to one of two causes. Either the problem of natural endowments returned to haunt us, or the entire equal allocation procedure developed above was not implemented. In the case of endowments, we saw that we are forced to make a difficult choice: compensating for endowments or ignoring their inequality. In the first case, we reach a forced labour result, and in the second, we accept a level of unfairness as unavoidable, as a price for living in an imperfect world. Similarly, if the entire equal allocation principle is rejected (or even the 'no gifts/no inheritance' principle Varian argued for), inequality is accepted as 'natural' and envy-freeness will never be complete.

With surplus division, the conclusion is similar: whatever inequalities remain prior to trade will affect the final result. Envy of the other party's surplus should be subject to the total bundle examination, but some envy will still remain (ie, some

[26] The test of *equality* of initial allocation rather than its *fairness* is based on the finding that fair but unequal initial allocations are unstable over subsequent trade, ie lead to *unfair* bundles. See Feldman and Kirman (n 6).

will want to 'trade places' with others). One may require commercial law to correct the distribution of surplus, but this seems to me misguided. First, the question of surplus is merely one of many factors affected by initial inequality. Correcting the symptom rather than the source again introduces second-best problems. It may bias other factors in unpredictable ways, resulting in either over-compensation or under-compensation, with no available means for approximation of the result. Second, the assumed inequality prevents any generalization as to the positions of the different parties. Even if we conclude that compensation is in order, and a certain surplus division is the correct method to achieve it, implementation would be impossible where different consumers purchase at the same price, each with his own background ('the hand he was dealt' during the initial allocation) and each with distinct subjective preferences leading to different levels of consumer surplus *at the same price*. The same, of course, goes for producers with different costs structures, etc. This is so, even before we deal with the problem of producing firms with multiple stakeholders, each deserving special consideration due to differing circumstances: in short, a nightmare of multiplicity impossible to tackle here.

We may conclude that where markets are perfectly competitive, fairness dictates allowing any trade by which a person improves her position (by definition, any trade she consented to), with initial allocation inequalities either accepted as inevitable, or demanding compensation of the sort best dealt with by more discriminating means than mere surplus division.[27]

B. Market Failures

Where market failures exist, we cannot assume equal opportunities or complete freedom of trade. Here, it may very well be that one party envies not only the surplus that another received in a specific trade, but would gladly trade places altogether. Equality of initial allocation aside, in the presence of market failure, trade may enhance the position of one at the expense of the other. In the case of monopoly, this means that market imperfections allow for extraction of excessive profits from consumers, justifying their envy of the monopolist's position, as well as limiting entry, justifying competitor envy.

The question to be addressed is whether such envy justifies intervention based on fairness protection of consumers. This turns out to depend on the source of market failure, as will be clarified through the example of barriers to entry:

1. *Barriers to entry exist independently of the monopolist.* In this case, the monopolist benefits from outside circumstances, similar to those 'born lucky' considered before, who benefit from their superior natural endowments. If there we accepted inequality as inevitable and avoided forced labour, why should we do any

[27] Eg, taxing the lucky or subsidizing the unlucky (luck meaning any unearned benefit considered), with trade to be carried out consensually thereafter.

different here? Limiting monopolists' right to trade on their own terms constrains their right to property and freedom of contract. What justifies such constraints? Envy of consumers (or other producers, unable to enter the lucrative market) granted, it is aimed not at the profit itself, but at the superior position granted to the monopolist by pre-existing market imperfections. True, the monopolist cannot argue to have *deserved* market power and its benefits, but this is true of anyone born smarter, stronger or with an advantage in any other trait considered beneficial in their society. The same goes for luck in being born into a wealthy family, if no limitations on gifts and inheritance are accepted. True, ex post equalization of positions may be argued for, but since our focus here is on envy, such equalization should be conducted in reference to specific individuals wishing to switch places, ie, with focus on total bundles. A focused attack on monopolists' profit through antitrust law ignores this total bundle perspective. While other fairness conceptions may discriminate enough to allow correction of one symptom separately from other considerations, envy-freeness analyzed here does not. In essence, the argument here is similar to the social justice argument raised before, that if some individuals deserve protection, they should be protected without 'taking along' others not entitled to the same protection.

2. *The monopolist creates or maintains barriers to entry.* In this case, the monopolist cannot argue that inequality is exogenous or similar to other inevitable inequalities. Where the monopolist actively precludes others from doing their best to switch places (or at least 'join the party'), he maintains positions generating envy beyond initial allocation. Dissimilarly from exogenous effects, here the monopolist alone is responsible for creating unfairness, and limiting his actions will have no forced labour effect. Thus, granted that envy-freeness is deemed a worthy value, intervention is justified.

The problem, as always, is in the detail. What constitutes 'creating' barriers to entry? How are we to treat predatory pricing, predatory innovation, vaporware? Is exploiting informational asymmetries a legitimate enjoyment of allocative inequality, or is it malicious and unfair? How about signalling to competitors through large investments in sunk costs? While the principle distinguishing wilful distortion of competition from enjoying benefits granted exogenously may be clear, implementation is far from clear.

C. An Alternative Conception of Surplus

Up to now we considered surplus as a good to be divided between consumer and producer, and focused on fairness in division. This was based on the surplus belonging initially to no one, as only trade brought it into existence. An alternative argument could be that the surplus never really exists as a good to be divided, since the very trade creating it is the one dividing it as well. Consider a seller and a buyer negotiating a sale. At no point do they reach an agreement to go through with the sale, 'with price to be determined later'.[28] Determining the price is an essential part of the sale itself, and trade will proceed only if both parties are satisfied by it. Thus, once surplus is created, *it has already been divided* to the satisfaction of all involved (otherwise they would not consent). Going back to the question of division of surplus now assumes it to be an independent reality, thus accepting the parties' decision to produce and trade, but ignoring their decision as to price. The producer may argue that this is akin to forced labour, since his consent to production and trade was conditioned on price. Changing price now (necessarily a part of redistributing the surplus) rescinds his consent on both matters, thus trade cannot be said to be voluntary.

A possible objection is that if antitrust law is in place *prior* to production, both sides are aware of its limitation ex ante, basically trading under a known regime constraining certain surplus divisions. Thus, engaging in production was a choice made freely, knowing full well the legal limitations constraining a firm with market power. This goes back to our implied consent argument assessed earlier.[29] Our conclusion there, applicable here as well, was that even if we ignore the problem of antitrust law retroactively changing producer expectations in some cases, advance knowledge is not akin to consent (especially where no viable options for exit from the legal regime exist), and therefore intervention cannot automatically be justified. Just as a thief does not gain immunity if his victim had advance knowledge (but no chance at avoiding the theft other than forgoing property in advance), so we require an independent justification for antitrust intervention (other than it being 'known in advance'), if we wish to call it 'fair'.

D. Conclusion

What is the bottom line regarding implementation of the formalization of fairness analysis? It seems that the hope for a quantitative criterion defining exact surplus divisions is quite a bit on the optimistic (not to say naïve) side, though no one could realistically expect a clear-cut answer to such a long-standing question in the first place. What we have witnessed, though, is that fairness analysis from a seemingly unrelated angle has much in common with our more well known analysis of fairness claims in antitrust. In both cases we saw that preliminary definitions of what constitute independent values determine much of the end result. If we decide that equality is a relevant criteria, we must then choose how far back to go in order to say what an 'equal division' really means.

[28] I focus on price for simplicity alone, as the clearest among the terms of trade. What is written here about price could easily be applied to issues of bundling, refusals to deal and other issues in which monopolists are constrained. The question of monopoly pricing as an independent issue is dealt with differently in the US and within the European Community; see ch 2.

[29] See ch 3, section I.B.iv.

The wealth transfer argument, so commonplace in antitrust scholarship, was shown to rely on conceptions of equal treatment of different consumers and of consumers in relation to the producers they contract with. When examining surplus as the focal point of discussion we saw that the standard argument raised on behalf of consumers is not an independent one, but must be distinguished according to the source of market failures. This is important for two reasons. The first is that different scenarios of how monopoly arose have special bearing on what treatment can be justified, and whether intervention in the division of surplus is warranted. The comparison of exogenously determined market failures to unequal initial allocation of resources is especially telling. If exterior market failures are akin to natural endowments, an argument for state intervention through antitrust law must withstand scrutiny as to its philosophical implications, and not merely its treatment of monopolists. We have become accustomed to regulation of monopolies, but not many of antitrust's supporters would so easily make the argument in support of taxing those born lucky in order to equate starting positions (and thus surplus attained) of different members of society.[30]

Even Varian's more palatable version of 'no gifts/no inheritance' as restricting society's growing inequality and unfairness, is unlikely to gain as many supporters as antitrust law has. Yet we have shown that coherence demands precisely such an extension of the same arguments made on behalf of antitrust law—at least in cases where market failures are not the result of the monopolist's own doing.

The second reason the formalization analysis is especially illuminating for antitrust is that the focus is moved towards the monopolist's involvement in 'cheating' the consumers out of their supposedly fair share. If we reject the demands of following strong equality laid out above, intervention is warranted only in cases of specific actions taken by monopolists in order to secure market power by creating market failures. This moves our analysis from the objective focal point of assessing market characteristics and relative market power, to specific cases and means employed by the relevant players. Thus, emphasis will be on the individual (rather than aggregate) effects of suspect business practices. This is very much in tune with the focus on fairness claims in general, and the separation of aggregate social interests from individual fairness claims in particular. This focus intuitively follows existing constitutional doctrine, and is thus in accord with our discussion above. This is exactly what should be kept in mind while developing the constitutional standard for balancing among competing claims, facilitating the discussion below.

[30] See discussion at ch 3, n 29 and ch 4, n 15.

7

The 'Clear and Present Danger' for Antitrust

Our foray into constitutional discourse and the analysis of fairness allows a distinctive purview from which to assess not just antitrust policy, but the often unstated philosophy which underlies it. In this chapter I hope to show that what makes sense in a broad perspective, applies to antitrust as well, and answer arguments which might be brought against the implementation of constitutional standards to the context of antitrust. I begin with relevant standards applying to conflicts of rights, show their application to the antitrust debate and assess critique and counter-arguments that might be raised. While implementation to current antitrust policy is discussed, specific cases are not, as my purpose here is to present the guiding principle and its overarching justifications. Where specific cases are concerned, 'the devil is in the detail' and context-specific analysis is necessary to argue for or against any court decision. Nonetheless, general trends can still be observed and commented on. Antitrust policy stems from assumptions of right and wrong and current consensus regarding (often implicit) antitrust philosophy ignores monopolists as independent bearers of rights. As shown above, those arguing for consumers' rights forget that these conflict with similar rights of monopolists, and those promoting an efficiency-enhancing antitrust policy effectively claim that public benefit supersedes the private—justifying regulatory takings without just compensation. Competition as a social process, on the other hand, has been relegated from a basic principle justifying the limitation of economic power, to a proxy position presumed to enhance efficiency. As shown above, competition is more than an economic-growth-inducing device: it reflects social values that underlie democratic ideals and promote individuality and self-expression.

My hope is that this chapter brings the point home—if we are to consider ourselves members of a just society, we must continuously balance the conflicting rights and social interests. If we wish for legislators and judges to apply a balancing test, we would be wise to employ one that is both familiar, and clearly delineates the rights and interests to be included. The governing standard must be based on the importance of the rights to be assessed, as well as the state's ability and obligation to intervene when necessary. Since it is a standard (rather than rule) we move towards, easy answers are not expected—it is the continuous balancing act that is paramount to ensuring a just process, and neither monopolists nor consumers (nor aggregate efficiency) are entitled to perfect protection.

I. PROTECTING MONOPOLISTS' MARKET ACCESS: THE LOGICAL FALLACY ARGUMENT

As shown above, justifications for state action to limit monopolistic practices are concerned stem from two types of argument: those of fairness as an individual right (of monopoly's victims) and those concerning aggregate benefits (societal goals, such as efficiency or the importance of the competitive process). Different arguments within the same societal goal (for example, competing claims as to the efficiency of relevant business practices) can be 'horizontally' compared (ideally, quantitatively) to reach relatively clear-cut conclusions. Obviously, 'clear-cut' conclusions are a theoretical ideal, not always achievable in practice. Economists of antitrust are very familiar with competing models as well as different empirical methods, and controversy over results is unavoidable. In these cases, though, agreement exists as to the *values sought* and the costs and benefits to be assessed—even if human limitations prevent perfect and unambiguous implementation.

Competing societal goals can be either lexically ordered (always preferring one over the other), or relatively weighted (granting them initial standing, though allowing for differences in relative importance). In any case, it is *society* which decides to accept a stated price in order to achieve a stated benefit. Even allowing for indeterminacy due to possible mistakes or professional disagreement (for example, would it be economically preferable to ignore predation altogether?), conceptually a 'correct' answer looms ahead, waiting to be discovered.[1]

Fairness arguments, on the other hand, are more problematic. Even assuming we are able to discern the multiple interests affected, 'horizontal' comparison is impossible, not only in practice, but even in theory—due to the problematic nature of interpersonal comparisons of utility and the issue of incommensurable rights. As seen above, both sides claim rights based on freedom of contract and property, both show potential harm to be visited upon them if their claims are ignored and both turn to basic constitutional models to prove their claim: the monopolists to protection from state tyranny, and their victims to protection from economic subjugation.

But is it correct to categorize our context as one of state interference with individual rights? At first glance, both sides show that their rights have been infringed upon, but while monopoly's victims argue for their right to participate in the marketplace, monopolists actually claim a different right. Framing monopoly

[1] Not all would agree. See, eg, WA Galston, *Liberal Pluralism: The Implications of Value Pluralism for Political Theory and Practice* (Cambridge: Cambridge University Press, 2002) 5: 'there is no common measure of value for all goods, which are qualitatively heterogeneous ... but, rather, a range of public goods and virtues the relative importance of which will depend on particular circumstances'. Some go further, to blame the worst social ills on the quest for a 'right' answer. See I Berlin, *Two Concepts of Liberty* (Oxford: Oxford University Press, 1958) 52: 'One belief, more than any other, is responsible for the slaughter of individuals on the altars of the great historical ideals ... the belief that somewhere, in the past of in the future, in divine revelation or in the mind of an individual thinker ... there is a final solution'.

as an extension of the freedom to trade ignores the fact that *underlying such a freedom* is an assumption of free markets. The right to trade means little when markets are non-existent. Thus, such a right presupposes a market where each party is able to choose whether or not to enter into transactions, and is the sole judge of their own welfare. In other words, claiming a right to free trade relies on free markets in which to trade, thus a competitive market structure is not just an interest claimed by society at large or those vying for antitrust protection, but is the basis of the monopolists' claim as well.

Framed in this context, the monopolist arguing for freedom from state interference is basing his claim on the very free market which he intends to destroy (or at least subvert) once his 'freedom' has been granted. Such a claim, then, is not merely for participation in the market (the claim raised on behalf of his victims and critically assessed in chapter three), but a right to *destroy* the very basis of the freedom claimed. Allowing monopolists to go unhindered will allow manipulation of market processes so that these can no longer support freedom of any kind (except the formal freedom to choose whether or not to enter into a transaction, typical of the Lochner era). Perhaps, then, the claim monopolists make should be categorized not as 'freedom of contract' but as a right to 'market manipulation'.

Logically, it seems problematic to allow a player reliance on terminology and arguments based on free markets, when actually claiming a right to destroy or manipulate them. 'Choose', we might say, 'either to argue from within the system while accepting its premises, or from without—but then find other means to substantiate your argument'.

II. LOGICAL FALLACY OR BALANCING ACT? TRADE AND SPEECH COMPARED

In order to assess the issue of monopolists claiming protection based on principles stemming from the very market they aim to subvert, we turn to a seemingly unrelated issue, though one where a similar problem arises: the debate over freedom of expression and the extent of its protection. There, individuals and groups claim protection for their right to promulgate their views, but one claim in particular stands out: the protection of those arguing against democracy itself. Such groups are usually small minorities within society (we hope), thus may be under constant threat of harm by intolerant majorities. Without protection of their right to free speech, the majority would often see their ideas as unattractive and dangerous, thus silence them using a variety of legal (and sometimes illegal) means.

Similarly to the (actual or potential) monopolist claiming protection from interference with his right to trade as he pleases, the anti-democratic group claims protection from interference with its right to free speech. Similarly to the monopolist considered above, there are those who would dismiss such claims, arguing that one cannot use democracy against itself, or use free speech in order to promulgate views against its very basis. Indeed, Justice Holmes noted precisely this conundrum when claims were made that the Sherman Act be held unconstitutional due to its infringement on the freedom of contract of those wishing to enter unlawful combinations: 'It is out of the very right to make what contracts one chooses, so strenuously advocated by Bentham, that combinations have arisen which restrict the very freedom that Bentham sought to attain, and which even might menace the authority of the State'.[2]

Nonetheless, the current consensus in constitutional debate is that freedom of expression is so important a right, that even those opposed to it deserve its protection.[3] This is not to say that *every* speech is automatically allowed. Some limitations are always necessary since freedom of speech, however important, cannot justify all harms that might result from its exercise. The important point for our context is that even when anti-democratic groups threaten democracy itself, this is not enough to *automatically* void their claim to free speech. In order to justify limitation of their right, a balancing test is performed between the right to free speech on one hand, and the interest or right threatened by the relevant expression on the other.

Legal history has seen several balancing tests and governing doctrines come and go, from the obvious and omnipotent right of a sovereign to determine the content of public expression, through assessments of relative harm such as the 'harmful tendency' test, or the more stringent 'clear and present danger' standard. The standard affording least respect to free expression is that of sovereign determination, popular in times when modern democratic government was still unforeseen. Up to the late seventeenth century, printing in England was subject to such restraints, and all manuscripts had to pass through a licensor and receive a 'stamp of approval' prior to print.[4] This system obviously led to strict content-based censorship, usually by the publisher himself, unwilling to risk a conflict which might cost him his licence. Moving a bit further up the road of history, we see a great deal of respect afforded to free speech, first in philosophical writings of the liberally inclined, and later in statutes and legal opinions.[5] In the US, 'freedom of the press' became one of the better known slogans of revolutionary thought, culminating in the First Amendment to the Federal Constitution. Despite this, actual protection of such freedom in the courts was less clear, as political sentiments and the need for 'social unity' sometimes dominated philosophical ideals.[6] Our discussion here will draw not on the history of speech protecting, but on

[2] *Carroll v Greenwich Insurance Co*, 199 US 401, 410 (1905).

[3] The extreme case obviously being *Village of Skokie v National Socialist Party of America* [1978] 69 Ill 2d 605, 373 NE 2nd 21.

[4] See JO McGinnis, 'The Once and Future Property-Based Vision of the First Amendment' (1996) 63 *University of Chicago Law Review* 49; WT Mayton, 'The Illegitimacy of the Public Interest Standard at the FCC' (1989) 38 *Emory Law Journal* 715, 720–27.

[5] See, eg, JS Mill, *On Liberty* (London: JW Parker & Sons, 1859) ch 2—expounding what will later become a focal point for legal and popular discussion of freedom of speech. It should be noted, though, that Mill is more noted for exposition of the benefits accruing *to society* from respecting freedom of speech, although he also urged respect of the individual on his own account.

[6] See LH Tribe, *Constitutional Choices* (Cambridge, MA: Harvard University Press, 1985) 189–90.

its methodology. Once a right is recognized as important, the focus turns to the appropriate *level* of protection, as witnessed by the different balancing tests employed over time. Since constitutional discourse over freedom of speech differs considerably from what we have become accustomed to regarding the rights to property and contract underlying my thesis, I begin with comparisons between the two as to their applicability in the antitrust debate, and then consider a variety of objections and counter-claims that could be made.

III. THE BALANCING TEST: FREE SPEECH AS A GUIDING FORCE

Different standards have been proposed over the years as guides for constitutional limitations on state infringement of individual rights and private interests. The common thread binding all these standards is their causal determination, ie, requiring some level of harm expected from the specific action examined by the court, and focusing on the level of probability that this harm will in fact occur. The *choice between standards* depends on comparing the values involved—how important the individual right claimed is versus the severity of harm expected, to society or individuals therein.

Perhaps one of the most illuminating aspects is in what all these tests (as well as their discussion and exposition by the courts) *do not do*: the standards demand determination of the harms that the specific expression might cause, but they purport to ignore its specific benefits, relying instead on a general assumption of the right's importance. Thus, a court will generally consider all speech as valuable, to be limited only if the specific case warrants it due to specific potential harms, but the harm to be caused will be balanced against the *generally accepted value* of speech, rather than the specific value of the particular speech being limited in this case.

This type of one-sided causal examination seems strange at first glance. If the purpose of a balancing test is to examine whether the harm threatened by allowing some expression is great enough to justify its limitation; why not go all the way towards utilitarian balancing, by weighing all potential costs and benefits? Moving to a fully-fledged cost-benefit analysis of each challenged expression as it reaches the courts, has both advantages and disadvantages.[7] On the upside, it would allow for more exact inspection of the specific expression's perceived effects, and for case-specific judicial determination. Thus, an expression with potential for significant social benefits would be limited only in cases of high probability of harm, whereas expressions of little social value might be limited with less circumspection.

[7] The 'cost/benefit' terminology need not require a focus on economic aspects. Just as the harms examined may be of different types, so can the positive implications accruing from the expression be multivariate. Both 'costs' and 'benefits' ideally include all relevant implications, whether of social or individual focus and whether or not measurable in economic terms.

The downside of such a specific expression analysis is that if a court must determine an expression's social value, the entire doctrine of speech as *inherently valuable* and worthy of protection might be endangered. The most important cases are precisely those where the majority inhibits minority opinion, not only due to conflicting opinions, but due to lack of respect for the content of another's opinion in the first place. In other words, in a society where a strong consensus exists on a certain issue, respect of pluralism and belief in the inherent value of fierce public debate might suffer. Such a dynamic is apparent in the fluctuations in free speech protection by American courts in times of turmoil. Especially when there was fear for the very existence of the Union, balancing tests were considerably relaxed, in practice if not in name. Notable occurrences include the Sedition Act 1798, limitation of anti-war expression during the First World War and the unfortunate 'McCarthy' era, where fear of communist influence caused public acceptance of restrictions on political expression, both real and imaginary.[8]

Requiring, or even allowing, judges to weigh potential benefits versus potential harms of the specific expression litigated may grant them too wide a discretion resulting in repression of minority opinion, either due to judges' human fallibility (inadvertently allowing personal opinion to influence assessment), or due to more conscious manipulation.

More generally, protection of speech should not rely on the case-specific benefits, since the main contribution of free speech is of a general character. The benefit of allowing an expression (or striking down its statutory limitation), is not in the actions or ideas that this expression seeks to promote, but in the fostering of popular and political debate in society—the famous 'marketplace of ideas'.[9] Limiting expression, even one of spurious nature, sends us down the 'slippery slope' of content-based censorship and befits totalitarian regimes more than the democratic ideal we strive for. While allowing any and all expression to go unhindered is a practical impossibility, the 'marketplace' view assumes that every single case of free expression practised contributes (indirectly perhaps) to a social good, thus any case of state intervention causes a clear yet indeterminate harm. This harm caused by limitation of speech must be justified by a balancing test that requires one form or another of causal proof that a greater harm is thus averted. Put simply, the benefits of speech are axiomatic, thus judicial standards need only examine its harms, choosing an appropriate balancing test based on the inherent worth of expression per se, and perhaps categories of expression as a 'sliding-scale' of importance (for example, affording political expression more protection than artistic or commercial).

[8] See JE Nowak and RD Rotunda, *Constitutional Law*, 6th edn (St Paul, MN: West Publishing, 2000) 1084–87.

[9] As Justice Holmes stated in *Abrams v US*, 250 US 616, 40 S Ct 17 (1919): 'The best test of truth is the power of thought to get itself accepted in the competition of the market place'. For discussion of the metaphor and harsh critique of its use, see S Ingber, 'The Marketplace of Ideas: a Legitimizing Myth' (1984) *Duke Law Journal* 1. See fns 1–2 therein for references to scholarly and judicial use of the term.

Similarly within antitrust, freely practised trade (difficult as that may be to define) creates the marketplace in which competition thrives, and monopoly is seen as constricting that freedom, limiting the rights of those wishing to buy or sell in the competitive market. For monopolists to argue for *their* freedom of trade is like the anti-free-speech party' arguing that state intervention limits their political expression; hence the comparison with the *Skokie* case in chapter five.

When choosing which standard to apply to antitrust, it is instructive to examine the evolution over time and competition between standards in the arena of speech. Early First Amendment jurisprudence contrasted two main standards: 'harmful tendency' versus 'clear and present danger'. The latter was first introduced in 1919 by Justice Holmes, and only gradually made its way into mainstream judicial terminology.[10] Even when finally accepted, the test was restricted in line with political developments, so that while the standard was formally retained, its content was severely abridged.[11] While the 'harmful tendency' standard seems more permissive of state intervention, there is little to distinguish it from some of the uses made of 'clear and present danger'. As one scholar has noted, 'this is simply the remote bad tendency test dressed in modern style'.[12]

It seems then, that balancing tests in and of themselves offer meagre true security to the rights they aim to protect. This is due both to courts' tendency to move back and forth between competing standards, and to the simple fact that even when literally using the same standard, the vagueness of its terms allows judges wide discretion in reaching what they see as 'the right decision', painting it in colours befitting the generally accepted rule. Such flexibility may cause exasperation with the whole endeavour of defining an appropriate standard in the first place, but I think the effort is well worth our while. In law, words are not merely tools, but the very basis of analysis.

While jurisprudence is far from an exact science, formulating a balancing test is the first step to achieving appropriate protection of important interests, and allowing for implementation that considers all relevant factors. Individual applications of any given test may indeed vary, but framing the debate within a clearly delineated verbal model adds expressive content to the law, guiding future courts to take heed of all the relevant perspectives. Put simply, discretion always exists, but verbal models impose at least some constraints on their users, and often more

[10] The original case was *Schenck v US*, 249 US 49, 39 S Ct 247 (1919), though it must be noted that despite the fact that Holmes wrote for the court, the 'clear and present danger' standard was his alone, with others agreeing to the ruling and not its justification. In *Abrams v US*, 250 US 616, 40 S Ct 17 (1919), Holmes elaborated on his test, while dissenting from majority opinion. His test was finally accepted in majority opinion only in *Whitney v California*, 274 US 357, 47 S Ct 641 (1927).

[11] In what is now known as the Vinson–Hand test, these two justices used the same words but stated that where danger is great, even remote possibilities might justify limiting speech; *Dennis v US*, 341 US 494, 71 S Ct 857 (1951).

[12] See MM Sapiro, *Freedom of Speech: The Supreme Court and Judicial Review* (Englewood Cliffs, NJ: Prentice Hall, 1966) 65, referring to the Vinson–Hand reformulation of 'clear and present danger'.

than just 'some'. Words may be manipulated, yet they offer guidance and judges (usually) take them seriously.[13]

The freedom of speech debate is illuminating, since balancing tests were developed therein in accordance not only with the *importance* of the relevant interests, but also based on courts' inherent suspicion of politicians limiting speech. Since speech may ultimately be used to bring a particular administration down from power, those in power at any present time are understandably inclined to hinder speech detrimental to them. Judges, then, correctly deem state intervention suspect, subjecting it to careful scrutiny. Of course, courts themselves are not immune from the influence of passing political and social tides, so at times the wording of a balancing test is all that stands to protect (albeit imperfectly so) the bearer of a right that populist conceptions would gladly limit.[14]

The 'danger' referred to in the *clear and present danger* standard does not specify its source, nor does it specify those who might be endangered. These are criteria left to legislators, enforcement agencies and ultimately the courts, to 'fill in' as necessary. While speech is important, other rights are as well, so that limiting speech in order to avoid danger to life or property is sometimes necessary. Perhaps the most common example is that one cannot shout 'fire' in a crowded theatre, as the physical harm potentially caused by the stampede outweighs the protection of speech in that context.

Speech is limited in much less life-threatening contexts as well. Consider the extent of protection granted to flag burning, pornography and cryptography. One is undoubtedly a method of expressing discontent with political reality, but perhaps causing emotional grief and harm to national solidarity that cannot be discounted. Another is less clearly 'speech' in the normal sense of the word, definitely not political in nature (except for the very few using sexual imagery to argue for social change). Pornography is used for personal gratification, yet perhaps harming individuals and society at large by debasing women and men as sex objects to be used and discarded at will. The last is not really 'speech' in its expressive meaning (except for the very few mathematicians who create it and find artistic beauty in its complexity). Cryptography is hailed as a vehicle for allowing speech

[13] See DAJ Richards, *Foundations of American Constitutionalism* (New York: Oxford University Press, 1989) 188, using a similar framework to argue the superiority of 'clear and present danger' over the 'ill tendency' test.

[14] See JH Ely, *On Constitutional Ground* (Princeton, NJ: Princeton University Press, 1996) 183–84. Ely proposes that the more technical the test, the less fear there is of administrative manipulation, preferring that harms not be examined at all. See also CR Sunstein, *The Partial Constitution* (Cambridge, MA: Harvard University Press, 1993) arguing for a two-tier test, granting strict protection of political expression similar to Ely's proposal, while relegating non-political expression to less stringent standards. This process-oriented view, of course, is not without detractors. There are those who argue that the very attempt at process-determined judicial intervention is a myth, and substantive, or political, considerations are present in any case. See RM Dworkin, *A Matter of Principle* (Cambridge, MA: Harvard University Press, 1985) 57–65 (interestingly enough, there he also argues with the same Ely, though as to a different matter). Finally, this is reminiscent of Daniel Crane's argument regarding antitrust, in favour of technocratic rather than substantive application; see ch 4, n 12 and related discussion.

unhindered by governmental 'snooping', yet at the same time allowing those who most threaten democracy to coordinate mass murder undisturbed. 'Speech' has been expanded to include almost everything, yet remains subject to limitation wherever one shows that the harm caused by its protection is unacceptable. The governing standard balances not only among those rights considered highest in normative hierarchy (such as political expression, public safety and the like), but allows also for relative discounting according to circumstances so that actual harm caused, and not abstract rights claimed, leads the way.

IV. IMPLEMENTATION TO ANTITRUST

Similarly to the speech debate, the context of antitrust is one of clashing rights, where both sides have convincing claims that can rarely be simultaneously respected. Also, the rights and interests claimed are of various types, ranging from straightforward protection of property, through claims of rights to participate in the bounties of free trade, to the social interest in aggregate efficiency and the benefits of competition. There is no way to distill these into one criterion, but allowing for balancing among them is possible. Similarly to the speech context, majoritarian sentiments would first limit those arousing little sympathy, here—the monopolists. Constitutional lawyers dealing with the First Amendment are familiar with the fact that court protection is sought, and standards formulated, in an increasing proportion to the public loathing of those seeking protection. Whether it be neo-Nazis, anti-war activists, or pornographers—free speech jurisprudence owes much to those derided by then contemporary consensus. Beyond historical fact and intuitive reasoning, even empirical research shows that rights claimed by less popular groups and individuals will inevitably be dismissed more easily (or protected less fervently) than similar claims made by those with more palatable ideologies.[15] In the context of antitrust, it is monopolists who bear this burden.

Protecting the rights of monopolists is thus appropriate. First, since it is justified by analysis of their claims and fully substantiated above. Second, because it carries out to the fullest extent the protection of property and contract, basic maxims in our society. By protecting the rights of those less 'inviting' trust and sympathy, we ensure full protection of others' interests in less extreme circumstances (the slippery slope argument). This again is reminiscent of the purpose that protection of anti-democratic groups serves in our society.

While fairness analysis, as carried out in chapters three and four above, shows that monopolists' claims merit more protection than commonly afforded them, it might be said that this is true in the abstract, but real world implementation

[15] See GE Marcus, JL Sullivan, E Theiss-Morse and SL Wood, *With Malice toward Some: How People Make Civil Liberties Judgments* (New York: Cambridge University Press, 1995).

shows that any harm they suffer pales in comparison with that generated by their market power. The proposed balancing test does not contradict this claim. If indeed substantial and otherwise unavoidable harm is expected, the clear and present danger allows for limiting a person's (monopolist) rights in order to protect others (consumers, society). What the standard does demand of us, though, is serious consideration of the harm averted, as well as that caused to those whose business freedom is constrained.

The analysis of abstract rights is an initial premise from which to begin, with implementation to be carried out thereafter. Incorporating a constitutional standard creates a general framework, allowing for arguments that certain monopolistic practices (or certain factual contexts) are so harmful that intervention is necessary. Where this is true, no objection will be made to stringent enforcement of antitrust law. Where effects are ambiguous, on the other hand, there is no reason to allow a trend of majoritarian despotism, subjecting monopolists' rights to the material interests of consumers and others, who have no better claim than: 'I want it, I want it cheap, and I want it now'.

Obviously, this black and white exposition has multiple shades of grey in between. In many cases, it will be difficult to argue for rights-based arguments of monopolists, while harm to consumers and others is obviously present. This is where judicial and administrative discretion step in. With the clear and present danger standard as a guiding principle, implementation can be carried out on a case-by-case basis, allowing for real life complexity. The standard will demand careful deliberation by authorities, and force them to *consider* monopolists' rights in a manner fitting with constitutional standards. This is a good thing, as absent this inclusive fairness analysis, decision-makers might ignore monopolists' rights altogether, in line with the implicit common view of monopoly as evil and monopolists as its perpetrators.

The societal goals examined in chapter two support this standard as well. The most prevalent argument in favour of antitrust law is made on behalf of aggregate efficiency. Chapter two showed many exceptions to the rule of monopoly as inefficient, and even where the rule stands, state intervention is not always an appropriate solution. Efficiency is enhanced only where the benefits of intervention outweigh its costs, including indirect costs, public choice phenomena, chilling effects and unavoidable mistakes of enforcement agencies. Even where intervention is warranted despite these qualifications, the legal standard should be one where the burden of proof is on those arguing for intervention, in line both with the fear of 'false positives' supported by the state's superior power, and the rights-based analysis reviewed above. The debate as to efficiency's moral value notwithstanding, preference should be given to proven and accepted rights arguments wherever possible, especially where efficiency effects themselves are ambiguous. The claim that society *deserves* efficiency was shown above to be problematic in that this subjugates monopolists' rights to societal needs, akin to uncompensated takings. Again, this is not to say that intervention is necessarily thwarted. Where arguments are clear, and harm to individual or societal concerns exists, the standard allows for needed antitrust intervention, albeit after consideration of those whose commercial freedom is to be limited. The argument for competition as a societal concern—not as a proxy for its efficient results but for its democratic appeal and limitation of economic power—grants a much stronger basis for intervention. Where monopolistic phenomena threaten the state itself, a clear and present danger to the entire framework protecting individual rights might be discerned, justifying limitation of those who would ruin the state-fostered public good for everyone.

Of course, speech is not profit, and political demonstrations have little to do with antitrust. Yet it must be stressed that the 'clear and present danger' standard is not essentially modelled for speech purposes, but embodies a level of protection that can be bestowed on any deserving right. Speech is considered to be one of the most protected rights, thus its limitation is justified not in any case of 'danger', but only where the danger is to rights and interests of comparable worth, or that the harm posed is so great that it corresponds with the extent to which speech is limited in the circumstances.

The difference between the flag-burning debate, for example, and the relatively undisputed ban on public nudity shows this dynamic. On one hand, emotional grief caused to some because of others' speech (existing in both examples) is usually discounted as not justifying limitation of expression. On the other hand, the centrality of the symbol embodied by the flag leads to a stronger sentiment than usual, as well as a public interest in maintaining national unity and comradeship. Public nudity may not affect national unity, but does arouse strong sentiment and resentment based on the majority's conception of morality. Were this the end of story, perhaps both would be treated similarly, either limited due to the indignation caused by public display, or allowed due to the preference of speech (as both arguably may be construed as speech in the social sense) over moral outrage. Despite this, we return to both cases to ask the extent of harm that would be caused to the right's claimants if such 'speech' were outlawed. Publicly burning a flag is easily construed as closer to the 'inner core' of political speech. Allowing it only in private settings would defuse its purpose, as shock and outrage are inherent in the act itself as a political statement. Public nudity, however important to its perpetrator, is considered to be more of a 'lifestyle' choice, possible in private (or special communities) and thus less justifying the externalization of harm onto unwilling observers. The 'clear and present danger' applied to both, yields disparate results, due to examination of the importance of the specific interest protected in each context.[16]

In antitrust we may be arguing on what is morally a lower ground. The right to property is a basic one in our society, but its embodiment in the right to profit from a monopolistic position is hardly the central interest so protected (to say

[16] Of course, if the nudists in question strive not for personal freedom, but for political action, the result may differ. This is possible where public nudity is seen as a political statement against contemporary standards, seeking to change public views on the subject, or protest legal action.

the least). The standard does evolve from the basic right, here property, while its implementation will incorporate the specific details and harms caused.

Employing the 'clear and present danger' standard in antitrust does *not necessitate* equal protection to that granted to speech, but only a strong default rule protecting monopolists *relative to the existing interests in their context*. Thus, the right to property of monopolists is compared to the similar rights of their victims, and cases where protecting monopolists seriously injures others will be assessed by balancing the rights each side claims. In the antitrust context, the balancing test takes into consideration that while property and profit are important (especially to those threatened), they may be justifiably limited due to more important concerns present, or graver harm to others holding similar rights. Most of antitrust law, though, deals with direct 'horizontal' comparison of rights of comparable worth. Consumers as victims essentially argue for their right to procure cheap products and benefit from consumer surplus—rather than allow sellers with market power to expand producer surplus at their expense. Competitors argue for their right to participate in the market in order to generate profit—rather than allow monopolists to limit market access through pricing tactics and anti-competitive agreements, aimed at keeping profits high for themselves. Where this equivalence breaks down is where monopolists use their power to compel others and to limit social institutions. Compulsion through threat of economic harm can be addressed through contract law, but the protection of democratic institutions from economic power is well within the confines of antitrust.[17] The balancing test is formulation precisely to allow courts to assess the dangers, to society, and individuals within it, that might arise if monopoly goes unchecked.

In short, the 'clear and present danger' standard will not constrain cases where the harm done by protecting monopolists outweighs the importance of their rights. It will, though, demand a strong show of merit in the claims of those asking the state's intervention in monopolistic conduct. There are a number of strong objections that will undoubtedly be made to my argument that antitrust must justify its intervention in this way, and these will be considered in turn.

V. OBJECTIONS TO THE 'CLEAR AND PRESENT DANGER' STANDARD

Applying a balancing test to antitrust, especially one formulated in such a different context, is bound to be contentious. In this section I thus consider possible objections to the standard's applicability, as well as counter-arguments justifying

[17] While historically this statement is correct, recent focus within antitrust scholarship is on market, rather than economic, power. In ch 2, I argued against this trend as overly narrow and forgoing one of antitrust's main justifications. For elaboration of the argument for antitrust enforcement against economic power, see A Ayal, 'The Market for Bigness: Economic Power and Competition Agencies' Duty to Curtail It' (2013) 2 *Journal of Antitrust Enforcement* 1.

its implementation. I state the objections starkly and consider their merits, and only after presenting the case against the proposed standard, do I return to counter-arguments justifying it.

A. Free Trade is Different from Free Speech

The first and most prominent objection concerns the analogy from which the standard is drawn. Free trade is not free speech, and the suggested standard seems to place the two on the same level. The 'freedom' of an individual to trade in the marketplace without outside interference may be considered important, but not as important as speech is in a democratic framework.[18] While up to this point few would argue, it is also possible to carry the argument even further. Protection of trade, some might say, is not due to its enjoying a 'basic right' status, but instead is based on one of the following two arguments.

First, freedom of trade is an extension of the right to property. The right to property itself is a secondary right, justified only because of its connection to life and liberty. A society ensuring these rights for all their members through a non-capitalistic system might find private property wholly unnecessary or limit its extent much beyond measures to which we are presently accustomed.[19]

Second, freedom of trade in capitalistic economic systems may be considered instrumental rather than an end in itself. Without exchange, the market does not exist. Exchange facilitates 'gravitation' of resources to their most efficient user, and free trade allows market forces to operate to society's benefit. Thus, while trade is

[18] This argument is important well beyond the antitrust context. See KM Sullivan, 'Free Speech and Unfree Markets' (1995) 42 *UCLA Law Review* 949, arguing the need for special respect for speech in face of economic inequalities.

[19] Eg, granting rights to the products of labour or innovation, but not to basic inputs (land, inherited capital, etc) or property that would preclude others' ability to create their own. See, eg, the discussion in ch 6, n 12, using models of envy-freeness to deepen our understanding of fairness and delving into the problems posed by inherited wealth. Some use the fact that the communist bloc has acknowledged failure and is undergoing serious upheaval, as an argument for the 'victory' of capitalistic ideas and dismissal of limited property conceptions out of hand. This is an unconvincing argument for several reasons: First, the failure of certain administrations is not the failure of the idea itself. Historically, control of states within the communist bloc was mostly in the hands of dictators concerned more with their own, or their faction's, interests than with following the ideological principles they advocated, a phenomenon not limited to communist states or modern times. Second, no society exists where socialist principles (or capitalist ones, for that matter) were followed completely; therefore no empirical test exists for their success or failure. Even in the 'kibbutz' communes in Israel, economic failure presently witnessed may have been caused by other influences, or human imperfections, rather than the impossibility of the ideas on which they were founded. The same type of argument is raised against capitalistic states. On one side, moral and social failures (homelessness, healthcare, ethnic discrimination, etc) are used to show the immorality of capitalism. On the other side, historic market failures (such as the Great Depression or the recent financial crisis) are used to show that the system itself is unstable over time. There also, other explanations may be at the root of the problems, rather than a failure of the idea itself. The lack of empirical proof for either side may be perceived as a weakness, but may also be perceived as proof of the correct nature for the debate: one of morality and ideology rather than hard science.

important in a market society, this may be due to aggregate considerations rather than individual rights.

Free trade could thus be argued to be ancillary to the right on which it is based or the interest it serves, and should be considered less important than the freedom of speech. It is only because of the latter's importance that such a stringent standard as 'clear and present danger' is used. Without grounds for considering monopolists' rights of similar importance, there is no justification for similar treatment. One should not, then, apply a standard based so distinctly on an individual liberty of primary importance to a legal right lacking a similar moral basis.

B. Monopolists have no Right to Infringe upon Others' Rights

Those claiming a right to free trade cannot extend that right to prevent others from exercising a similar right of their own, beyond the fact that the 'right' claimed by monopolists is inferior to that claimed by their victims. Monopoly's victims claim a right to participate in the market, to exchange their property with others through mutual agreement based on free will and to innovate using their own resources and ideas. Monopolists, on the other hand, claim a right to accumulate market power—subverting the economic system that allows others to exercise their own rights, to block others from access to inputs necessary for their own manufacturing and innovation and to determine prices—subverting others' free will underlying the exchange process. It is true that monopolists may claim a right similar to that of others, a right to trade *within the free market*, but this is not their argument. Were we to acknowledge market trade as a universal right, monopolists would be indistinct from others, but this would do nothing to justify their *taking control* of the market. In other words, the right to *free* trade justifies state minimalism but that claim cannot be extended to monopolists' *manipulation* of trade or the market system it depends on.

C. The Standard Discriminates in Favour of Monopolists

Even if we accept the contention that monopolists' rights operate on the same level as those of their victims, the standard is not yet justified. The 'clear and present danger' standard prefers non-intervention in most cases (where such a danger was not proven). This gives the monopolist in question the benefit of the doubt, to the detriment of his victims who are unable to fend for themselves (assumed to be economically less powerful). Since monopolistic practices create market failures, state intervention is the only help these victims can hope for. The proposed standard removes this hope, except in the most extreme cases.

Accepting the need to balance the interests of all players involved does not necessitate giving one party a preference over the other. To the contrary, if the rights of all involved are considered of equal importance, the standard adopted should reflect this equality, for example, by preferring the party to whom the potential harm is greater. As monopoly's victims stand to lose much more by non-intervention than monopolists lose from state-imposed antitrust law, the victims should be the ones benefiting from rights-protection, with the state shifting away from this baseline only in the most extreme cases.

D. Antitrust Law must Prevent rather than Operate 'Ex Post'

The proposed standard would have antitrust enforcers limit their intervention to cases where the danger posed was both clear and present. This would diminish the role of preventive enforcement, since in many cases the standard could not be satisfied, resulting in lessened antitrust scrutiny and great harms that might have been avoided. Ex post litigation is not as effective as ex ante prevention, and sometimes harms caused cannot be undone.[20]

While the proposed standard aims at a fair solution that takes into account the rights of all relevant parties, following it may cause both inefficient and unfair results. The monopolists gain not only a standard working in their favour (as the previous objection noted) but one allowing them to establish facts by acting first and facing consequences later, if at all. In cases where ex post litigation is an insufficient deterrent, monopolists will get away with harming others in ways that would have been prevented under current doctrine.

E. Current Antitrust Law Already Considers Monopolists' Rights

The final argument against adopting a new standard in antitrust law is that its aims are already achieved by current standards. Antitrust law is not a system for discriminating against monopolists, but for protecting others from monopoly's excess. Monopoly as such is not forbidden, but its exploitation in harming others is. Monopolists' rights are already taken into account, and the detailed analysis by enforcement agencies and courts attest to that fact. Were this not so, no 'rule of reason' and the like would be used. Instead, intervention (indeed divestiture) would be the automatic response to monopolistic practices and monopoly itself. The standard, therefore, may be unnecessary.

[20] This is especially true in network markets, where 'tipping' effects, market lock-ins and path dependencies cause market failures difficult to undue in retrospect. Merger policy, as well, rests on the assumption that 'scrambled eggs cannot be unscrambled', preferring prevention over ex post litigation.

VI. ANSWERS TO THE RAISED OBJECTIONS

The objections raised are certainly not without merit, but may be answered as follows.

A. Free Trade is Different from Free Speech

Indeed, the distinction between these freedoms is self-evident and was attended to above. My proposition is not that the two are identical in content, but that they may be *treated* alike in context. While some view freedom of trade as instrumental, a means to the efficient result sought by the market mechanism, this is far from the only possibility. Here is not the place to conduct a philosophical debate as to the superiority of private property capitalism over common ownership socialism, or vice versa. Instead, the argument shall be constrained to our topic of choice, *within* the currently accepted social system. In our society, property is accepted as a basic and inalienable right. The legitimacy of governmental intervention or taking depends on the merits of the case, with a clear bias for respecting individual rights (including property) wherever possible. It is within this context that I deal with the objection as to the analogy from free speech to antitrust.[21]

Antitrust deals with power within the economic arena, power to limit the activities of others. Regulation of monopolists is deemed important because of the rights of those harmed by monopoly, whether consumers, competitors or others. The question dealt with here, then, is not the relative importance of property rights in general, but the relation between the monopolists' claims to that of their victims', as *both sides rely on their right to property in their claim for protection.*

Thus, in our discussion, we must compare the rights of (and the harms to) both sides of the equation as equally deserving bearers of rights. If property is considered an ancillary right, undeserving of extensive protection, this pertains to the claims made by monopoly's victims as much as to those made by monopolists. If, on the other hand, property *is* a basic right—again, both sides may claim protection. The standard's applicability is due to the comparison between these claims made on both sides, taking into consideration their relative strengths as assessed in chapters three and four above.

B. Monopolists have no Right to Infringe upon Others' Rights

Two facets of this objection bear mentioning. The first is the claim that those infringing on others' rights lose their standing as deserving protection for their

[21] There is much more to be said on the topic, some of which I reference in ch 4, nn 16–19, and accompanying text. The point made here does not depend on these distinctions between property systems and their justifications.

own rights. This must be dismissed immediately. In chapter five I discussed the necessity of examining the rights of *all* those involved before judgment is passed and one party preferred over the other, referring to the extreme example of even a criminal being afforded rights regarding the punishment imposed. Indeed, were it not so, no balancing test would be necessary—neither here, nor in any other case of clashing rights.

The second facet of this objection is the distinction between the right to trade *within* a free market framework, and the right to *distort* that framework. The monopolist, it is argued, claims the second, while his victims claim the first. The question here is whether the free market is truly the basis for monopoly's victims' claims. I think not.

The protection sought from antitrust enforcement is not limited to players in markets free of imperfections (indeed, almost no market is). Regulated markets, those with informational asymmetries, prohibitive transaction costs and so on, give rise to antitrust litigation just as well. Indeed, flawed markets are *more* problematic, since market power is more durable and victims of monopoly will be harmed over longer periods of time and to a greater extent. Perhaps the clearest example is the law's treatment of the dominant firm. The existence of monopoly power is in itself not an antitrust offence;[22] it is the abuse of monopoly power, or its wilful accumulation, that is seen as an evil to be prevented by antitrust enforcement. Thus, antitrust law is traditionally seen as 'protecting competition', but in practice it does not necessarily maintain competitive markets. Victims of monopoly, while perhaps wishing for perfectly competitive markets, are not regarded as *entitled* to such. What they are entitled to (according to current law), is protection from a dominant firm abusing its market power by wilfully engaging in harmful practices that would increase its power over the market and push out competitors or limit their entry.

The right to trade within a competitive framework is thus not a vested right that victims of monopoly may rely on to justify legal intervention wherever markets fail. The law protects them in a different way, sometimes narrower and sometimes broader: narrower, since a person or firm may find themselves within a monopolized market with no legal recourse (if the monopolist does not engage in forbidden practices); broader, since even in a relatively competitive market, it is possible for an antitrust offence to be committed (and penalized).[23] The basis for the victims' protection is their right to property or their right to trade, and not a

[22] See generally, ch 1, outlining legal frameworks for antitrust in the US and the EU. While conceptions of monopolization differ, both jurisdictions allow for legal monopolies, limiting only its use in purposefully constraining competition. American antitrust jurisprudence goes further in limiting *the pursuit* of monopoly, while European monopoly doctrine (as distinct from agreements or mergers) comes into effect only once a dominant position has been attained (and is more restrictive in limiting its abuse).

[23] The most obvious examples are practices forbidden per se, ie, without requiring proof of intent or actual harm. See ch 1 for examples and comparison of legal treatment in the different jurisdictions and ch 2 for discussion of circumstances when such forbidden practices are harmless (or indeed aggregately efficient!) due to specific circumstances.

right to a specific competitive framework. These are precisely the rights claimed by monopolists as well.

If two parties claim the same types of rights, each justifying state action in itself, but conflicting with the other, the state may not a priori prefer one over the other. The nature of monopolists' claims does not rule out the need for balancing. On the contrary, it is exactly what requires it.

C. The Standard Discriminates in Favour of Monopolists

This objection accepts the need for a balancing test, but argues that the 'clear and present danger' doctrine is overly restrictive of state intervention. That this standard gives the benefit of the doubt to monopolists is true, but justified. The relevant difference between the two parties involved is that the monopolist operates within the private sphere, potentially harming others by her behaviour. A monopolistic practice here may significantly harm others' rights and interests, but this is only so long as the perpetrator enjoys market power. Admittedly, in some cases this may be a very long time, though we must remember that circumstances differ, and many of those limited by antirust law are far from the powerful paradigmatic monopolists commonly intuited.

The harm caused *to a monopolist*, on the other hand, would not be directly at the hands of her competitors, but at the hand of the state—acting on their behalf. The introduction of the state into the 'game' changes the appropriate rules and effects. Two central reasons exist for a more stringent standard on state action than on private action, however detrimental to others.

First, the liberal state perceived as appropriate in our society is based on individual liberties, to be interfered with in special cases only. The protection sought by monopoly's victims is state protection. Accepting the premise that the state operates under more stringent constraints than private parties, it is not surprising the appropriate standard 'discriminates' in favour of the party subject to state regulation. This discrimination is not out of love of monopoly, but fear of state power. Of course, there are cases where monopoly power may be just as harmful (or repressive) as state power. It is precisely because of this fact that the standard *allows* for state intervention—since such cases will definitely pass the 'clear and present danger' guideline.

Furthermore, we need not limit ourselves to cases of extremely powerful and all-repressing monopolies. In any case where the harm potentially caused by monopoly is such that the guideline is 'activated', state intervention is warranted. Thus, it may be that even small and local monopolies will be regulated due to their effect on a segregated market or especially vulnerable victims. The flexibility of the standard, allowing circumstances in any given time and place to determine what constitutes 'clear and present danger', allows for differential treatment of monopolistic practices with varying effects. The strong and powerful monopolies that dominate intuitive reasoning regarding antitrust law may be forcefully repressed if necessary, or allowed to practise freely in cases where their actions are less contentious. The smaller and less repressive monopolists on the other hand (such as Tom, our entrepreneur from chapter four), may be allowed more lenient regulation. What is important to remember, is that the focus is not on the monopolists themselves, but on the results of their actions, and the need and justification for protecting others who might be harmed. In other words, the standard focuses on contextual analysis rather than providing all-encompassing rules that create an illusion of uniformity while actually creating disparate effects depending on the circumstances of their implementation.

Second, state regulation is intrinsically different from private action. When the state intervenes in business practices, it sets boundaries on the parties' freedom of action. This is true of some monopolistic practices as well. The monopolist may constrain his competitors' choices, or force them into deals they deem unfair. The difference is that when a monopolist holds market power, he is constantly under pressure of existing *or potential* competition. Such competition places constraints on his ability to exploit his power and protects his victims (at least to some extent). This 'protection' is not complete, otherwise monopoly would pose no problem and no 'victims' would exist.[24] But this effect must be taken into account when arguing for state intervention and the proposed standard would do just that in its consideration of monopoly's harm in the specific circumstances. More importantly, even in markets where a monopolist is currently unconstrained, it may be expected that circumstances for potential competition may arise in the future. Circumstances may change as to barriers to entry, the nature and economic power of relevant competitors, or even developments in other markets influencing consumers' elasticity of demand. Such changes may reduce the current monopolist's market power, making state intervention a moot point.

In short, market characteristics are subject to fluctuations and the current monopolist/victim definition may be annulled or substantively changed as a result. Even where markets cannot *replace* state intervention, one important distinction stands out: *state intervention is much less dynamic and self-correcting than the market.*

While market dynamics may not correct a monopoly situation, it leaves room for new competitors to arrive and threaten the current status quo. If the government steps in, an administrative or judicial decree is final, at least until legally overturned. A relevant change of circumstances may not reach the appropriate agency, or will almost certainly be slower to do so than the market may respond to such changes.

[24] The theory of 'contestable markets' makes this exact argument, though again it need not go to the extreme of arguing for *no* harm whatsoever. If no barriers to entry exist, potential competition alone will constrain an existing monopoly to competitive standards. If such barriers exist but are relatively low (a more realistic contention), the constraints on monopolists operate in inverse proportion to the barriers' level. Thus, the level of state intervention necessary should be assessed taking contestability into account. See ch 2, n 24.

This argument was made before in support of legal minimalism in antitrust.[25] This is not the path followed here. My argument goes beyond the *effects* of false positives and negatives, to the philosophical distinction between private market power and state legal power. Not only will state-sanctioned mistakes linger longer than market power imperfections, but state action limits individual freedom and carries social stigma in a way that monopoly does not. Thus, when society uses its collective power through law, it is subject to harsher constraints and must live up to higher standards. In a nutshell, it is not that the standard discriminates in favour of monopolists at the expense of their victims, but that it discriminates in favour of individual freedom at the expense of state power—and this is an appropriate bias, to be overcome only when circumstances demand it. The fact that antitrust law often bestows criminal status, with both legal and social connotations, solidifies the need for precisely such a bias.

D. Antitrust Law must Prevent rather than Operate 'Ex Post'

This objection is misguided, mixing two separate arguments. If prevention is a key element of effective antitrust and ex post enforcement is not enough, this may be taken into consideration when weighing the 'clear and present danger' involved. It is true that in cases of doubt, the standard operates in favour of the subject of potential state intervention (here, the monopolist), but the 'doubt' involved has nothing to do with prevention versus ex post litigation. If antitrust operates more effectively ex ante than ex post, evaluating the 'danger' posed by monopolistic practices will include the potential harm caused by lack of prevention. In cases where this is justified, the state may act decisively *ex ante*, so that these harms are avoided. This is not different from similar arguments within constitutional law, from which the standard was drawn. There, also, it may be argued that prosecuting one who has publicized a particularly inciting article calling for the use of violence is no remedy once the article has reached its audience. This is even more obvious when the speech to be limited includes bomb-making instructions (or a particularly effective encryption algorithm).

The debate between those favouring ex ante prevention and those arguing for ex post litigation alone, is therefore in full force with or without the standard we propose here. If the standard is justified, both sides may embrace it, and each may use it according to their own interpretation of the severity of the harm monopolists' pose. Ex ante prevention may be justified by showing the imminent danger that must be avoided, and ex post intervention may be used for correction of wealth transfers via compensation. Both types of intervention have deterrent effects as well, since ex ante litigation (if successful) precludes the harm altogether,

[25] See ch 5, nn 13–15.

and ex post intervention (when made public) serves as a deterrent to others contemplating similar practices.

E. Current Antitrust Law already Considers Monopolists' Rights

The standard proposed here is not a priori in favour of, or against, monopolists. It is also not based on the premise that current antitrust law is wrong and must be changed. The focus of the discussion is on justification and criteria, aiming for coherence of the theory justifying antitrust law, along with the limitations thereof.

When examining current doctrine, it seems that monopolists' rights are taken into consideration, especially when using rule of reason analysis rather than per se prohibition. But upon further reflection this is not completely true. The rule of reason is not a standard for examining the monopolists' rights and balancing them with their victims' rights; it is a standard for examining just *one side of the equation*—the harm monopolists cause. The rule of reason was developed as an alternative to forbidding per se certain practices, examining the harm that these practices actually cause instead. If a monopolist can show that on balance the challenged practice does more good than harm, it will be allowed. The main point, though, is that the harm and benefit assessed are *aggregate rather than personal.* For example, assessing efficiencies as a justification for allowing a merger potentially enhancing market power, maintains focus on society's benefit from more efficient business concerns, rather than the potential monopolist's profit expectations. Furthermore, the use of pass-through rates (the level of savings passed on to the consumer) as relevant criteria for approval of mergers emphasizes this tendency, here not only preferring aggregate concerns over those of the monopolist, but directly preferring consumer over producer welfare.[26]

The result is that even suits dismissed due to rule of reason analysis do not necessarily show respect of monopolists' rights, but rather treat them instrumentally as proxies for societal concerns. Antitrust jurisprudence has moved away from per se rules due to their excessive limitation of efficient business practices, forbidding what may actually help consumers—not due to monopolists gaining favour in public debate or case law. Of course, this does not mean that monopolists' rights were never considered to date, but merely that a coherent and full theory for incorporating them into a fairness analysis, necessitating balancing between their and their victims' rights, has not been proposed.

On the other hand, the standard proposed here may justify *more limitation* of monopolists, rather than less. The focus on societal concerns with economic

[26] See JA Hausman and GK Leonard, 'Efficiencies from the Consumer Viewpoint' (1999) 7 *George Mason Law Review* 707; JB Baker, 'Developments in Antitrust Economics' (1999) 13 *Journal of Economic Perspectives* 181.

power and its accompanying dangers for democracy and individual freedoms, poses a serious problem to be dealt with by antitrust agencies, limiting monopolistic phenomena even where direct victims might have no claim.[27] Where society deems the integrity of the market process to be threatened, aggregation of power might be limited in and of itself, even where the specific markets involved are not monopolized or their consumers directly exploited. This focus on societal goals, including but not limited to efficiency, is an essential part of the 'clear and present danger' society ascribes to monopolistic phenomena, and may call for more intervention than currently practiced.

VII. A REBELLIOUS THOUGHT

Proposing the 'clear and present danger' standard as a criterion for state intervention in antitrust shifts the discussion in a new direction—equal consideration of all those involved, including the monopolists. Under this standard, dismissal of antitrust litigation may be based on the classic efficiency analysis that 'the practice does more good than bad', but it may also be based on the appreciation of the monopolist's rights. Thus, even if on balance a business practice *is* harmful (from either a fairness or societal goals viewpoint), it may be allowed since the harm does not satisfy the 'clear and present danger' criterion and thus does not justify limitation of individual rights.

Perhaps the aim at constitutional coherence is appropriate in general, but misguided in direction? Is it not better to reverse the 'clear and present danger' doctrine, so that instead of monopolists enjoying the benefit of the doubt, their victims will? This would be possible by considering the harm monopolistic practices cause as justification for their regulation (as currently practiced) and allowing a defence for monopolists in cases where a protected interest of theirs is shown to be endangered. For example, we may accept the argument that commercial activity is an extension of the right to property, justifying protection from intervention where this right would be harmed. Monopolists would thus be able to claim protection when their rights are 'clearly and presently' endangered, but the default rule would grant initial protection to those most needing it—the victims.

While this reversal of the standard's application may better conform to common intuition and current practices (preferring the victims to the monopolist), it is seriously lacking. The main point of antitrust law is to protect the rights of victims of monopoly, who cannot do so themselves. The right most often protected is the victims' right to their property. It is the realization that the same right applies to monopolists, and that the interests (as well as the types of

[27] See ch 2, section II.A.

individuals and groups) involved are similar, that justified the proposed standard in the first place.[28]

Furthermore, the main point of granting the benefit of the doubt to the 'perpetrators'—the monopolists—was an acknowledgement of *the state's superior power* and the need to limit it and protect individuals and private parties from possible irreversible mistakes. As in constitutional law, it is the special and unequal relationship between the state and its subjects that calls for a standard granting the benefit of the doubt to those subject to regulation.

The standard, if justified at all, must remain a constraint on state intervention. That monopolists would enjoy its protection is perhaps counter-intuitive, but coherent with their standing as bearers of rights given equal standing before the law.

What bears remembering here (and is elaborated in chapter three), is that regarding most interests commonly espoused in favour of intervention, antitrust proved to be too large a hammer for that specific nail. Conceptions of social justice and protecting 'the little guy' have coloured our analysis with virtuous, but misplaced, sentiments. Antitrust law benefits a wide class of affected individuals whose claims merit less protection than is afforded them in practice. Beneficiaries are often firms (competitors or otherwise) and 'the little guy' is far removed from the real world application of antitrust. While some of the benefits of competition trickle down to final consumers, pass-through rates and multiple levels of production make quantification of such consumer benefits difficult to assess. Monopolists, on the other hand, are limited directly by antitrust law, thus any state action targets them specifically and infringes upon those of their rights shown to have merit by the analysis above. An acceptable balancing standard should thus reflect this fact by focusing on initial protection to monopolists' interests, subject to overruling in specific cases.

The discussion of 'formalization of fairness' in the previous chapter shed a different, yet complementary, light on monopoly's victims' arguments. The wealth transfer argument, so central to antitrust doctrine today and especially its public appeal, was shown to exhibit considerable weaknesses when assessed in a broader context of what constitutes surplus, how we define the 'transfer' of wealth, and how division between a seller and buyer in a monopolized market interacts with principles of fairness. While no clear-cut solution emerged (unsurprisingly), the intuitive protection of monopoly's victims and the commonplace disdain for monopolists suffered a substantial blow.

Aggregate societal goals, including economic efficiency commonly perceived today as the main target of antitrust, do nothing to bolster the claim for reversing

[28] Chs 3 and 4 showed that on both sides we find firms (necessitating the discussion of applicability of rights analysis); workers (some harmed and some benefiting from monopolistic phenomena, or conversely, intervention); local communities (harmed by outside monopolistic domination, or harmed by breaking up a local monopoly) etc. Consumers, the long-standing symbol of helpless individuals to be protected, also turned out more often than not to be other firms or producers buying inputs for their own commercial enterprise. This, notwithstanding the lack of convincing rights-based arguments that consumer protection claims produced for antitrust intervention.

the standard's direction. According to the aggregate view, society should benefit and antitrust is a means towards that end. But once monopolists' rights are taken into account, we see that this returns us precisely to the main justification for the 'clear and present danger' standard *in favour of monopolists*. It is precisely in cases such as these—where the majority seeks to use state power in order to limit the minority—where a governing standard protecting the latter is necessary. Governmental agencies limiting one party's business freedom in order to allow others access to the market, employ the state's superior power and reverse economic disparities which justified intervention in the first place. It is precisely cases such as these that necessitate constitutional protection, charging the courts with restraining majoritarian tendencies. The default rule should thus be that intervention is allowed only when clearly necessary—after passing an appropriate balancing test.

The costs of intervention, direct and indirect, monetary and otherwise, need to be taken into account as well. As shown in chapter three, these might be substantial, and only a minority of them can be precisely assessed. Perfect competition is a textbook fantasy, unattainable in practice—though guiding antitrust rhetoric. It is not monopoly and competition that governmental agencies must compare, but *realistic* outcomes that fall somewhere in between. Public choice effects, fear of false positives and litigation costs of all parties involved, must be taken into account when assessing the appropriateness of antitrust intervention. While exact data are lacking, assessment of the social benefits of antitrust should be along these lines:

$$\Delta W = W_c - (W_m + C_e + C_m)$$

with ΔW denoting addition to total welfare accrued through antitrust, W_c—welfare within *realistically* competitive markets (those we expect to achieve, not those we wish for), W_m—welfare within realistically monopolized markets (including market correction and interim effects), C_e—costs of enforcement (including indirect costs and public choice effects) and C_m—costs of mistakes in realistically expected enforcement (including 'false positive' effects). Optimization requires that if ΔW is positive, antitrust intervention is employed, if not—we would be better off without it. But even this formulation still makes a fatal assumption: *to argue that our society follows an optimization principle, assumes that state intervention is the rule rather than the exception, that aggregate welfare inherently supersedes the protection of rights.*

This view has government aiming at enhancement of societal welfare regardless of extent of intervention made necessary, since state intervention is regarded as good a method as gradual market self-correction, with only relative costs to guide the choice between them. One need not ascribe to the extreme libertarian view in order to find such a conception troubling. Are we so tolerant of governmental intervention that the only question to ask is 'will it do good'? Or perhaps modern liberal democracy prefers state minimalism, at least until shown intervention is necessary. Between two extremes lies a continuum of possible formulations, with no need for us to choose at this point. Since even the extreme interventionist viewpoint above turns out to be sceptical of antitrust at times, it is only necessary to point out that the further we move down the scale (towards state minimalism), the more substantial the proof required for justification of antitrust. Thus, if state intervention is considered a last resort than a primary tool of fine-tuning society, the burden of proof should lie on those arguing for it in each case—monopoly's victims.

Conclusion and Future Implementations

Put bluntly, the thesis put forth in this book may be stated thus: monopolists, the current 'bad guy' in antitrust jurisprudence, have not received a fair deal. Vilified in public discourse, they are seen as exploiters of the weak and destroyers of the free-market system. Historical resistance to monopoly by political decree and royal grant has seeped into current antitrust discourse through stereotypical examples such as *Standard Oil* and similar economic behemoths that used their economic power to subvert both competition and democracy. This created a popular conception of monopoly as evil, a malignant growth of economic power that the state must constrain. Juxtaposing consumers with monopolists leads the former to be considered unwilling victims of the latter, which leads to an almost automatic acceptance of (often unstated and unsubstantiated) assumptions regarding consumers' right to 'a fair deal'.

Modern antitrust jurisprudence, with its reliance on technical economic analysis, fares no better. While it avoids pejorative and emotionally-laden metaphors, economic analysis constrains our view to issues of efficiency—implicitly assuming that if society as a whole is better off, the individual freedoms hampered in the process do not count. As a society we have allowed ourselves the comfort of assuming antitrust is both right and fair, promoting efficiency as well as fairness. Inherent collisions between these values are considered almost only when consumers (or some other protected group of monopoly's victims) are harmed while aggregate welfare is not, leading to 'fairness trumps efficiency' arguments in favour of intervention. Monopolists' rights are ignored altogether, under both conceptions.

This book took the unconventional route, arguing that as we go back to basics and open-mindedly assess the underlying rights and interests of all those involved in the antitrust debate, monopolists and their victims alike have strong claims to be made. Fairness entails the protection of all involved, or at least the consideration of their rights and ensuring that public policy does not trample them unnecessarily. Efficiency is a societal goal (among others), but it too is limited by morality. Bettering the circumstances of society as a whole cannot automatically justify limitation of the rights of the few. As claims for each party to the debate were raised and assessed, it became clear that a balancing test is in order, one which would take into account not only those clamouring for state protection, but those seeking protection from the state as well. Learning from constitutional debate regarding similar issues (albeit in a different context), I argued that there should be a 'clear and present danger' standard for antitrust, protecting monopolists from excessive intervention while ensuring the harm from their conduct remain minimal. Efficiency was placed in the broader context of societal goals, which include not merely aggregate wealth, but also value-laden judgments regarding the type of society we seek, the role of competition in ensuring democracy, and the economic price to be paid for prevention of economic power and subversion of the political process.

Some would take the arguments proposed here to argue for limitation of antitrust enforcement as such, as further basis for constraining state intervention in economic matters. Taken as such, the arguments have a political connotation, infusing the 'left versus right' delineation common in American politics, or the Chicago versus Harvard (or post-Chicago) schools in antitrust discourse. I see things differently. My purpose is not in constraining antitrust or freeing monopolists; neither do I think that the practical implementation of current antitrust jurisprudence is necessarily mistaken. But I do think that we have allowed ourselves to be complacent, to rest on our intellectual laurels regarding common conceptions of monopoly and antitrust—and I believe a deep revision is necessary. By focusing on efficiency, antitrust aficionados enjoy a false sense of contentment, relying on economic expertise and professionalization, which mask the fact that our societal interests do not always justify limitation of others' business conduct. Equating fairness with victims' rights allows for focusing on one side of the debate: overlooking viable claims on behalf of those relegated to the position of 'enemies of the state'. We have, in essence, become too used to the idea that monopoly is a social evil and competition a virtue, while relegating our conception of competition to a market-by-market assessment. This technocratic focus has downplayed the importance of economic power and the democratic values intertwined with competition as a process of rivalry. The quest for efficiency thus masks both overly zealous intervention blind to property rights and under-enforcement where short-term economies of scale and scope override long-term protection of democracy and social values.

Essentially, the 'clear and present danger' criterion proposed above forces us to take account of the various individual liberties and societal goals involved in the antitrust debate. Contrary to rule-of-reason analysis, which focuses on economic effects and micro-market competitive issues, the balancing test broadens our perspective to include non-economic issues and constitutional rights. Similarly to the speech context from which it is drawn, this type of constitutional balancing focuses on protecting the competitive process rather than specific end results thereof. Monopolistic phenomena subverting competition and preventing entry or innovation will be treated as more of a danger to protected societal interests than those merely raising price. Individual consumers suffering from monopolistic pricing will have to show why their claims to a larger share of the surplus exceeds the counterclaim brought by producers. Arguments as to efficiency will be analyzed as a social good to be contrasted with the rights of those whose business conduct is to be limited. In both speech and trade, there are horizontal comparisons between those who are party to each claim for intervention, and there are vertical comparisons between the individuals and the state. Horizontally, monopoly's victims and perpetrators will argue for their interests and constrained rights. Vertically, those to be limited will argue for constitutional protection from the state's superior power. In all cases, balancing is necessary to avoid the intuitive trap—forgetting that the 'bad guy' has protected rights, and that our system's claim to justice relies on their protection.

The focus on process rather than result applies both to competition itself, and to the debate and legal implementation infused by internalizing the need for a balancing test. By seriously taking note of initially counter-intuitive arguments and forcing ourselves to consider both pros and cons, victims and perpetrators, we strengthen our true moral resolve. It is not the end result which should guide us, but the belief in a just process, in the moral clarity which is the result of constant balancing and reassessment. A society which continually takes account of the unpopular protects itself from the natural tendency to 'protect our own', to identify with those in which it is easier to find reflections of ourselves. It is this purpose which a true balancing test serves: keeping alive the difficult question of justice and the conflicting demands of complex issues. If antitrust is to be invigorated with such deliberation, those considering the competing claims will be challenged and bettered by the process. If such analysis leads to reconsideration of other fields, re-thinking where an inherent preference for one side has plunged the other into normative invisibility, the lesson will truly have been learned.

Implementation of the balancing test proposed here will undoubtedly require much thought and deliberation. What constitutes 'clear and present danger'? When is the 'danger' to efficiency sufficient to justify state intervention? A balancing test such as that, I propose, opens room for contextual analysis, allowing judicial and regulatory discretion which pushes antitrust away from clear-cut per se rules and towards standards to be applied on a case-by-case basis. There are those who would argue that this detracts from the prescriptive power of antitrust, from its use in guiding business behaviour. I believe this is false. Per se rules in antitrust have been in decline for decades as economic analysis matured and cases previously considered clear became recognized for nuances hitherto overlooked. Instilling monopolists' rights into the debate will undoubtedly call for reassessment of criteria for intervention, continuing the case-specific focus courts have been using on other grounds. I believe antitrust jurisprudence will gain as a result, and moreover, legal analysis more broadly construed will rise to the occasion and we as a society will take one more step towards true morality—constant reassessment of the grounds for our actions.

What does this mean for the practically minded individual? First, a demand on the courts to substantiate decisions to intervene based not only on economic analysis, but on respect for the affected parties. Consider merger policy, for example. Econometric analysis of economic data is often used to show when prices are likely to rise post-merger. Side-by-side comparisons of local markets are often used to drive the point home—a merger might raise prices and we can predict where and by how much. But standard analysis ignores the firms' interests in maximizing profit. The public, it is implicitly assumed, has a right to lower prices which places an obligation on the firms to compete, or at least negates their right to cooperate in reducing the significant overhead costs associated with multiplicity of infrastructure and logistics. Reducing costs is a legitimate issue—but only insofar as such savings are to be passed on to the purchasing public. A person's right to run their business is thus implicitly assumed to be merely instrumental in securing a consumer's right to a good product at a low price.

Considering mergers through the lens of the proposed balancing test does not necessitate their approval, but it does place more stringent requirements on the agencies seeking to block it. A claim might be made:

> Show us not just that a merger raises prices, but show that the problem is severe, that the consuming public is so threatened that the state justifiably inhibits business freedom. Or show us that the competitive process, which society relies on, is seriously curtailed.

Where harm to consumers is sufficient to surmount harm to producers, a state-sanctioned enforcement agency might rightly step in. Where firm size and economic power is sufficient to threaten the political process, agencies might limit growth. 'Clear and present danger' sounds overwhelming, but it is a standard known to allow judicial flexibility. A balancing test applied to merger review does not guarantee any specific outcome, but it does guarantee that firms seeking to collaborate be afforded a similar respect in antitrust litigation that courts afford them in other circumstances. Just as firms may sue for breach of contract, and judges anthropomorphize them and protect their rights just as any individual, those served by firms should be able to say: 'the merger may raise prices, and it may not, but please take into account my interests also. Afford me the respect of curtailing my activities only when *really* necessary'.

In relation to unilateral conduct, new and complex pricing mechanisms cause economists and lawyers to ask whether these are legitimate business plans, or mechanisms for pushing competitors out and monopolizing the market. Selling goods bundled together (or rebating them accordingly), granting loyalty discounts, slotting arrangements in supermarkets and department stores—all have become of interest to the antitrust community. Pricing has the potential to allow one firm to outmanoeuvre another, or build upon a pre-existing advantage. Thus, a firm with market power might well be using pricing and discounts to monopolize a market. Economic analysis suggests conditions where such pricing may be anticompetitive, in the sense that it might result in monopoly (or at least increase concentration). But applying models to the real world is a difficult and ambitious enterprise, and the truth is we never *know* when a preventative measure is really necessary. This does not mean that intervention is never warranted, since avoiding mistakes is impossible. False positives and false negatives abound in antitrust discourse, and the terminology is often used to warn from overly zealous enforcement. Employing a balancing test reminds us that false positives are not merely potentially more harmful to efficiency, but are a euphemism for harming specific individuals, curtailing the plans and ambitions of many business people congregated (usually) within a firm. Requiring that 'clear and present danger' be shown ensures that this harm is taken into account: not just what is better for society, or consumers, but what standard of care should be taken so that we as a society do not trample our peers; that we consider *all* aspects, including those of firms we suspect as monopolists.

The fact that firms are involved, much more often than individuals, is emblematic of the economic size that antitrust deals with. This could be used to argue against the rights-perspective—that firms are merely instrumental, non-human. But then we remember that most consumers are firms as well, and most of antitrust takes place deep within the commercial world; that most firms sell to other firms, who sell to other firms. Even when pass-through is shown towards end users, it is often meagre, or difficult to quantify. And firms are afforded legal respect in every other legal arena; their having rights is almost universally accepted.

The balancing test does not necessitate that we agree that firms have rights, or that we prefer those of monopolists to those of consumers—but it does require we state our assumptions clearly. A strong consumer-protection policy is still possible within the standard as well—but it will have to be defined explicitly, clarifying what the danger is and why we think it is so important.

We have become used to the 'antitrust for the consumers' mantra for too long, and neglected to examine its philosophical underpinnings. The question we should be asking, and the balancing test forces us to ask, is 'is it worth it?'. What level of limitation are we willing to impose upon others running their businesses so that we get our low prices? Since we are all consumers, and public-spirited regulators and judges like to think they are acting on behalf of 'the people', our consumer-preferring bias is understandable. But just as a majority in a constitutional democracy imposes upon itself restraint and limitations protecting minorities, a marketplace 'belonging' to consumers is not necessarily a good thing.

The professionalization of antitrust led to utilization of quantitative models and increasing focus on narrowly-construed 'antitrust markets'. This causes us to miss the forest for the trees. Economic models are useful in quantifying effects, but tell us nothing about meaning and morality. Consumer-centric rhetoric, coupled with efficiency analysis, lead to ignoring both monopolists' rights and society's concern with economic power. The anti-democratic nature of large firms and conglomerates exerting political power, moved out of focus due to market delineation and its contribution to precision of analysis. The fact that political markets are often localized allows similar problems to arise even where the firms involved are far smaller than the huge multinationals usually considered problematic. The issue of economic power should thus be examined in context, focusing on the relevant democratic process and preventing localized harm just as much as national effect.

It is true that quantitative models lead to more certainty in application, but only within narrowly-confined markets, and at the expense of allowing agglomeration of economic power and political influence. Antitrust has moved away from its initial purpose, leaving the field open for conglomerates to avoid scrutiny while subverting the marketplace. 'Bigness', not in firm size but in political and economic effect, should be considered within the clear and present danger framework, as an important societal concern worthy of antitrust protection. The market should be protected as a public good, a commons for all to meet in and enjoy—though as chapter six showed, who gets what share of the surplus is indeterminate. Rather than focus on prices, we should focus on process; rather than protect consumers, antitrust should protect all market participants—limiting those threatening public participation while allowing for profit maximization.

In the end, it is the balancing which keeps us honest, the process of examining rights on both sides and the interests of society in one cohesive framework. It is a demand society should make of itself to ensure that rights are not curtailed unnecessarily. As with economic analysis, mapping out the rights affected in any type of dispute is a fact intensive endeavour. Some cases will justifiably lead to intervention, but those calling upon the state's superior power to protect their own interests (even if they are the majority and include 'us'), will need to admit the interests of those they aim to curtail. 'I want it now, and I want it cheap' is not always a good enough reason.

INDEX

www.ingramcontent.com/pod-product-compliance
Ingram Content Group UK Ltd.
Pitfield, Milton Keynes, MK11 3LW, UK
UKHW020140290926
15471UKWH00003B/611

9 781509 907069